ULTIMATE SPARRING
Principles & Practices

BY
SHIHAN JONATHAN MABERRY

ORIGINAL PHOTOGRAPHS BY ROBERT PATRICK O'BRIEN

Strider Nolan Publishing, Inc.
68 South Main Street
Doylestown, PA 18901
www.stridernolan.com

Printed in Canada

Library of Congress Catalog Card Number: 2002114919
ISBN: 1-932045-08-2

First Edition Paperback 2003

Design by Mary Wilsbach Katz

Strider Nolan Publishing, Inc.
68 South Main Street, Doylestown, PA 18901
www.stridernolan.com

DEDICATIONS

This book is dedicated to my stepson, Sam West-Mensch…with all my love and respect.

And to the memory of Rich Spadaro, who will always be remembered as the kindest of men and the best of students.

ALSO BY THE AUTHOR

From Strider Nolan Publishing:

Ultimate Jujutsu: Principles & Practices

The Martial Arts Student Log Book

From Other Publishers:

Judo And You

Effective Survival Methods

ACKNOWLEDGEMENTS

This book would not have been possible without the generous help, advice, encouragement, and support of many wonderful people in and outside of the martial arts. The following list is alphabetical rather than in any order of importance because each and every person has been equally vital to the creation of Ultimate Sparring. Thank you all!

- Art Bourgeau and the students of the Philadelphia Judo Dojo
- Asian World of Martial Arts Supply Company (www.awma.com)
- Avenida dos Estados Unidos da América
- Batuque Capoeira Group of Holland
- Benny "The Jet" Urquidez and Stuart Sobel
- Bill "Superfoot" Wallace
- Bill Durant of the United Seated Armwrestling Association (USAA)
- Bill Kent
- Brad Daddis of Extreme Martial Arts & Fitness Academy of Philadelphia
- Capeda-Abueg Martial Arts; Bryson Kim, Photographer
- Chris Amberger
- Christopher Matthews and Tom Lancaster
- Chuck Lee, Susan Holbrook, Valerie Ross, Trevor White, Maria Mora, Larry Hambrecht a.k.a. Team Moral Support
- Chuck Norris
- Coordinadora de Colectivos Tradicionales de Juego Del Pal Canario de Tenerife
- Cory Schaefer of the International Sport Karate Federation (ISKF)
- Daryl "Nitro" Croker
- Dave Pantano and the students of Counterstrike Kenpo
- Doreen Simmons
- Dr. Edward Andujar
- Dr. Guy Mor of the W.P.O/I.F.P.A
- Dr. Martin Sewer of the Martin Sewer Kung Fu School of Zurich, Switzerland
- Eric Legret and Fédération of Gouren
- Fred Apple and Rick Lombardi
- Gloria T. Delamar for her editing assistance
- Grandmaster Chiu Chi Ling and the Chiu Chi Ling Hung Gar Kung-fu Association
- Greg Stea, Vinny Avalon, Mike Boryla, Chip Hand and Stan Nigro
- International Chinese Kuoshu Federation (I.C.K.F.)
- International Muay Thai Federation (IMTF)
- Jamal El
- James Petro of Jim's Chop Shop in Columbus, NJ
- Japan Aikido Association, USA, Sean Flynn Marketing Director
- Jared Weiner, Lloyd Irwin and Leo Dalla of the Brazilian Jiu-jitsu United of Philadelphia
- Jeff Larson, Dave Cvet, Bill Wilson, Brian Price, Jain Shuster, Nicole Allen, Paul McDonald, Tim Ruziciki & Michael Cawelti of the Western Martial Arts Workshop (September 2002); Gilda Pasquil, photographer

- JCC Northeast Philadelphia
- Jeff Loper-Bey
- Jeff Smith
- Jim Winterbottom
- Joe Frazier
- Joe Lewis
- Kancho Robert Taiani
- Kyokai
- Len Solomon, Fitz "The Whip" Vanderpool and Kosta Tszu
- Loren Lalli
- Maria Daniels of the University of Pennsylvania Museum of Archaeology and Anthropology
- Mark & Lara Masters of the Fencing Academy of Philadelphia
- Marlena De Carlo
- Matthew Nichols
- Mestre Doutor (Adenilson Jose dos Santos), Zen One (Ron Wood) and the students of the Associação Santista de Capoeira Areia Branca (ASCAB)
- Nick Cione
- Patience T'ai Chi Association
- Paulo de Oliveira of Universidade de Évora
- Prof. M. Gene Holden Kancho of the Mibukan Goju-Ryu and the Okinawa Karate-do Goju-ryu
- Professor Ronald Duncan (www.wayofthewinds.com)
- Ramon Lawrence & Georgie Thompson of the Shingen Academy; Bruce Powell, photographer
- Randall "Tex" Cobb
- Ray Minger
- Robert McLaughlin of the Philadelphia Center for Well-Being
- Roy Kleckner
- Sammo Hung
- Sensei Robert Klotz
- Sifu James D. Angielczyk & the Depew, New York school of Hung-ga Gung-fu
- Sifu Pete Buckman, Maynard Espansol, Teresa Buckman & Luba Andreeva
- Southern California Naginata Federation (www.scnf.org)
- Stephen D. Hyers
- Stu Shames
- Su Bayfield of www.egyptsites.co.uk
- Tan Shin Kai Kendo Dojo of Philadelphia, Shoji Okutani founder & Chief Instructor
- Temple University
- The Pennsylvania Renaissance Faire
- The students of the Shinowara-ryu Jujutsu Dojo of Philadelphia: M.S. Katz, Max Schmidheiser, Sam West-Mensch, Bob O'Brien, Mike Mazzoni, Andy DiViny, Paul Scott, Mischa Wheat, Zac Rubino, Matt Kirsch, Jason Miller, Sam Adels, Jason Lukridge, Jill Katz, Hector Osorio, David Lent, Nick Cione, Jim DeGeus, Sean Gallagher, and Rich Tang.
- Tony Cecchine of www. catchwrestle.com
- Toshiro Yamato and Andy Collins
- United States Chinese Kuoshu Federation
- University of British Columbia
- USA Amateur Boxing Federation (USA/ABF)
- Vince Volker, Robert S. Clarke, & John J. Hyland, III, photographers
- World Eskrima Kali Arnis Forum (WEKAF.com)
- The World Shuai Chiao Society and Dave Pickens

ABOUT
The Author

Shihan* Jonathan Maberry holds a 7th degree black belt in Shinowara-ryu Jujutsu and a 5th dan in Yu Sool Hapkido. He is a former bouncer and worked for several years as a bodyguard in the entertainment industry. From 1969 through 1984, Shihan Maberry competed in point fighting and full-contact matches. As a colored belt he fought 171 matches, with a record of 157 wins, 12 losses, and 2 ties. As a black belt he fought 108 full-contact matches with a record of 104 wins (including 53 KOs or TKOs), 2 losses, and 2 ties. He has also competed in amateur wrestling, boxing, and sabre fencing.

Shihan Maberry is the author of over 500 articles on martial arts, sport fighting, and self-defense, and has written a number of books including *The Martial Arts Student Log Book*, *Judo and You*, *Ultimate Jujutsu: Principles and Practice*, and *Ultimate Self-Defense For Women*.

Shihan Maberry also taught martial arts history for fourteen years at Philadelphia's Temple University. He currently teaches Jujutsu, traditional Japanese weapons arts, and Family Safety at various dojos in Philadelphia.

---

* *Shihan*: 7th dan or above.

CONTENTS

PREFACE
How To Define Sparring

In *Ultimate Sparring: Principles and Practices* we use the word "sparring" rather loosely.

According to *Webster's Online Dictionary*, sparring means:

1. To fight with an opponent in a short bout or practice session, as in boxing or the martial arts.

2. To make boxing or fighting motions without hitting one's opponent.

3. A motion of attack or defense in boxing.

4. A sparring match.

For the sake of convenience we are using this word in a somewhat broader sense, stretching it to include all methods of competition that use simulated combat. This broader category includes fencing, dueling, ring fighting, comparing, and a number of other areas. Sparring is a common term to boxers and martial artists and no one takes exception to its use, but weaponry arts like Historical Fencing and Kyudo do not, by literal definition, "spar." These arts are included because they preserve beautiful and historically important weapons arts and the practitioners sometimes compete against one another. This is not intended to slight or diminish practitioners of any art, but is used to create a smooth flow of information throughout this book.

Ritualized fighting, such as Limited Step Sparring used in Karate and Taekwondo, and choreographed fighting, such as that used in stage combat and movie fight direction, are likewise included and gathered under the category of "sparring" for use in this book.

INTRODUCTION

The martial arts have existed in one form or another since mankind first dropped out of the trees. In a nutshell, "martial" arts are really practiced methods of efficient fighting. The "art" comes from remembering and passing on those battle skills that have proven themselves effective in combat. The first time a caveman in a bearskin told his friends how he knocked someone out with a stone, the tradition of martial arts was born. It really was about as simple as that. Something works, you tell anyone else whom you feel needs to know and they try it. If it works for enough people over a long enough period of time, it becomes a tradition. These traditions were handed down from father to son, from brother to brother, from tribesman to fellow tribesman.

Sparring through the ages: (l to r) ancient Egyptian boxing, Greek wrestling, and African Maculele.

It was not until the earliest days of Indian, Egyptian and Chinese cultures a few thousand years B.C.E.* that these combat skills began to be organized into a form similar to what we practice today. As tribes grew into towns, then into city states and then into nations, warfare grew as well. Much as we'd like to believe otherwise, the spread of humanity around the globe was not a non-violent process. Aggression was the chief national export of most countries for much of history. However, as wars became more complex and sophisticated, so did the warriors themselves. With the rise of the first advanced cultures came the first advanced thinkers--warriors who

* B.C.E. stands for Before Christian Era, meaning the same as B.C. A.D. is now commonly called C.E., or Christian Era.

thought about what they were doing, what it meant, how it worked, why it was done, and the moral implications. The status of warriors in a culture changed so that the warrior was not just a brutish guy with a cudgel but a member of society who was expected to demonstrate civil graces as well as physical prowess.

As empires expanded, "peace" spread across the conquered lands. Thus, there were often long stretches of time with little for soldiers to do. Training methods had to be developed that would allow the soldiers to practice their fighting skills to a high degree without killing their fellow soldiers.

This is where sparring came into play.

The Egyptians developed several competitive forms of martial sports including boxing, wrestling and fencing with both swords and sticks. As far as historical records can verify, these were the first organized combat sports.

The cultural influences of Egypt upon later cultures is immeasurable, and certainly fencing is one of the most enduring exports; but not all combat sports evolved from the land of the Pharaohs. Many hundreds of cultures developed their own combative sparring, though these evolved later and in incredibly varied forms.

Medieval jousting.
Photo courtesy of Pennsylvania Renaissance Faire.

Sparring has been used for a number of purposes over the years, and many of those uses are still in force today. It has long been a common part of military basic training, allowing soldiers to practice and improve their skills. Methods of sparring as training drills can be found throughout history, from the days of the Roman army practicing with hardwood versions of their Gladius short swords, to the Pugil Sticks used by the U.S. Marines to teach how to fight with the barrels and stocks of their rifles.

Combat play as a matter of establishing prowess in times of peace has been a major factor in the training of young nobles all over the world, from the jousting and melee matches of the Middle Ages, to the wrestling method known in Brittany as Gouren, to the wooden sword Bokken matches of the Samurai in training.

Japanese Kendo.

Sparring has been widely used to settle disputes, and every country has had its forms of dueling, either with pistols at dawn, flashing rapiers, or fisticuffs.

By far, the most significant use of sparring over the last century has been pure recreation. For the viewers it is a chance to live vicariously through the champions, to be (at least for the length of a bout) a heavyweight boxer like Muhammad Ali, a Karate point-fighting champion like Chuck Norris, or an Olympic wrestling gold medalist like Brandon Slay. Viewing competitive combat sports is intensely personal…for the duration of the match we ARE the fighters. We feel their punches hit home, we grunt when they get hit, and we are on top of the world when they win.

Joe Lewis (r) vs. Chuck Norris (l) two of the greatest Karate fighters of the Twentieth Century.

Participating in combative sports is exhilarating. It opens up all of the senses, gets the vital juices flowing, and allows us to step outside of ourselves and become true brothers to the warriors from all those centuries ago. This is important because as martial artists we seldom (thankfully) have the opportunity to use our skills. As the old Jujutsu adage goes: "In the martial arts we train ten thousand hours in order to prepare for a single moment that we hope will never come." Sparring allows us to test ourselves, to find out how good we really are (or, in some cases, are not, which is also important to know). It makes us train harder, become faster, stronger, sharper, better.

The Twentieth Century saw many significant changes in the approach to sparring, with a tendency toward safe practice rather than encouraging or even allowing injuries. Boxing is no longer fought in an unlimited number of rounds and with bare knuckles. Muay Thai kickboxing is no longer fought to the death. Greek Pankration no longer allows crippling techniques in the ring. In terms of safety and a greater compassion for our fellow athletes, we truly have evolved.

Likewise, the sciences of physics, exercise physiology, nutrition, and sports medicine have substantially improved all of the combat sports. Athletes are stronger, faster, and have more endurance than ever (despite the somewhat inflated stories of the prowess of many legendary heroes and champions).

Sparring in the Twenty-First Century is about pushing back the accepted standards of what is possible. New records are set all the time, and the level of sportsmanship, ability, intelligence, and fighting skill has reached a peak never before paralleled in history.

Bill "Superfoot" Wallace, one of the first world champions of professional kickboxing.

This book, *Ultimate Sparring Principles and Practices*, has two parts to it. The first part, Principles, talks about the ABCs of getting ready to spar: fitness, nutrition, safety, first aid, skill development and theory. The second part, Practices, presents an encyclopedic array of hundreds of sparring styles from around the world and throughout history, offering information on their history and how they are played.

Many of these combative sports exist in great variety, such as Karate and Wrestling; and in those cases the rules which are presented are common to the majority of the styles and organizations supporting these methods. This book is not intended to replace or supersede the Official Rules of any competitive organization, and a smart player will always check the "House Rules" to learn the particular Rules of Play for whatever tournament he enters.

Like most encyclopedias, this book is more likely to be read in a random fashion, checking back and forth, instead of a straight cover to cover read. To that end some of the information is repeated in those sections where it is necessary for clarity and convenience.

Now let's strap on the gloves and climb into the ring!

PART ONE
Sparring Principles

Legendary kickboxer Benny "The Jet" Urquidez in action against former
Japanese Champion Shinobu Onuki, circa 1978.
Photo courtesy of Stuart Sobel.

CHAPTER ONE
Safety First

**Modern Ninjutsu master Professor Ronald Duncan
demonstrating self-defense sparring.**

Sparring is not fighting. Sparring is a game. Fighting has no rules, sparring has plenty of rules, and they are sensible rules of safety and fair play.

Unless you are engaged in one of the less common forms of full-contact fighting where the only means of victory is a knockout, the goal of sparring is not to injure your opponent at all, but to simulate injury; and even in the roughest of rough-house sparring there are limits to what one can and should do to the other player. No matter how much pre-game hype is used to make it seem like the players are bitter rivals, when it comes right down to it the competitors are really part of a brotherhood of select athletes with quite a lot in common.

All good fighters know this, and the knowledge makes them very concerned for the overall safety of the sport.

On the other hand, sparring competitors are fighters. This may sound like a contradiction, but it is not. Even though a sparring match simulates fighting, the contestants who compete are true fighters. Whether boxer or kickboxer, Kendo swordsman or epee fencer, Judo player or Greco-Roman wrestler, the players in competitive combat sports are all trained to be real fighters. It is only the fact that modern urban man is not called upon to fight for his life on a regular basis that keeps these fighters from having to prove just how deadly they are. It is a further test of their skills to control their skills during a match so that neither partner is injured.

In order to spar safely, there are a number of necessary precautions to be taken because overall fitness and conditioning are of absolute importance. Sparring puts heavy demands on muscles, tendons and bones. It helps to be strong, and it is vital to be flexible, in order to spar safely; and this fitness should be complete, not just specialized to a few areas of the body. Even a kicker can sprain a shoulder, just as a grappler can pull a leg muscle.

Training before a match—and the demands of an actual contest—require so much physical exertion that injury and illness can occur unless martial artists eat sensibly, stay sufficiently hydrated, and practice fitness as diligently as they hone their fighting skills.

DRESS APPROPRIATELY

Certain styles of sparring have a dress code that is often related to safety concerns. In Taekwondo for example, a complete dobok is generally required, a uniform that is loose and durable and allows the legs to move without restriction. In Judo a sturdy Judo-gi is needed, to provide body padding for throws and to allow a safer grasp of one's opponent than would be possible when wearing t-shirts. Make sure that you have the proper clothing and that it is in good repair for whatever style of sparring you choose.

WEAR PROTECTIVE PADDING

Unless it is forbidden by contest rules, adequate protective equipment is necessary. Start with the vitals. For men, an athletic supporter with durable

A gi must be sturdy yet unrestrictive for grappling arts such as Judo.

groin cup is a must for any match that involves trading blows (although the cup does become something of a liability in grappling and wrestling). For women, sports bras are sensible, as are the reinforced chest protectors available through all major martial arts equipment suppliers. There are tuck-under groin protectors for women as well.

Plastic mouth guards are highly recommended for everyone. It is too easy to lose a tooth, and even easier to accidentally bite your own tongue.

Other equipment should be purchased based on one's own judgment, as well as the particular dangers of a chosen style of sparring. A competition that focuses on striking and kicking may warrant forearm or shin padding, whereas such equipment is not necessary for a grappling match.

Protective padding is recommended for intense sparring, even between fellow students.

A final factor in choosing protective equipment is the contestant's own physical condition. A fighter with a bad knee may want to wear a protective brace. Someone with bad eyesight may want to wear protective goggles over eyeglasses or contact lenses.

LEARN THE RULES

Rules of competition are as much about safety as they are about structure. Know them going in and abide by them at all times. Someone who cannot (or will not) follow the rules presents a serious danger.

DRINK PLENTY OF WATER

Staying hydrated eases breathing, keeps muscles and tendons flexible, rids the body of toxins, and generally balances the body's systems. Water is essential for rigorous training.

A referee going over the rules for two Pankration wrestlers.

EAT BEFORE TRAINING

Balanced meals before (but not immediately before) training help the body stay strong and energized. Make sure your diet includes foods that provide electrolytes and minerals, including potassium. Be cautious of sports drinks: they are often very high in sugar and sodium. Dietary supplements are useful, but natural vitamins with minerals are best. Avoid sugars and fatty foods because they can lead to an energy drop. If protein supplements are taken, water intake must be increased accordingly.

REST AFTERWARD

After a sparring match, help your body settle down. After a competition, drink plenty of water and make sure you replenish your electrolytes. Dehydration can lead to muscle cramping, nausea, or worse.

PREVENTION IS BETTER THAN CURE

Pay attention to any aches or pains you have before, during, and after sparring. Learn to recognize and manage minor injuries, and keep them from becoming serious. The primary goal of safe fitness training is to prevent injury.

WHEN IN DOUBT ... REFER

If you are injured, stop. Immediately discuss the injury with your instructor and/or a physician. All athletes should recognize their limitations and understand the importance of seeking proper medical attention when any injury is suspected.

Always discuss sparring injuries with your instructor and seek medical attention if necessary

CHAPTER TWO
The Benefits of Sparring

Sparring is a vital part of martial arts training. It offers a tremendous variety of benefits. It builds the body, sharpens the mind, hones the reflexes, and cultivates the qualities of good sportsmanship and fair play.

The term "sparring" includes hundreds of methods of competitive but simulated combat. Even boxing and full-contact Karate are simulated, because no matter how intense they get, in the ring they (sensibly) do not allow things such as eye-gouging, leg-breaking, and neck-twisting.

Is sparring the same thing as street fighting? Of course not. Actual martial arts fighting is far less structured and far more brutal. Many techniques that might be used in self-defense cannot (and indeed would not) be used in a sparring match. You might try to dislocate a mugger's shoulder or run a would-be rapist head first into a wall, but you wouldn't use those skills on a sparring partner.

So if sparring is not "real" fighting, can it be used to prepare for self-defense on the street? Definitely. Sparring develops strengths that can only be cultivated in the down and dirty, close quarters immediacy of a competitive match. Classroom defense simulations, valuable as they are, cannot impart a sense of actual competition. Opponents in a fight (on the street or in a sparring match) act much more randomly and are much more determined. They are unpredictable and tricky, and unlike classroom training partners, are not the least bit cooperative. The random nature of sparring is worth its weight in gold for the development of combat reflexes.

A potentially fatal palm strike against a would-be rapist is not a technique to be used, even in self-defense sparring, unless heavily modified for safety.

The following are some of the major benefits of sparring.

BALANCE

Learning proper balance is fundamental to all of the fighting arts because the body has to be ready to move immediately and without hesitation. In sparring you are constantly moving, shifting weight, lunging, evading, leaping, kicking, pivoting, punching. Proper balance allows you to perform each of these maneuvers with grace, speed, and efficiency.

Ideally, the body's weight should be canted slightly forward. This helps to work against the body's natural propensity to lean back onto the heels of the feet. To enable a person to move quickly, weight must be taken off of the heels and kept on the balls of the feet. with the toes used as stabilizers. If the feet are flat, then the body's weight becomes settled and has to first be lifted by the leg muscles in order for any step, kick, or evasion to be performed. This creates lag time, which makes a person slow off the mark, easy to hit, and clumsy.

Fighting Cranes is an excellent Kung Fu sparring method for increasing balance. See Chapter 14.

Ball-of-the-foot balance is immediate, efficient and very fast. Tennis players and boxers are encouraged to stay in this posture at all times, and this advice is echoed by all good martial arts instructors. This is precisely the source of the expression "keeping on your toes."

The knees should always be slightly bent to allow the muscles in the legs to act as springs as well as shock absorbers. When the legs are slightly bent the body's weight is essentially in suspension, which means that it is hoisted off the ground and capable of being shifted instantly.

CONFIDENCE

A martial artist's fighting abilities are, for the most part, hypothetical. Only in rare cases does a person ever have to use the exotic kicks, strikes, blocks, and throws in a

Short of using one's skills in a real fight, sparring is the best way to build confidence.

real self-defense situation. You certainly can't go out and pick a fight just to see how well you'd do. But it does make it difficult for a serious martial arts student to determine if he (or she) can really fight.

When you spar you get to test your combat judgment, your timing and speed, your reactions and reflexes, your ability to withstand pain, your focus, your capacity to endure hardship, your control, and your basic fighting ability. Even though sparring is not street fighting, it is still a demanding test of your abilities as a fighter. A person who has trained in martial arts and never sparred simply cannot be as confident in his abilities as someone who has.

Experience is the best teacher. For example, if in one match you try a move that is blocked and you get tagged by the counterattack, you now know something about the move you chose, the way in which you performed it, the method by which it was countered, and the circumstances that may have contributed to the technique not working (how tired you were, the comparative sizes, strengths, and skills of you and your opponent, etc.). That is a lot of information. If you accept this and process the information in a purely analytical way —instead of getting upset for not succeeding with your technique and/or getting hit—then you can grow in your abilities. You may choose to drill your technique to make it faster, sharper, and better timed. You may choose to try the technique on a variety of training partners to get a sense of how different body types and skill levels react to it. You may refine the technique so that next time it will work. Or you may decide the technique is impractical and remove it from your arsenal.

You may even focus on the counterattacking move and add that to your own repertoire. A wise fighter learns as much from his opponent as he does from himself.

The bottom line is that the more experience you gain, the more your understanding of your own skills will grow. The better you understand your skills, the more confident you'll be.

COORDINATION

Physical coordination allows a person to do many things well. Martial arts training, boxing, fencing, wrestling—all of these arts enable a person to become very coordinated, to be able to do several things simultaneously and skillfully. Much of a student's training time is taken up with learning how to move seamlessly from one skill to another and even perform techniques that are downright acrobatic. Sparring pushes that envelope even further by forcing you to block, evade, shift, duck, kick, grapple, escape, slip, dodge, jump, and lunge—sometimes simultaneously. Since sparring keeps you in constant motion and demands so many things at all times, coordination grows rapidly, far more so than with the routine repetition of skills.

Sparring also teaches you to coordinate your brain and your body. Successful sparring requires the ability to think, strategize, and psych-out your opponent while at the same time utilizing blocks and counters with reflexive speed. In this way, sparring harmonizes the conscious and the subconscious minds.

ETIQUETTE

Despite all appearances, sparring is not a violent confrontation between two people. It is intended to be an exercise, a test, or a sport. To reinforce this in the minds of everyone who steps onto a mat or into a ring, there is an acknowledgement: a nod, a bow, a touching of swords or of gloves. Sometimes this is done with ancient rituals, as with Sumo; sometimes with a sober solemnity, as with traditional Karate; sometimes with a rougher and simpler acknowledgement, as in boxing. But in all cases the message is the same: "We are in this together."

The formal ritual of bowing before a match helps players remember that sparring is a game shared by equals, not a fight with an enemy.

The ways of etiquette should always be a serious and heartfelt acknowledgement of the other person's life, skills, knowledge, and basic humanity.

We may train to fight in order to learn how to survive in a potentially violent world, but when we spar we must understand that our opponent is coming from the same perspective. He's worked just as hard, sweated as much, felt the same frustrations and endured the same hardships. Because of that there should be a kinship, not an enmity. That is the nature of respect.

When you and your opponent step onto the mat, there should always be a moment where the human and humane connection is addressed. The bow should never be token, the tap of gloves should never be a mere formality. A person who shows poor etiquette has lost the match before it has even begun. No award or trophy can ever mark him as a champion.

On the other hand, a person who shows and feels the proper respect for his partner, and for himself, is a champion every day of his life.

FITNESS

Many people spar for the sole purpose of getting fit. Others simply enjoy that benefit as part of their overall martial arts training. Either way, sparring burns calories, works the cardio-vascular system, builds stamina, and tones the muscles. Sometimes the demands of in-class sparring encourage students to make sensible lifestyle changes, such as quitting smoking, changing diet, and learning about nutrition.

HONOR

Honor is one thing that really can't be taught. A teacher can explain it and can live his life in a way that teaches by example, but true honor has to be accepted by a student for it to be real.

It would take a whole book to explain the concept of honor, but the short definition is this: Honor is the commitment to the underlying values martial artists (and society) have accepted as correct, in order to give them a place of importance in our thoughts and actions, and to be faithful to them in all areas of our lives.

To be an honorable person is not just to do the right thing, nor simply to give basic moral considerations a central place in our lives. It is also the desire to be known and trusted by others—especially other honorable people —as this sort of person. And honorable people will go to great lengths to maintain these bonds of trust or to re-establish them if they are ever broken.

Honor is important in the ring because lives and health may depend on it. Bowing to your opponent demonstrates that you accept the rules and safety considerations implied in that action, and you are "honor" bound to follow those rules to the letter. Any errors

Some martial arts bow while making eye contact (left), others with the eyes averted (right).

must be made on the side of caution, compassion, and consideration for the other person's safety.

Honor is not something you put on with your uniform and belt. You carry it with you everywhere you go, 24/7. Honor is a constant; if it doesn't touch every area of your life then it isn't real.

Cheating, dirty tricks, bad-mouthing your opponent, or ignoring the rules will not only lead to injury (for one of you or both), but will destroy your honor. You can come back from a loss in a tournament, but re-establishing honor can take a lifetime.

SELF-ESTEEM

Building self-esteem is the first step toward happiness and a better life. Self-esteem increases confidence and self-worth, and allows you to respect your own wishes, realize your desires, and grow as a person. If you respect yourself you can respect others, so building self-esteem can help you improve your relationships.

Keeping a log book helps a student keep track of what he has learned and shows him just how far he has come.

Low self-esteem causes depression, unhappiness, insecurity, and poor confidence. A common side effect is inner criticism, that nagging voice of disapproval from inside that causes you to stumble at every challenge. As a result, you'll find it much harder to begin new or challenging projects, improve your skills, or win at anything (in or out of the ring).

The first step to building self-esteem is to identify your goals and then make a plan to achieve them. In martial arts training, it is not the black belt that we should strive for, but the development of a variety of skills. Once the skills are acquired, the rank will come. In sparring, it is not the trophy, belt, or certificate that should matter. What really matters is growth as a competitor, as a fighter, as a technician, and as a person.

Keeping a log book of your sparring matches is an excellent way of monitoring your progress. You can record how your skills have changed, from those first awkward matches in the dojo where you were pretty sure you were going to get your head handed to you (but which didn't actually happen), to your first trophy match, to advanced sparring contests. Looking back will show you the upward slope of your progress, and act as a great boost to the ego. Every time you complete a match—whether in school or in a national title fight—the rush from knowing that you've faced up to a challenge and weathered it is also good for the ego.

Both fighters must use focused force and controlled contact in order to avoid sparring injuries.

FOCUS

Mental focus and physical focus are of equal importance in competition.

Physical focus is the easier of the two to develop. In sparring, this includes the control in striking specific targets, the amount of power used, and the depth of penetration. Each of these varies based on the type of sparring. In point fighting you have to make limited contact without losing any stinging speed; but in a full contact match you'll need to pack every ounce of power into each blow.

And yet in both cases you have to stay away from any targets that could cause genuine harm, such as the eyes and throat. This requires practice as well as presence of mind even in the heat of battle. Therefore, mental focus is of equal importance. Mental focus is the combination of drive, strategic awareness, common sense, and good sportsmanship that allows you to better yourself and at the same time helps you to be a tough and honorable opponent.

SPEED

Speed is the most essential element of fighting. It is the difference between successful self-defense and becoming a crime statistic, the difference between blocking a sucker punch and getting dentures.

Speed is vital in sparring, for blocking and evading if nothing else, so you should do plenty of speed drills to enhance your sparring performance. Luckily, sparring itself places such a demand on your reflexes that it acts as a natural accelerator.

This is a very important point to know about sparring, and about speed. When asked to throw a punch, most people (even well-trained fighters) will often deliver the blow with only a portion of their available speed. It may take athletes a few "practice swings" to get to top speed; with beginners it seldom happens until they at least reach intermediate stage.

Believe it or not, our advanced human brains are at fault here. Animals do not need to practice in order to move instantly at top speed. Try swatting a fly or catching rabbit; they go from zero to sixty at once. On the other hand, humans have lost touch with their reflexes because our technical sophistication shelters us from having to do anything immediately at high speed. Most people have no idea what their own top speed might be, having never done anything to test or measure it. And when they try to do something fast, they exert way too much mental control over it, often concentrating on the wrong muscles, or tensing instead of relaxing; as a result the blow is often far slower than it could be.

In martial arts training we have to learn to relax and to move with reflexive speed. We must learn about momentum and impetus and snap. Animals already know this instinctively, so much of martial arts training is designed to teach our instincts to take more active control over our actions. The results are often surprising.

Since sparring involves constant surprises (you never know what your opponent is going to do), the conscious mind should not be given a chance to get in the way too much. Sparring forces you to rely on instinct and reflexes. Practice enough sparring and you'll increase overall reaction time and performance speed for every technique you perform.

Bill "Superfoot" Wallace, a champion kickboxer who epitomizes speed ...

STRENGTH

Sparring requires muscle control to deliver fast, accurate techniques to precise targets, and muscle control requires strength. Sparring is not for the weak, although a weak person may spar. This is not a contradiction; strength is relative. A fifteen-year-old girl does not have to be as strong as a twenty-five-year-old man in order to be successful. Each person's strength is measured according to his or her weight, sex, age, body type, physical limitations (if any), and overall health. It is important for each person to be as physically fit and strong as he or she can be. Sparring may be a contest, but fitness is individual.

Strength training is just as important as flexibility, speed and endurance. Training by sparring increases strength in numerous ways: leg strength not only improves kicking power but helps with evasion and power generation; abdominal strength allows for better punching, improves respiration, and protects internal organs; neck strength allows you to take a shot and also reduces headaches and tension. Most important, both leg and abdominal fitness improve posture which in turn strengthens and protects the lower and mid-back. Thus, the strength that is acquired in order to fight successfully in the ring also helps you live well while outside of it.

... and strength in the martial arts.

TIMING

Timing is vital in sparring because no technique takes place in isolation. Each move occupies a beat of time and these beats create a rhythm. Even the most apparently random clash of fighters has some rhythm that can be picked out by a discerning eye. By watching other people spar it is easy to spot these rhythms and discover how the spaces between beats and half-beats create opportunities for counterattacks. Wise fighters pay very close attention to this combative rhythm so they can better time their own techniques, decrease the number of points scored against them, and thereby increase their victories.

By studying the timing of fights, as an observer as well as a participant, you'll also learn how to find openings that were previously invisible. This not only helps you in the ring, but on the street as well.

In Capoeira, where the object is to come as close as possible without making contact, timing is critical. See Chapter 9 for more on Capoeira.

CHAPTER THREE
Preparing the Mind and Body for Sparring

3.1 PRE-TRAINING PHYSICAL EXAM

Before beginning any kind of fitness program for martial arts or competitive sports, it is vital to get a thorough physical examination from your physician. You need to know what is going on inside your body just as you need to know the condition of your muscles, bones, and tendons. Most people believe that if they feel fine, then there cannot be anything wrong with them. This is a fallacy that allows unhealthy conditions to become serious before medical treatment is obtained.

Ask the doctor to check everything, including your heart, hearing, vision, reflexes, and joints. Many martial arts schools require this level of examination, and nearly all regulated sports demand it as well.

An exam serves another purpose as well: it gives you a baseline to work with so that you can more easily measure your progress in terms of fitness, strength, speed, and flexibility.

3.2 BASIC FITNESS

Fitness training is as much an integral part of any martial art as it is a part of all competitive sports. Being a martial artist of any kind means being an athlete first. Being a competitive martial artist, whether in a major tournament or a sparring match at the dojo, requires an even higher level of athleticism.

Getting fit and staying fit is fundamental to martial arts because of the heavy demands placed on the body in both training and competition. During the drills done before a match, the body is put through extreme rigors: performing movements over and over again while increasing speed and power, twisting the torso, throwing complex combinations, leaping, falling, rolling, and countless other extreme movements.

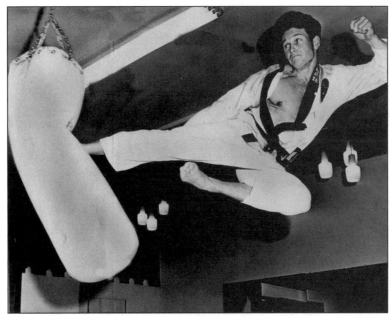

Former kickboxing world champion Joe Lewis – one of the leading advocates of sensible fitness training.

Some quick fitness rules to follow:

3.3 FIVE SAFETY TIPS FOR EVERYONE

1.   Warm up and stretch properly for activity.

2.   Wear non-restrictive clothing appropriate for a particular style of sparring.

3.   When shoes are allowed in competition -wear good shoes and avoid worn-out shoes. If you are required to train in bare feet, make sure you have had your feet checked by a doctor to evaluate your arches. People with arch problems or other foot conditions might only make them worse.

4.   Modify the intensity level of the exercises to your level of fitness.

5.   If an activity causes dizziness, stop and consult the instructor for modifications.

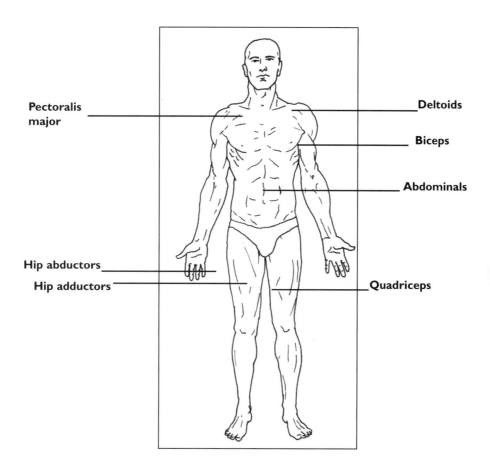

Pectoralis major

Deltoids

Biceps

Abdominals

Hip abductors

Hip adductors

Quadriceps

3.4 THE MAJOR MUSCLE GROUPS

It is very important to understand basic anatomy in order to know which parts of the body should be developed and improved. Here is a quick reference guide to the major muscles used in martial arts:

Gluteals, often referred to as 'glutes', come into play for lunging, jumping, and kicking. There are a number of gluteal muscles, including the gluteus maximus, the large muscle in the buttocks that contracts when delivering certain types of punches.

Quadriceps are the group of muscles in the front of the thigh. They are vital for kicks, jumps, and stance work.

Hamstrings are the muscles in the back of the thigh, involved in kicking, especially high kicks, and all postural movements.

Hip Abductors and Adductors are the muscles of the inner and outer thigh. The abductors are on the outside and make the leg move away from the body. The adductors are on the inside and pull the leg toward or across the centerline of the body. Naturally these muscles are vital for kicking, especially crescents, roundhouses, and jumps; but they are also used heavily during throws, especially techniques like hip sweeps, reaps, and scissors.

Calf muscles are on the back of the lower leg, and include the gastrocnemius and the soleus. The gastrocnemius is what gives the calf its strong rounded shape. The soleus is a flat muscle running under the gastrocnemius. Without well-developed calves, the ball-of-the-foot skipping movements so critical in boxing would not work.

Lower Back muscles are called erector spinae. These muscles extend the back to its proper width and help establish good posture. They give grapplers the power to lift and turn their opponents.

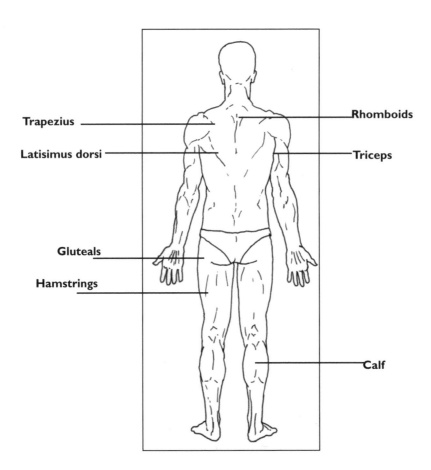

Abdominals are an important set of muscles. They include the rectus abdominus, a large flat muscle that runs the whole length of the abdomen, and the external obliques, which travel along the sides and front of the abdomen. Most punching techniques rely on the abdominals for power and to help push out breath during exertion and ki-ai. Well-developed abdominals also provide shielding for punches to the body. The rectus abdominus, if properly developed, can even withstand a punch to the xiphoid (solar plexus).

Pectoralis Major, the large fan-shaped muscle that covers the center of the upper chest, is the keystone of all punching power. Both a shield for the chest wall and a power generator, the pecs provide massive power for striking and blocking, and help grapplers generate short-range power even in the tightest clinch.

Rhomboids are small but crucial muscles in the middle of the upper back, between the shoulder blades. They help support the arms when doing any kind of full-range motions (such as blocks, punches, grabs, and throws).

Trapezius muscles, known as 'traps', form a portion of the back. The upper trapezius runs from the back of the neck to the shoulders and acts like a suspension bridge for the arms. The traps support lock-outs and bridges while grappling, help in all arm movements, and provide steady power for throws, rolls, and falls.

Latisimus Dorsi are the large v-shaped muscles of the mid-back. The "lats" provide power for lifting, pushing, and pulling, as well as blocking and striking.

Deltoids are made of three sections, or "heads": the anterior deltoid (the front), medial deltoid (the middle), and posterior deltoid (the rear). The deltoids provide the speedy power to make jabs hit like stinger missiles.

Biceps, the "apples" on the fronts of the upper arms, are the nuclear reactors of punching. They provide the main force for techniques as varied as uppercuts and fingertip flicks, and are used in every aspect of grappling and matwork.

Triceps are located on the backs of the upper arms. They help to power pushes, parries, and rolls, as well as techniques which involve bracing and resistance.

3.5 FITNESS RULES OF THUMB

Many martial artists supplement their training with membership in a gym (home or otherwise) or adherence to a regular fitness program. The following are some rules of thumb for successful fitness training.

FIND A FITNESS PARTNER

There have been hundreds of studies on fitness regimens. One point on which they all agree is that people get in shape better, faster, and safer if they have a fitness partner. Someone to keep you honest, share ideas and advice, act as a spotter, and simply "be there" for you.

START AN EXERCISE LOG OR JOURNAL

Maintaining an exercise journal is a great way to keep track of your progress. It provides ongoing motivation. Opening it and seeing how far you've come is a great boost to ego, confidence, and drive.

An exercise journal can be as simple as a notebook that records dates of workouts, sets, and reps, or a more detailed log that tracks body dimensions, increases in weights lifted, or inches of stretch. The specifics are up to you; just pick one that you'll remember to update constantly.

SCHEDULE YOUR WORKOUTS

The only way to get fit is to make exercise and fitness true priorities in your life. They must become part of a regular schedule, even if that means setting aside extra time besides that spent in martial arts classes.

THROW OUT YOUR SCALE

Fitness is about improvement and health, not about little numbers on a scale. Weight varies hour by hour and day by day, and obsessively checking the scale is a fast way to become deeply frustrated. Be patient.

DRESS FOR ACTION

Always wear clothes appropriate for exercising. Physically, it is important to allow freedom of movement. From a psychological standpoint, dressing for exercise makes you feel better, and helps you remember why

Different kinds of uniforms are needed for different martial arts. The gi may be too restrictive for kickboxing, but the simple Muay Thai shorts do not provide any protection during grappling.

you're there. There is a lot of truth in the old saying "clothes make the man."

Organized competitions generally have a dress code (gi, boxing trunks, etc.). In-class sparring is usually done in the formal uniform, but recreational sparring or out of class sparring is up to you. Some thought has to be given to what to wear in order to maximize safety and freedom of movement.

Jewelry should never be worn during any sparring. Rings, earrings, watches, and necklaces can cause injury to both partners.

Eyeglasses can be extremely dangerous and are generally not allowed in sparring. However, some tournament rules allow contestants to wear soft contact lenses.

Clothing should be in good repair. Tears or holes can catch fingers or toes. Poorly maintained clothing can tear in the middle of a match, occasionally creating an enormously embarrassing moment in the middle of an otherwise serious event.

FIGHT BOREDOM

Let's face it, exercise can be dull after a while, especially repetitious and time-consuming training like treadmills and exercise bikes. Take a Walkman to the gym (books on tape are an excellent alternative to music), read a magazine or newspaper, or switch on the TV if training at home. Expand the mind while strengthening the body.

DON'T MAKE EXCUSES

Exercise is not something you can do occasionally and still achieve maximum benefits. You have to work it into your lifestyle so that it is as regular as taking a shower, brushing your teeth, or sleeping. Unless fitness becomes a true habit, you'll likely drift away from it.

STRETCHING

Muscles come in all shapes and sizes, and each one serves a different purpose. There are muscles that lift and muscles that push, muscles that pump blood and muscles that help us breathe. Each one is unique in its structure and purpose, yet they are all basically the same at a microscopic level.

Stretching before a match can prevent injuries.

Muscle is made up of strands of tissue called fascicles, the fibrous strands you see on body charts of the muscular system. Each fascicle is composed of numerous fasciculi, bundles of muscle fibers. These muscle fibers are in turn made up of tens of thousands of thread-like myofybrils, which variously contract, relax, and lengthen. Myofybrils are in turn composed of millions of bands, called sarcomeres, laid end-to-end. Each sarcomere is made of countless overlapping filaments called myofilaments. These thick and thin myofilaments are made up of contractile proteins, primarily actin and myosin.

The stretching of a muscle fiber begins with the sarcomere, which is the basic unit of contraction in the muscle fiber. When the sarcomere contracts, the area of overlap between thick and thin myofilaments increases. As the sarcomere stretches, the area of overlap decreases, allowing the muscle fiber to elongate. When the muscle fiber is at its maximum resting length (meaning all sarcomeres are fully stretched), then any additional stretching will exert force on the surrounding connective tissue. As this tension increases, the collagen fibers in the connective tissue align themselves in the same direction as the tension. In short this means that when you stretch, the muscle fiber is pulled to its full length, sarcomere by sarcomere, until the connective tissue takes up the remaining slack. When this occurs, any disorganized fibers are realigned in the direction of the tension. This realignment is what helps rehabilitate scarred tissue back to health.

During stretching, not all muscle fibers are stretched; some remain more or less at rest. The current length of the entire muscle depends upon the number of stretched fibers.

Even though the muscles of a competitive athlete are strong and generally limber even in the morning, the precautions of safe stretching are never to be ignored. Stretching should be slow, never hurried. Athletes should stretch before training or competing and afterward as well. And ballistic stretching, such as bouncing while in a stretch, is never advised. It can create micro-tears in the muscle fiber leading to injury. The best approach to stretching is to bend slowly until you feel moderate resistance, and then hold the stretch for at least twenty seconds. Slow repetitions help increase stretch using this approach.

3.6 DRILLS

Drills are an integral part of martial arts training, but are especially important for ring fighters and competitive fighters. Drills not only build basic skills (balance, timing, speed, and power), they develop combat reflexes that are vital in the heat of a match. Ring fighting is often so fast and furious that there isn't time to work out a combination while blocking, evading, and moving. By drilling specific combinations over and over, these moves become second nature and will show up without much conscious thought.

One approach to drills is The Dozens. These are combinations designed to be practical and effective. They are drilled a dozen times each, right side then left side. Below are a few sets of drills of tried-and-true ring combinations. Drilling them repeatedly at top speed will add a lot of "oomph" to your competitive arsenal.

Naturally these combinations are suggestions and may have to be modified to suit the type of sparring you are doing. Creating your own drills is both easy and sensible, because you know what you can do best and what you need to work on most.

SET I: BASIC KICKS / NON-COMBINATION

1) Front Snap Kick – Standard and Reverse

2) Front Thrust Kick – Standard and Reverse

3) Side Snap Kick

4) Side Thrust Kick – Standard, Reverse, and Back Reverse

5) Shuffle Side Thrust Kick

6) Roundhouse Kick – Standard and Reverse

7) Jump Roundhouse Kick – Side Spring, Jump Reverse, Advancing, Retreating, then Fake and Kick

8) Leaping Side Knee

9) Jumping Front Snap – Springing and Reverse

10) Jumping Front Thrust – Springing and Reverse

11) Hook Kick – Low then High

12) Back Kick – Standard and Turning

Front snap kick drill done against handheld targets.

Roundhouse kick drill focused inches from the body.

SET 2: BASIC STRIKES / NON-COMBINATION

1) Backfist – Snap, Shuffle, and Lever

2) Jab

3) Cross

4) Reverse Punch

5) Overhand

6) Uppercut

7) Hook – Standard, Short, and Cutting

8) Cutting Palm

9) Palm Heel – Thrust, Folding, and Roundhouse

10) Forward Elbow

11) Knife Hand

12) Hammerblow

Block and counter-punch drill.

SET 3: HAND COMBINATIONS

1) Jab – Cross

2) Double Jab – Cross

3) Jab – Cross – Hook – Cross

4) Cross – Hook – Cross

5) Hook – Cross – Hook

6) Right Uppercut – Left Uppercut – Right Uppercut – Hook – Cross

7) Jab – Cross – Left Uppercut – Right Overhand

8) Jab – Hook – Cross – Left Uppercut – Cross – Double Jab

9) Rear-handed Backfist – Overhand Backfist

10) Left Uppercut – Left Hook – Right Hook – Right Backfist

11) Jab Fake – Right Cross Fake – Left Uppercut – Right Overhand

Combination: right hook ...

... into left uppercut.

12) Left Backfist – Right Overhand – Right Reverse Elbow

Crescent kick drill.

SET 4: KICK COMBINATIONS

1) Reverse Low Roundhouse – High Roundhouse

2) Reverse Low Side Thrust – High Side Thrust

3) Reverse Low Roundhouse – Spinning Back Kick

4) Side Medium Roundhouse – Spinning Roundhouse

5) Lead Leg Front Snap – Reverse High Roundhouse

6) Inside Crescent – Spinning Hook Kick

7) Side Snap – Back Reverse Side Thrust

8) Front Snap – Shuffle Front Snap – Roundhouse

9) Low Roundhouse Fake – High Outside Crescent – Low Roundhouse sweep

Side Medium Roundhouse.

SET 5: RINGFIGHTING COMBINATIONS

1) Hook Block and Grab to Punch – Hook Kick over Arm – Roundhouse Kick

2) Jab – Cross – Grab & Knee

3) Jab Fake – Back Spinning Leg Sweep

4) Grab and Knee – Leg Sweep Takedown

5) Shuffle Backfist – Jumping Wheel Kick

6) Lead Leg Front Kick to Body – Cross to Head – Left Hook to Head

Parry to set up Combination Punch Counterattack.

7) Left Jab – Left Lead Leg Side Kick – Right Cross to Head – Jumping Roundhouse to Knee

8) Double Left Jab to Face – Right Cross to Head – Hook to Body – Back Leg Roundhouse

9) Front Thrust Kick – Jab – Cross

10) Side Snap – Backfist – Cross – Side Thrust

11) Rear Side Knee – Elbow – Push – Front Kick

12) Front Thrust Kick – Palm Heel to Face – Y-Hand Strike

Side thrust against kick shield.

3.7 MEDITATION AND SPARRING

Meditation is an integral part of most martial arts systems. Slow, regular breathing, proper positioning of the body, and reduction of external stimulation do wonders to focus the mind before a match and calm the mind and body afterward.

Studies have found a direct correlation between meditation and the performance levels of sports professionals. Meditation strengthens the mind, and a controlled mind is better able to guide the body, whether preparing for a match, calming down afterward, or analyzing the match clearly and unemotionally.

**Seated (left) and kneeling (right) meditation postures.
Perfect form in meditation leads to perfect calm.**

CHAPTER FOUR
Setting The Rules

The best way to maximize a positive sparring experience is to set the rules before the first punch is thrown and then follow them to the letter. That way the risk of injuries is reduced, the risk of fouls is reduced, and the overall quality of the activity is elevated.

Obviously all competitive sparring has preset rules. But there are scores of in-school or drill-oriented sparring methods with rules that are up to you, your partner, and/or whoever is running the class that day.

Some guidelines for safe and productive sparring:

1. Sparring should only take place in the presence of an instructor or coach.

2. Appropriate protective equipment should be used for all contact-oriented sparring, and is actually recommended for all sparring.

3. Light contact is better. Skills can be tested and developed with light contact. Unless you are in a competitive match there is no reason for heavy or full contact. The idea is to share the learning experience and the fun of it, not to bash each other into rubble.

4. Scoring areas should be clearly designated before-hand.

5. A clash is not a point. If both of you land a hit at the same time, just break and start again. It's a waste of time to try to sort out who had the better hit during a clash.

6. Only righteous points score. Sloppy techniques or questionable hits should never be counted. Set a high standard and always strive for it.

Don't waste time arguing over who scored first in a clash. The object is to learn, not to win.

7. Spar in a controlled manner. Learn to focus your blows, even at high speeds. This increases safety for your partner and refines your own skills.

8. Adjust your skills to suit your partner. Sparring techniques should be adjusted to the level of the lowest ranking participant. Nothing is gained by trying that Jump Spinning Axe Kick on a white belt stepping onto the sparring mat for the first time.

9. Report injuries immediately to the exercise leader, referee, instructor, or coach.

10. Be cautious of blood. If either partner is bleeding, the match should be stopped and the blood cleaned up immediately. Once the injured person has received First Aid, a bandage must be used to cover the injury. Anyone getting blood on them should thoroughly wash it off.

11. Respect your partner. Always.

12. *Enjoy it.*

Respect your sparring partner.

CHAPTER FIVE
Sparring Categories

There are a lot of different sparring methods and each of these is grouped into three Major Categories, three Style Categories, and finally eight Method Categories.

5.1 MAJOR SPARRING CATEGORIES

1- COMPETITIVE SPARRING

These are the sparring forms, like boxing, wrestling, point-fighting and fencing that are designed and practiced specifically as matches to establish champions. Though often used for recreation, fitness, and entertainment, Competitive Sparring is a race for the trophy.

2- Drill-Based Sparring

These methods of sparring are designed for improving combative skills such as striking, kicking, balance, timing, endurance, courage, coordination, and so on. Though Competitive Sparring often accomplishes many of these same goals, Drill-Based Sparring is far more selective, often working one specific aspect, with the improvement of skill as the goal rather than a trophy or title.

3- MOCK COMBAT

These are forms of nonviolent fighting used to preserve an aspect of culture either for entertainment purposes of posterity (as with the case of jousting or swordfighting found in Renaissance Faires), or fighting that is choreographed as part of a stage show, TV program, video game, cartoon, or movie. Though these "matches" have predetermined outcomes, they are often fought at high speeds and require many of the same qualities necessary for top-ranked tournament fighting.

Photo courtesy of Pennsylvania Rennaisance Faire.

5.2 SPARRING STYLE CATEGORIES

1- STAND-UP FIGHTING

Stand-up fighting is any method of sport combat that does not permit takedowns, wrestling or grappling. Stand-up Fighting arts include Karate, Taekwondo, boxing, fencing, and most weapon arts.

Taekwondo has always been a well-known Stand-Up Fighting art.

Judo is famous for grappling techniques and throws.

Brazilian Jiu-Jitsu has become an extremely popular form of combination fighting.

2- GRAPPLING

Grappling arts are those which allow some combination of wrestling, matwork, takedowns, throws, or locks. Grappling arts include Judo, Aikido, Jujutsu, and all forms of wrestling.

3- COMBINATION FIGHTING

These are arts which begin as Stand-up fights and generally progress to the floor. These include arts like Pankration, Varmannie, Brazilian Jiu-Jitsu, and Japanese Jujutsu. Combination fighting falls into both the Sparring Style Category and the Sparring Methods Category.

5.3 SPARRING METHOD CATEGORIES

1- PRE-ARRANGED (LIMITED STEP) SPARRING

Pre-arranged sparring, also known as Limited Step sparring, is one of the oldest methods of testing skills in the martial arts. The idea is to allow a student the chance to practice a specific defense with as much realism as possible.

Many pre-arranged sparring techniques are extracts from much longer forms (kata, poomse, etc.) that a student would normally practice solo. In pre-arranged drills, the student's partner acts as an attacker, but is only to deliver a specific attack and not to counter the defense. The attacker must use as much speed, force, and accuracy as possible, so even though the defender knows what is coming, he has to defend against it as if it is real. This is not as easy as it sounds, and is an excellent way to build an understanding of individual techniques and a competence in performing those techniques.

Karate, as demonstrated by Goju-ryu master Gene Holden, utilizes a great deal of Limited Step Sparring to allows its practitioners to perfect their techniques.

In Free Sparring, anything goes (within reasonable limits).

The different levels of contact sparring include no contact (top), semi-contact (middle), and full contact (bottom).

Depending on the technique and the student's skill level, the pre-arranged spar could be a simple one-punch/one-defense response, or a more complex attack with a defense that combines various blocks, strikes, kicks, or takedowns.

2- FREE SPARRING

Free sparring is just that: a match (either formal or informal) with no pre-arranged techniques. The school's "House Rules" apply, but the purpose of free sparring is not so much competition as the exploration of one's own skills. This means discovering which techniques work and which don't, at least at the moment; experimenting with new skills; testing strategies and tactics; and trying to find a balance between conscious control and true combat reflexes.

3- SEMI-CONTACT

Semi-contact sparring is designed to be challenging but at reduced risk. Targets are selected and often awarded a point value. Light contact is allowed to the selected targets and prohibited elsewhere. Face, throat, groin, ears, and knees are often off-limits in semi-contact fighting, though this will vary from one organization or art to the next.

It is not uncommon to permit focused blows to certain areas in semi-contact sparring. This means that a blow must be stopped within a few inches of the target, such as the face, for a point to be awarded. Any contact will result in a point being taken away.

4- POINT FIGHTING

Point fighting is a popular variation on semi-contact sparring. Contact while blocking is permitted, but no punches or kicks may make contact. Points are given for fast, accurate blows that stop within the prescribed distance from the target. Points are often removed for making contact, even if accidental.

A point is awarded for a blow that could have landed but was withheld using control, but not for a blow that was thrown in such a way (badly aimed, overextended) that it would never have scored in a real fight.

Full Contact Sparring, seen here with kickboxer Benny "The Jet" Urquidez against former Japanese Champion Kunimatsu Okao, circa 1977.
Photo courtesy of Stuart Sobel.

5- FULL CONTACT

Full contact fighting has been a crowd favorite since the days of Roman circuses, though modern martial arts tournaments don't end with a thumbs-up or -down decision. Full contact allows both combatants to actually hit each other, but (quite sensibly) a large number of techniques are not allowed, and certain targets are off limits.

Even in the most extreme full-blown battle ending in a knockout, there are rules. Attacks to the groin, eyes, and throat are not allowed, nor are techniques that could break the neck or shatter bones. But even with these restrictions, full contact fighting is dangerous, exciting, and demanding. It requires years of preparation and conditioning for safe practice.

In Combination Sparring players can use a great variety of holds, locks, kicks and strikes.

6- WRESTLING

Wrestling has been around as long as there have been people. In ancient India and China, in the Greece of the Spartans and the Rome of the Legionnaires, in the Old West and the

Far East, there have been forms of grappling. Many current martial arts (such as Jujutsu, Kung Fu, Varmannie, Judo) are based on ancient wrestling arts.

There is great variety in the rules and techniques of competitive wrestling. For example, Judo uses very few of the techniques that are favored in Greco-Roman wrestling, so cross-discipline matches are rare. Most (but not all) wrestling competitions do not permit strikes and kicks.

7- COMBINATION SPARRING

There are two types of Combination Sparring. One involves matches featuring arts that do both Stand-up fighting and Grappling in the same bout; and the other is an in-class drill-based exercise that matches disparate skills together for mutual expansion of knowledge, such as matching hands-only against grappling, or feet against hands. The upshot of these drills is that the participants are forced to think outside the box, to adapt quickly, and to use their imaginations for immediate problem solving. All of these skills create stronger, faster, and sharper martial artists.

Combination Sparring: grappling versus kicking.

8- WEAPONS SPARRING

Fencing is probably the oldest method of weapons sparring still actively practiced. It exists in a remarkable variety of forms, from the slither-and-rasp of European foil fencing to the clash-and-stamp of Japanese Kendo.

There are a number of other weapons-based sparring methods, some of which are classical and competitive, others designed for developing skills in the martial arts classroom. These include sparring methods for sticks, swords, staves, whips, flails, pugil sticks, and knives.

Weapons Sparring: Chinese three section staff vs. ring.

CHAPTER SIX
Principles of Safe Sparring

Following are some tips for making sparring both safe and productive, whether in the ring or in the gym.

PROTECTING YOUR JOINTS

A well-trained martial artist or boxer can pack an amazing amount of power into a punch. Martial arts kicks can be devastating. Performed correctly, the force from each technique is channeled outward, against a heavy bag, a stack of boards, or an opponent in the ring. Performed incorrectly, however, much of that destructive force can remain internalized and injure your own body.

Elbows, wrists, ankles, and knees take the brunt of poorly delivered techniques, but these injuries can easily be prevented. The small joints (the wrist and the ankle) should be straight

Small joints, such as the wrist or ankle, should be kept straight to avoid twisting injuries.

Extreme angles during forceful kicking can cause as much injury to the kicker as to the opponent.

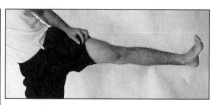

A completely straight elbow or knee can be easily damaged when delivering blows of even minimal force.

and tight on impact. The larger elbow and knee joints should never be straight at any time. A simple way to remember how to safely position these four joints is SSBB: Small and Straight, Big and Bent.

The elbow is amazingly strong when it is bent and its muscles locked. The muscles and tendons are in much better alignment to deliver force, withstand shock, and resist impact. But when the arm is completely straight the elbow breaks (at the base of the humorus) at approximately eight pounds of pressure per square inch of bone. Since the area in question is two square inches in size on average, a mere sixteen pounds of pressure can break the arm. The knee, when completely straight, is only a little stronger. Both will break much easier than a one-inch pine board. This is why locking techniques such as the Arm Bar work so well.

The wrists and ankles, on the other hand, are very fragile joints and bend easily. When the force of a punch or kick is transferred through these complex joints, the joints tend to want to bend, a movement that would result in breaks, sprains, or tears. When training for sparring matches, much care should be given to building up the muscles and tendons around the wrists and ankles so that they will stay locked and strong when hitting or kicking.

STAYING MOBILE

One of the oldest (and wisest) martial arts adages is, "The best block is to not be there." Mobility in the ring is smart and safe. It allows you to stay away from the opponent while giving you a constant source of momentum that can be used to create force. Muhammad Ali had it right when he said: "Float like a butterfly, sting like a bee."

The key to mobility is to stay on the balls of the feet, like tennis players do. This keeps the weight from settling on the heels during the match. It requires more effort to lift the body's weight once it has settled than it does to remain on the balls of the feet.

Remember to "stay on your toes" and "don't be caught flatfooted." If you stand flatfooted when you get hit, your body will not be able

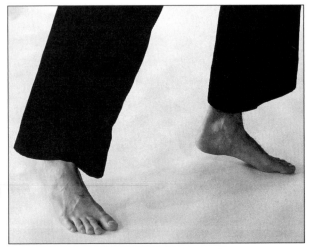

The key to mobility is staying on the balls of the feet.

to evade or roll with the punch. Every ounce of force in the incoming blow will be felt. But if you were on your toes you could duck and dodge, bob and weave, roll with a strike or absorb it, then be ready to fire off a quick and powerful counterattack.

BREATHING

Breathing is key to endurance. It cools the body, helps to exert force, and relaxes the mind and the muscles. Staying relaxed is important to achieving optimal performance in any endeavor, not only sports. Relaxation permits the integration of mind and body that is necessary for peak performance.

You can use breathing skills at all stages of sparring: before, during, and after. Breathing exercises clear the mind and relax the body prior to sparring, so you don't bring stress and tension into the ring. During a match, breathing skills help to maintain focus and keep tension from burning up energy you'll need to go the distance. After the match, proper breathing helps you cool down and return to a balanced physical state.

Proper breathing is something that should be explored with your trainers. Relaxation and breathing skills improve circulation (blood flow), which can reduce the risk of injury and allow the body to more quickly return to its normal state.

SWEATING

Sweat happens. Perspiration is a natural and essential process that regulates the body's temperature and eliminates waste products. Even during moderate exercise, heat production can be ten times greater than while at rest. When you exercise, the temperature of the blood in the brain increases, causing the body's thermostat to stimulate the millions of sweat glands into action. When sweat reaches the surface of the skin it evaporates. Evaporation cools the surface blood supply. Evaporation accounts for about 80% of heat loss during activity, compared to 20% at rest. Otherwise you'd burn up (and burn out) during a "heated" match.

It is commonly believed that people who sweat a lot are out of shape, but the opposite is true. Your sweat glands respond to exercise by growing larger, allowing them to release more water and thus cool your body more effectively. This means that as your level of fitness increases you sweat more, and more quickly. This lessens the risk of overheating.

It is important not to let sweat become a liability during a fight. A sweatband or bandana (if the rules permit) can keep stinging, blinding sweat from getting in your eyes. A dab of petroleum jelly over and under your eyes helps prevent sweat from blinding you. It is not water soluble, so sweat won't wash it away. It also acts like a sealant for minor cuts, and keeps blood from streaming from small cuts to the eyebrows (which can bleed profusely).

TAKING A HIT

Sparring is all about trying to hit one another, and unless you have reflexes like the Flash, you're going to occasionally take a hit. Getting hit isn't the same thing as losing, however. If you spar enough in class, first with body armor and later without, then you will learn how to take a punch, absorb it, roll with it, and generally deal with it. In fights of all kinds it is more often the surprise from being hit than the actual damage from the hit that causes a person to lose the fight. If a fighter is not experienced in getting hit, then the shock and surprise will jar him for a moment, making him hesitate. Hesitation opens the door for the next hit, and the next. On the other hand, a ring fighter experienced with taking hits will not be startled by one, probably not even slowed down by it, but will know to instantly respond with a counterattack.

One way of taking a hit is to absorb it, allowing the force to pass closely and the opponent to be pulled off balance.

FINGERS AND TOES

Except for fencing and boxing, toes and fingers are often exposed, and frequently injured, during sparring. In Judo matches, for example, fingers are notorious for catching in collars and sleeves. In Point fighting, toes seem to get snarled in an opponent's pants cuffs. Sprains and breaks happen all too often, and the level of pain from a sprained little toe is out of all proportion to the degree of actual damage.

Generations of ring fighters have taken to wearing little strips of tape to wrap the little fingers and little

Many fighters "buddy tape" their toes and fingers to protect them from getting bent back or caught in clothing.

toes to the next digit. This method of "buddy taping" can protect these joints, but should only be worn during a match, not during regular training. Otherwise these muscles may atrophy from disuse.

SPEED AND POWER

While it is basically true that martial arts should work as well for a small person as a large one, this does not hold true in ring fighting, especially where contact is involved. A person of one hundred and fifty pounds would find a twelve round full-contact match with a two hundred and forty pounder to be a very painful and disappointing encounter. Rules limit the number of damaging techniques in a small fighter's arsenal which could otherwise even the odds. Street fighting is, of course, different. On the street you can stamp on toes, break knees and kick groins, techniques that anyone of any size can do. Luckily, these are not allowed in the ring.

Speed is the most important element of good fighting...

This is why we don't generally mismatch people. Ring fighting is designed to match weight for weight, which means that the level of each participant's physical strength will be approximately the same. In an equal contest, the edge will come to the person who has spent the most time cultivating speed.

Speed is the most essential element of good fighting. This is true of all kinds of fighting. Power, good form, accuracy, and timing are all important, but it is quickness that generally wins a fight.

Speed drills should be done for hitting, blocking, moving, evading, trapping, and countering. Effective speed is acquired by drilling moves over and over again so that the reflexes will eventually select a technique and fire it off long before the conscious mind can even think of it.

...and can even help smaller fighters overcome larger opponents.

63

One last and very significant point: when you hit faster, your strikes and kicks will land with much greater force. These are the results of simple physics, and can turn an otherwise equal fight to your favor.

GOING THE DISTANCE

You can have the fastest kicks and the most bone-crunching punches, be able to duck any blow and hit like a Stinger missile, but if you can't go the distance you won't get much of a chance. This is especially true in point-based matches where you can't try to overwhelm and knock out an opponent in the last second before the bell.

Luckily there are a lot of good ways to build stamina: jumping rope, aerobics, high-speed drills, jogging, and swimming are a few examples. And then there's sparring.

A fighter must maintain a fitness regimen in order to keep in shape.

CHAPTER SEVEN
Sparring Theory

Fighting is a give and take; sometimes you are the aggressor and sometimes you're being assailed with a flurry of hands and feet. If you find yourself on the defensive there are some important strategies and tactics that can help you evade and counterattack.

7.1 OFFENSE

BE DIRECT

Nothing is more effective than a direct counterattack, especially if you launch it while the opponent is still launching the attack, rather than waiting until he's completed his move. Done right, this falls somewhere between a preemptive strike and a jam, allowing you to head them off at the pass and, quite often, catch the attacker off guard.

The best defense is to counterattack before the opponent's strike can land.

TAKE A CHANCE

Unless the world championship is at stake, sometimes it's good to try out new things and see what happens. Next time someone plows into you using the kind of technique you usually get nailed by, try something totally different and radical (but within the rules!). You might discover a new tactic that can turn a lost point into a counterattacking win.

LOOK FOR OPENINGS

Remember that the same arms that are throwing punches at you are what the opponent would normally use to defend against your attacks. That means that in order to attack, an opening must be created. This leaves a hole for a counterattack. Be ready for it and move!

An attack will frequently create an opening for a counterattack. Here, once the attacker has swung the club, the defender must be ready to jump into the opening made by the swing.

CHARGE A KICKER

For the most part, kicks are long-range attacks, so block the kick and get close. By getting in close, you avoid much of the power from the kick, which had been intended to connect with full power at a greater distance from the attacker. The kick itself leaves the attacker with some natural vulnerabilities: open targets and questionable balance. Once you are inside the attacker's guard, the attacker may still be balanced on one foot and therefore find it difficult to evade.

Charge a kicker before he can regain his balance.

JAM IT

When in doubt, or if you're not ready to launch a good counter, then just plow forward whenever your opponent attacks. Going to short range spoils most attacks and allows you to disrupt his balance and set up a flurry of incoming hits.

CIRCLE BEATS A LINE

Don't try to oppose force with force, even when jamming. Turning around an attack works as an evasion. Turning is also a method of creating power through torsion, using hip to add force to a block or counter strike.

LINE CUTS A CIRCLE

When faced with a circular attack such as a spinning kick, drive straight in and slam body to body against the attacker. Your balance will be far greater in that situation, so your mass in motion should easily be able to upset his mass, which will be posted on a single rotating leg. Furthermore, a spinning kick is a fairly long-range technique, so a straight line, close-body counter brings you well inside the arc of attack and therefore out of reach of the foot.

Using circular techniques against a head-on attack is easier than meeting force with force. Here, the defender simply evades a straight punch by stepping around the attack.

ALWAYS ATTACK

Even though counterfighting is a great strategy, the best defense is often a strong offense, especially in the ring. If you spend too much time waiting for the opponent to give you an opening, you might find that the clock is working against you and you're down by points because you haven't taken the initiative. So if your opponent doesn't give you a break, just go for it.

Conversely, a circular attack, such as a round kick, should be charged head-on before the attack can make contact. This also gives the defender a wide open target.

To win a fight you have to think like a winner, and that means thinking like an attacker. In the animal world, the tiger is the ultimate predator. He does not worry about defense; he just attacks with total ferocity. If there were tigers in Africa there would be a new king of beasts (lions, by the way, sit back and let the lionesses do the hunting). Tigers - male and female - just go for it.

Consider this: if you are solely counterfighting, then all the attacker has to do is concentrate on his attacks. But if you take the initiative, your opponent has to divide his time between thinking up fighting strategies and analyzing your attacks. That limits his thinking and his overall fighting abilities.

The attacker sets the pace and controls the fight. Do that. Set a pace that works toward your end (victory) and control the fight so that you maximize your points and force the opponent to be purely defensive.

Understand that this doesn't mean you toss out all of the advice on counterfighting; you keep those tactics in reserve. If you develop aggressive and counterattacking skills equally, then the other guy is going to think he stepped into a ring with, well … a tiger.

7.2 DEFENSE

USE YOUR ELBOWS

These are big knots of bone that often come in handy. Nothing is better for saving your ribs than keeping your elbows close to your ribcage. Also, a few hook punches into defending elbows can make your opponent pull back some throbbing fists, and be a little less willing to throw the next shot.

A shot from an elbow will not only help to block a strike, but cause pain and possible injury.

PROTECT YOUR FACE

Don't pull a Rocky Balboa and try to block every punch with your face. Head shots do damage every time, and a lot of them will do a lot of damage, some of which can be permanent. Head shots also limit reaction time, cause pain, create distraction, and can disorient you. Use evasions as a first line of defense, then back this up with slap parries and forearm blocks. In direst need, use a bridge block: place your clenched fists against your skull and take the shots on your forearms, upper arms and elbows.

When using a bridge block, keep the hands against your head. Otherwise you may wind up getting hit and then hitting yourself.

TUCK YOUR CHIN

Ideally you should evade or parry a punch, but if someone smokes a hook into your open side, keeping your chin and shoulder together allows you to stop that punch with a mass of muscle rather than just your jaw. There is no sense in getting your chimes rung when your beefy shoulder can take the hit without much effort. Watch professional boxers very closely and you'll see the way they use their shoulders. Fewer hits actually connect with their faces than might first appear.

Fistfighters keep their chins tucked to protect the jaw.

KEEP YOUR REAR HAND UP

If a strike comes from your outside you can easily bend and roll under it. However, if it comes to your open side you are probably going to have to block. You'll want that rear hand up to protect your throat and face in case your block is not successful, or to use it as a quick follow-up technique so it takes less time to counterattack.

Never drop your hands or you leave a wide open target for a follow-up strike.

The hand that is not being used should be ready to throw up a block in a split second.

DEVELOP A SET OF RELIABLE COUNTERS

Select a number of practical, energy-efficient counterattacks and drill them until you can do them without thinking. But remember: the only way for skills to work with reflexive speed is to drill, drill, drill. And then drill some more.

NEVER RETREAT IN A LINE

Backing up in a straight line against a driving attack will do nothing more than get you hit or run you out of room to move. It also allows the attacker the greatest amount of balance, control and comfort when charging, because he does not have to make any changes in his posture or his choice of attack. Go left or right, spin away, rush forward, duck and dodge, leap to one side … do whatever it takes to evade the freight train power of a linear attack.

BE AWARE OF FOOTWORK

The way in which your opponent moves will often tip you off to what he's about to do. A rear cross-step, for example, often signals a side kick. A quick ball-of-the-foot inward pivot suggests a roundkick. Watch how your opponent moves during the early part of the fight and when you see footwork patterns repeated, launch your counterattack just as he makes his approach. Jam him or hit him during a step, while his weight is not set.

A rear cross-step …

… often signals a side kick.

DRILL YOUR DEFENSES

As important as it is to drill your attacks, it is equally vital to drill your defensive moves. Evasions, parries, covering techniques, traps, and slips should all be drilled until they are automatic.

A quick ball of the foot
inward pivot …

… suggests a round kick
will follow.

7.3 MOVEMENT

STAY ON THE BALLS OF YOUR FEET

Never stand flat-footed with your knees straight. That's just asking for a knock-out punch. Anyone with a fast punch can tag you before you can move away. The arm travels so fast that the effort of lifting weight and stepping out of range will not be possible in the available time. Standing poised on the balls of the feet, however, allows one to dodge and evade with much greater ease and effectiveness.

MOVE LIKE YOU ARE ON SPRINGS

Keep your knees bent and your leg muscles coiled like springs. This allows you to move in any direction immediately.

PRACTICE TIMING

Timing is crucial. If you evade or slip too soon all you will accomplish is having your opponent track you and hit you while you move, like a hunter leading its prey with a shotgun. If you evade too late you get nailed. Timing takes practice: drill it in the gym, don't try to pick it up in the ring.

7.4 MENTAL ASPECTS OF SPARRING

PUT ON YOUR GAME FACE

Fighting is not just a physical game but a head game as well. Much strategy is dedicated to psyching out an

Stay light on your feet, then be ready to move in as soon as an opening is made. Don't delay your counterattack or the opponent can reset himself.

opponent. Flicking your eyes at an obvious target and then faking a shot toward it can trick the opponent into covering up or blocking; then if you check your attack and change up you can hit a different target. You can also use facial expressions to intimidate or to lure an opponent into a trap. Looking injured, uncertain, or scared can spur an opponent into a rush if he thinks he has you at a disadvantage. A fierce face can sometimes stall someone who may be looking for the right moment to attack. For the most part you want to maintain a neutral expression, varying it to suit the moment. This is often called a "game face," and it works.

A savvy fighter can psych out his opponent.

KEEP HIM IN YOUR SIGHTS

You don't have to make direct eye contact (unless you are good at using eye-flicks and trick glances to psych out an opponent), but you should always be looking at some part of him. Some fighters like to focus on a point midway between the shoulders, or at the center of a box formed by the two shoulders and the hips. Whatever works for you is fine, but if you take your eyes off your opponent, he will hit you. Look at him and you'll likely see any move coming and have time to block. When doing a lot of moving, such as with jumps and spin kicks, make sure you use your peripheral vision to check for his feet and hands, to observe the shift and cant of his hips, and to see his shoulders move. All of these clues indicate an attacking movement. The smartest fighters make a visual box of the shoulders and hips and stare at that. In this way all punches and kicks will be seen as they are launched instead of when they are ready to hit.

EYES: The opponent's eyes can help you and hurt you. An inexperienced fighter will often look where he is about to hit, which tips you off; but a wise fighter will use that as a trick, pretending to look at a target and luring you into an attack that he'll counter. Also, some fighters know how to project an intimidating amount of intensity through their eyes. Most good fighters know better than to make too much eye contact during a fight.

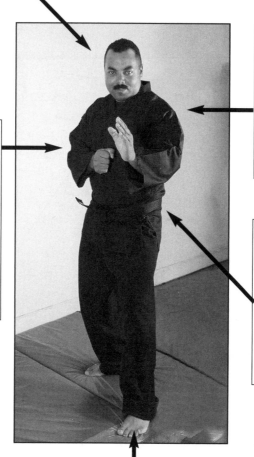

SHOULDERS: The shoulders are suspension systems—the muscles have to contract in order to lift the arms. Watching a fighter's shoulders is one of the most reliable ways to see a strike coming when it is still far away.

HANDS: Watching a fighter's hands is often a bad idea. By the time they are moving the blow is often already well on its way. Watch the shoulders instead. When blocking, move to intercept the arm, not that hand, so that the blow will be stopped short of completion.

HIPS: In kicking arts the hip tilts before a leg is lifted and the kick thrown. This makes a nice early warning system. Also, in grappling, the hips often tilt forward when a player is about to rush forward for a tackle. Watch for it and use it against him!

FEET: Footwork should be a constant, so the opponent's feet will often be in motion. Watching the feet is as distracting as watching the hands, because they can be used to deceive by "fancy footwork." By the time a foot is seen moving, the kick is already on its way. Watching the hips is smarter.

NEVER SHOW FEAR

Unless you're doing it as a trick (as described above) you should never show fear in a fight, either in the ring or on the street. Fear appeals to the predator lurking in every human heart and can incite a vicious onslaught. You have to be careful even when intentionally using this as a tactic because sometimes the face you wear can inspire a sympathetic physical reaction in your own body and mind. There is a strong biochemical link between attitude and actual mood. Frown too much and your mood drops; throw on a silly grin and your mood lifts. So when in doubt keep that game face on. If you look relaxed and confident it will make your opponent less relaxed and less confident.

KEEP IT SIMPLE

Don't waste time and energy trying to impress the crowd with your most clever moves. Do whatever you need to do to win the fight with the least possible effort and in the shortest possible time. Like the old boxing adage says, "Just win it and go home."

Simplicity is vital, especially in self-defense sparring where no movement can ever be wasted.

CHAPTER EIGHT
Types of Fighters

There are many different approaches to fighting, different styles that people either naturally adopt as an instinctive expression of their skills and mental attitude, or intentionally adopt as fighting strategies. It is important to know what kind of fighter you are. Knowing your fighting style lets you accurately assess your own strengths and weaknesses. Once you do that, you can start analyzing other fighters and gain useful insights into their strategies.

The most common fighting styles are Slugger, Blitzer, Counterfighter, Road Runner, Sharpshooter, and Change-up Fighter.

8.1 SLUGGER

Sluggers are tough, resistant fighters who are willing to stand their ground and trade blows shot-for-shot with their opponents. They rely on their own ability to take a hit in order to wear the other guy down. Sluggers are often physically very strong, as they would need to be in order to endure the punishment needed to win a pounding match.

Sluggers rarely use complex or fancy moves, preferring simpler and more direct power shots, like hook punches and uppercuts, or front kicks and knee thrusts. Sluggers are usually good in-fighters and, rules allowing, will use every part of the body to hammer away at their opponent's elbows, forearms, fists, hips, head, shins, and knees. During grappling matches, Sluggers like to quickly grab,

The Slugger relies on pure power.

then use a simple turn-and-drop to get the opponent down on the floor as fast as possible, and then promptly mount the opponent for a muscle-powered pin or (in percussive grappling matches) a barrage of short, hard hits.

8.2 BLITZER

Blitz is the German word for lightning and that pretty accurately describes how Blitzers fight. From the instant the match begins they charge in, all guns firing, throwing everything they have at their opponents. Blitzers love winning a fight right off. None of the typical sparring and pawing back and forth to get to know their opponents: the Blitzers just want to win now.

The Blitzer (left) attacks as quickly and as directly as possible, hoping to overwhelm his opponent.

There are pros and cons to that attitude. The upside is that if the Blitzer is deeply trained, highly conditioned and has worked his drills so that punches and kicks are going to fire off without thinking but with great efficiency, then they have a chance at winning right at the outset. In fact, many fighting styles praise the immediate win, citing it as true proof of who would have won the fight if it had been a real battle. Opinions vary on the subject, but a lot of Blitzers have won a lot of fights.

On the other hand…. If the Blitzer either overestimates his own skills or just comes mindlessly barreling in, he is opening himself up to a hard dose of reality. Many martial arts stress how to turn an opponent's weight and momentum against him. An unwary Blitzer can find himself suddenly part of a demonstration of passive resistance.

8.3 COUNTERFIGHTER

Counterfighters are observant fighters who wait for the right moment, then launch their attacks with speed and directness. Rarely aggressive, the Counterfighter by his nature waits for the opponent to make his move and then blocks and counters, or attacks the inevitable opening left whenever anyone launches an attack.

The best Counterfighters are very observant: they read their opponent's body language to look for physical triggers, such as a hip shift before a kick or a postural change before a specific kind of rush. Counterfighters look for opponents to telegraph their moves, and watch for any kind of pattern. Few people can fight without falling into some kind of rhythm, so a Counterfighter looks for repeated techniques or repeated combinations, and then attacks just as the opponent makes his move.

The weakest kind of Counterfighter is the counter-puncher. This is a very defensive fighter who strikes back only after blocking or evading, instead of looking for an opening and attacking. Blitzers generally overwhelm counter-punchers.

The grappling Counterfighter is a fearsome opponent who will coax his partner into totally committing his weight and momentum, and then just twist and steer, taking command of the movement and slamming his opponent down hard.

The Counterfighter waits for the opponent to attack first, looking for an opening.

8.4 ROAD RUNNER

Road Runners are timid fighters who generally would rather flee than fight. In matches they are usually very good at slips and evades, but seldom counterattack with more than token resistance. They often avoid confrontation by matching their opponent's movements, step for step: as the attacker moves in, they move back. It is like trying to fight your own reflection.

The Road Runner (on the left) would rather stay out of the way than take the initiative and go for an opening.

Road Runners tend to be of slighter build, and they rely on their inferior weight or size to help them move out of range in the blink of an eye.

8.5 SHARPSHOOTER

Sharpshooters fall somewhere between the Road Runners and the Counterfighters. Like the Road Runner, the Sharpshooter tends to avoid contact, evading or slipping his opponent's attacks; but unlike the Road Runner, the Sharpshooter likes to hit back. Rarely using combination hits, but often with great speed

77

and accuracy, the Sharpshooter dodges, dodges, dodges —and then snaps off a shot.

Sharpshooters like to tease their opponents, sometimes coercing them into unwise attacks so they can dart into an opening and hit.

8.6 CHANGE-UP FIGHTER

The most difficult fighter to defeat is the one who understands all other styles and can switch from one role to another throughout the fight. One minute Blitzing to confuse the opponent, the next a Road Runner avoiding a counter-attack, then a Sharpshooter moving in for the kill.

Change-up fighters pay attention to other fighters, not just the ones they are fighting. They watch how different people spar, and they learn. When it is their turn to fight, they adapt to each situation rather than using just one predictable style.

A Sharpshooter waits patiently for a perfect opening before he strikes.

The Change-up fighter is the ideal fighter. This is what a serious study of martial arts should instill in a person: a great variety of skills and the judgment to know when to use, and how to choose, the right techniques.

The Change-Up Fighter uses any techniques necessary to fit his (or her) opponent.

PART TWO
Organized Competition Sparring

Professor Ronald Duncan (left).

Part II of Ultimate Sparring deals with the many and varied practices of sparring around the world. There are sparring methods for every person and for every purpose. There are sparring methods for major international competitions such as Boxing, Olympic Wrestling, Kickboxing, Judo, and Pankration. There are sparring methods designed to teach down and dirty self-defense and others designed purely for fun. There are sparring methods that have become extinct except for ancient historical records, like Egyptian Stick Fencing, and others that have been brought out of obscurity into a new acceptance, like Scottish Backhold Wrestling. There are even sparring methods for show and entertainment like Tournament Jousting and theatrical stage fighting.

In short, there is a sparring method for every taste and talent, every need and desire. So get ready to climb into the ring!

CHAPTER NINE
Sparring Methods of the Percussion Arts

9.1 BOXING

GREEK BOXING

Boxing has been an important sport in Greece since the Olympic Games of 668 B.C.E. It was one of three combative sports demonstrated in the Olympics, the other two being wrestling and Pankration.

Nowadays boxing can sometimes be a brutal sport, but back then it was far more dangerous. Neither wrestling, grappling, kicking, nor biting were allowed, but fierce blows of the hand were used and the contest ended only when one of the contestants admitted he was beaten. Death was not uncommon, although it was forbidden to kill an adversary and would result in a loss for the surviving boxer.

Greek boxers did not wear padded gloves like modern boxers. They wrapped their hands with leather

Diagoras of Rhodes was the champion boxer of the 79th Olympiad, which was held in 464 B.C.E. (Photograph by Maria Daniels, courtesy of The University of Pennsylvania Museum of Archaeology and Anthropology).

strapping. This was first used as a method of protecting the knuckles from damage, but as time went on the boxers began using thicker and stiffer leather that turned the protective padding into fierce weapons.

Boxing skills gave a man a certain stature in Greek culture, and boxers were celebrated in song and verse. The famous Greek poet, Pindar wrote about Diagoras of Rhodes, a boxer he felt embodied every quality of the noble ancient athlete. Other celebrated heroes of Greek boxing were Theagenes of Thasos, Glaukos of Karystos, Melankomas of Karia and, according to legend, Hercules.

BAREKNUCKLE BOXING

In one form or another, boxing has existed since the days of ancient Greece. But boxing as we know it today was developed in England, with significant refinements beginning in the early Eighteenth Century. In those days, boxing gloves were used only for practice and sparring, and real contests were fought with unprotected hands, hence the nickname "bareknuckle" boxing. Boxing in those days also permitted grappling and wrestling as well as hitting.

One of the greatest Eighteenth Century boxers was John "Jack" Broughton, who was England's champion from 1729 to 1750. Broughton was the pupil of James Figg, who is regarded as the first heavyweight champion in the sport's history. A boxer at fairs and on feast day celebrations, Broughton quickly earned a reputation as a man who could not be beat. He was a sophisticated fighter, understanding the rules of movement and timing as well as carrying a great deal of brawn and the speed to make his hands a deadly blur. He won the championship title in 1738. In 1741, during his first championship match, he accidentally killed his opponent. This eventually led to the creation of the first official set of rules for boxing. After retiring from active competition he went on to teach boxing at his own arena, known as Broughton's Amphitheatre. The gym was opened in March 1743, at which time Broughton introduced his rules of boxing.

JACK BROUGHTON'S ORIGINAL BOXING RULES

1) That a square of a yard be chalked in the middle of the stage, and on every fresh set-to after a fall, or being parted from the rails, each Second is to bring his Man to the side of the square, and place him opposite to the other, and till they are fairly set-to at the Lines, it shall not be lawful for one to strike at the other.

2) That, in order to prevent any Disputes, the time a Man lies after a fall, if the Second does not bring his Man to the side of the square, within the space of half a minute, he shall be deemed a beaten Man.

Bareknuckle boxing.

3) That in every main Battle, no person whatever shall be upon the Stage, except the Principals and their Seconds, the same rule to be observed in bye-battles, except that in the latter, Mr. Broughton is allowed to be upon the Stage to keep decorum, and to assist Gentlemen in getting to their places, provided always he does not interfere in the Battle; and whoever pretends to infringe these Rules to be turned immediately out of the house. Every body is to quit the Stage as soon as the Champions are stripped, before the set-to.

4) That no Champion be deemed beaten, unless he fails coming up to the line in the limited time, or that his own Second declares him beaten. No Second is to be allowed to ask his man's Adversary any questions, or advise him to give out.

5) That in bye-battles, the winning man to have two-thirds of the Money given, which shall be publicly divided upon the Stage, notwithstanding any private agreements to the contrary.

6) That to prevent Disputes, in every main Battle the Principals shall, on coming on the Stage, choose from among the gentlemen present two Umpires, who shall absolutely decide all Disputes that may arise about the Battle; and if the two Umpires cannot agree, the said Umpires to choose a third, who is to determine it.

7) That no person is to hit his Adversary when he is down, or seize him by the ham,* the breeches, or any part below the waist: a man on his knees is to be reckoned down.

Marquis of Queensbury Boxing Rules

In 1866 England, the Marquis of Queensbury, a prominent figure in British sporting circles, developed a new set of rules for boxing that eventually supplanted Broughton's. Notably, he

---

* "Ham" was slang for buttock.

introduced gloves to professional fighting, where they had previously been used only for practicing. Likewise he removed all grappling and wrestling from the sport. The Marquis also structured matches so that they were fought in three minute rounds, with one minute rests in between, and allowed for a specific period of time to recover from a knockdown (the basis for the standing eight count used today used to determine if a player is capable of fighting; as opposed to the ten count that counts him out if he cannot rise at all).

John L. Sullivan (left), one of the greatest of the Bareknuckle boxers of the late Nineteenth Century.

There was a fair amount of resistance to these changes because they made the sport far more civilized and less overtly violent. Blood and violence were a big draw; but in time the new rules allowed fighters to have longer and healthier fighting careers and thereby generate larger followings. This also allowed for a better system of gambling, and when money began to flow in greater quantities the grumblings went away.

The rules for boxing as written by the Marquis of Queensbury are as follows:

Governing Contests for Endurance (1865):

1) To be a fair stand-up boxing match in a 24-foot ring, or as near that size as practicable.

2) No wrestling or hugging allowed.

3) The rounds to be of three minutes' duration, and one minute's time between rounds.

4) If either man falls through weakness or otherwise, he must get up unassisted, 10 seconds to be allowed him to do so, the other man meanwhile to return to his corner, and when the fallen man is on his legs the round is to be resumed and continued until the three minutes have expired. If one man fails to come to the scratch in the 10 seconds allowed, it shall be in the power of the referee to give his award in favour of the other man.

5) A man hanging on the ropes in a helpless state, with his toes off the ground, shall be considered down.

6) No seconds or any other person to be allowed in the ring during the rounds.

7) Should the contest be stopped by any unavoidable interference, the referee to

name the time and place as soon as possible for finishing the contest; so that the match must be won and lost, unless the backers of both men agree to draw the stakes.

8) The gloves to be fair-sized boxing gloves of the best quality and new.

9) Should a glove burst, or come off, it must be replaced to the referee's satisfaction.

10) A man on one knee is considered down and if struck is entitled to the stakes.

11) No shoes or boots with springs allowed.

12) The contest in all other respects to be governed by revised rules of the London Prize Ring.

AMATEUR BOXING

In 1880, the Amateur Boxing Association (ABA) was founded, bringing non-professionals into the sport for the first time. Eight years later the Amateur Athletics Union (AAU) was founded and since then annual national championships among amateurs have been conducted.

A few decades later (in 1926) the Chicago Tribune paper created the "Golden Gloves" amateur competitions, instituting a new level of national championships. Along with the AAU, rules for the safest possible practice of the sport were put into action and this drew boys and men from every quarter and income level.

Amateur boxing spread like wildfire, flaring up in nearly every country. International tournaments were created to organize matches between fighters from all over the globe. International boxing games are now conducted as part of the Olympic Games, European Games, Commonwealth Games, Pan-American Games, All-African Championships, World Military Games, and many others.

Amateur boxing has earned a solid reputation as a tough sport...

... and a fair game.

In 1978, the United States passed a law forbidding the AAU to control more than one Olympic sport. This resulted in the creation of the USA Amateur Boxing Federation (USA/ABF) establishment, which now controls all of American amateur boxing.

PROFESSIONAL BOXING

Professional boxing is a multinational, multi-billion-dollar sport. Past champions like Muhammad Ali, Sugar Ray Leonard, and Joe Frazier have become cultural icons.

BASIC RULES OF PLAY

Boxers are matched in weight classes.

Boxing rounds are three minutes in length.

Before a match begins, the referee must check that both boxers are properly attired and the ring is clear of obstructions.

A round begins when the bell sounds. During the match the boxers attempt to score points by landing good hits on their opponent.

A hit is deemed to be good if it lands on the target area with force and is a clean shot undiminished by a block, deflection, or evasion.

A point is gained whenever a hit connects if three or more of the five judges press the proper button on their computer score pads within one second of each other.

At the end of the bout the boxer with the most points is declared the winner.

If both boxers have an equal score at the end of the bout, the computer performs a recalculation of the judges' individual scores, dropping the highest and lowest scores.

Boxing is a popular international sport. On the left is Fitz "The Whip" Vanderpool, Trinidad-born Canadian and former Canadian Professional Welterweight Champion. On the right is Kostya Tszu, Russian-born former World Super Lightweight Champion. This picture was taken in Australia where Fitz was helping Yszu prepare for a fight held in Texas.

If the score is still even the judges will be asked to press the red or blue button (designating the different fighters) on their computer score pads.

The criteria they use to decide the winner are:

1. Leading off

2. Style

3. Defense.

KNOCKOUTS

Boxing is fought either to points, counted by rounds, or to a knockout.

A boxer is considered to have been "knocked down" if any part of his body, aside from his feet, hits the canvas.

If a fighter is knocked down and can't get up before the count of 10, the fight is over.

If a boxer gets up from a knockdown, he has to be given an eight-count by the referee.

If the referee feels the boxer hasn't been hurt badly the fight continues.

A boxer can also be considered "down" even if he has not fallen and is not lying on the ropes. This usually happens after a boxer has been dazed from a strong punch, or punches, to the head. The referee can give the boxer a standing eight-count to see if he's fit enough to continue. A boxer is also considered "down" if he is in such a distressed state that he cannot, in the opinion of the referee, continue the bout.

If a boxer takes three eight-counts in a round or four in a bout, the referee must stop the bout.

If a coach thinks his fighter is taking too much punishment he can stop the match by throwing a towel in the ring.

If a competitor is cut, the referee can check with a ringside physician to see if the fight should continue. The doctor can stop the bout at any time.

If deemed unfit to continue, the referee ends the match and the other player wins by a Technical Knockout (TKO)

If the referee calls for the advice of the ringside doctor he must then take the doctor's advice if the doctor says stop. He will give the decision as RSC (Referee stopped contest).

A match is also ended if a player is knocked unconscious.

FOULS

If a boxer commits a foul, he is given a caution. If he gets two cautions for the same offence he will get a warning, which could lead to a point deduction. Three warnings mean disqualification. Fouls in boxing include:

Hitting below the belt.

Kicking.

Holding.

Hitting with an elbow.

Hitting with any part of the glove other than the knuckles., including using an open glove (slap), the inside of the glove (heel of palm), or the edge of the glove (chop or thumb jab).

Hitting on the back of the head or body.

Ignoring the referee's instruction to break.

Using offensive language.

9.2 CAPOEIRA

Only feet, hands, and head can make contact with the floor.

A Brazilian martial art of West African descent, Capoeira (pronounced ka-poo-e-da; the tongue rolls on the last syllable to create a "d" sound) has a rich and fascinating history. Slaves brought from Angola taught their native fighting skills to other slaves, but disguised the combative movements as dance and gymnastic techniques that were even used to "entertain" the slave masters.* Eventually, in the 1850s, the slaves rose up in violent revolt and gave the slavers a different demonstration of Capoeira's uses.

---

* Capoeira skills demonstrated by Mestre Doutor (Adenilson Jose dos Santos), Zen One (Ron Wood), and the students of the Associação Santista de Capoeira Areia Branca (ASCAB).

Capoeira techniques are characterized by dynamic leaps, jumps, cartwheels, and tumbles. It is still practiced in dancelike forms.

Capoeira is often referred to as a *jôgo*, or game, and has a wonderful sense of fun and play to it. It is also a powerful and effective fighting system useful in self-defense. However, in Capoeira classes, or in competition, the jôgo de Capoeira is the primary source of play and practice for the students.

There are three main styles of this art:

The Capoeira "roda" is exciting to watch and physically demanding to perform.

Capoeira Angola: a traditional form emphasizing individuality and learned by emulation. This is closely linked to the African-Brazilian religion of Candomble.

Capoeira Regional: a form with a heavy emphasis on dancelike movement sequences. It uses standardized curricula and is used primarily for self-defense.

Capoeira Atual: a relatively new style which attempts to merge the other two styles.

THE CAPOEIRA RODA

A *roda* (pronounced "ho-da") is a circle formed by all of the players in the class. The combat game is played within the circle while the members of the roda clap in time to the music (usually performed live by class members) and sing traditional Capoeira songs. The Capoeiristas take turns playing three instruments particular to the art: the berimbau, the pandeiro, and the atabaque.

The players grip hands before they begin, demonstrating their comeraderie.

Two players mutually agree when they are ready to begin. They meet at the opening of the roda, grip hands, and then enter into the circle, usually by means of a cartwheel or similar turn. The players spin and kick and jump and dodge, but attempt to avoid making contact. During the match players are allowed to touch the ground only with their hands, head and feet.

No contact is made during the match, except where necessary to restore balance, or a light touch here or there. For much of the play the Capoeristas are not trying to win but to have fun, sometimes lapsing into demonstrations of gymnastic ability (called *floreios*) that are a thrill to behold.

The participants yield to blows by rolling with them or under them, or leaping or cartwheeling away just at the point where it seems a blow must land. The play continues until someone wins, then the players embrace and step out as the next pair comes in. In some cases a third player may "buy a game," entering the circle by cutting in on another player with a ritual called "*comprar de jôgo.*"

**Players often experiment
with new moves...**

**...but eventually engage in a serious
combative competition.**

RULES OF THE GAME

Only hands, feet and head may make contact with the floor. If one or both players fall to the ground, the game is restarted.

Only two players at a time can enter the *roda* (circle).

Strikes to the groin area and rear are not valid, even if contact has not been made. Strikes to these areas are considered dishonorable.

Players enter the roda at a point near the berimbau, which is the lead instrument being played.

The playing of the berimbau controls the game. When this instrument begins to play, players may enter the roda. When it stops playing, the other instruments stop, as does all physical play in the roda.

The participants fight until one has scored a point. Because contact is supposed to be avoided, a point is scored when one player delivers a blow that the other could not have evaded.

9.3 KARATE

Kickboxing exists in a great variety of forms around the world, some steeped in ancient tradition, some maintaining a fierce non-traditionalism, and hundreds of variations in between. The oldest form of kickboxing is Muay Thai, which originated as a battlefield art in Siam (now Thailand) and is now practiced worldwide as one of the roughest but most respected ring sports.

In the Twentieth Century, with Karate spreading around the world and arts like Taekwondo and Kenpo flourishing, students of many disciplines began seeking ways to test their skills in hard-core matches. Many of these fighters did not want to go the route of light contact or no contact sparring methods such as Point Fighting, but it was clear to the masters of the various arts and the promoters of fighting tournaments that Karate-type techniques could not be used in a ring for sport. Borrowing elements from Muay Thai and professional boxing, these men developed a new and modern form of contest: Full Contact Karate, also known as Professional Karate and Full Contact Kickboxing.

It was decided, for the sake of safety as well as entertainment value, that kicks would only be allowed above the waist. This saved a lot of knees from early retirement, and also gave the art more of a dynamic look - something appealing to the back row of a stadium as well as people ringside. Competitors took to wearing gloves designed to allow knuckle punches and some open handed blows, like the ridge hand. Foam-padded boots were designed to allow the bare soles of the players' feet to make contact with the mat while still providing padding for the instep and ankle.

The first International Championship for this sport was held in Los Angeles in 1974. Many leading Karate (In this regard "Karate" is used as a general term to include the various percussion-based disciplines that are structured similarly to Karate, such as Taekwondo, Kenpo, etc.) masters came out in open support of Full Contact fighting, and soon the sport had its first crop of top level champions such as Joe Lewis, Bill Wallace, and Jeff Smith, all of whom have become legends in the martial arts field.

Various national and international organizations were founded to help promote Full Contact sparring, including the PKA (Professional Karate Association), WKA (World Kickboxing Association), ISKA (International Sports Kickboxing Association), each cultivating a fine crop of champions and each contributing to the growth of the sport to the point that it eventually gained worldwide respect.

FULL CONTACT KARATE RULES

Full contact matches are fought in a 17-foot-square ring bordered with ropes, similar to a boxing ring. The fighters wear colorful karate pants or Thai boxing shorts, with foam gloves and boots. Groin cups are required for all male competitors.

Amateur matches are fought in two-minute rounds, with an entire bout lasting a maximum of five rounds.

Top amateur welterweight kickboxer Daryl "Nitro" Croker commanding the ring in a bout from the early 1980s. (Photos by John J. Hyland III).

Regional and state title bouts for professional fighters are set for eight two-minute rounds. National title matches last ten two-minute rounds and world title matches last twelve two-minute rounds.

In Professional Kickboxing competition there is a minimum kick requirement of eight kicks per round.

ALLOWED TECHNIQUES

Punches only with the knuckle part of the glove; no hammer blows, palm heels, etc.

Some tournaments allow open-handed blows such as the knife-hand and ridge-hand, while others strictly forbid them.

Kicks using the ball of the foot, instep, heel, side of the foot, or the shin from below the knee to the instep.

Kicks to the inside or outside of the leg, excluding the knee.

Sweeps to the inside or outside of the leg, excluding the knee.

Former professional kickboxing World Champion Roy Kleckner sets up his opponent with powerful combination punches...

FOULS

Spitting.

Biting.

Head butts, knee strikes, elbow strikes, palm-heel strikes, or clubbing blows with the hands.

Using the thumb to gouge or jab at the eyes.

Attacks to the groin, spine, throat, collarbone, a woman's breasts, or the kidneys.

Using scraping blows or rabbit blows (an illegal punch to the back of the player's head or body, usually the kidneys, generally delivered when the boxers are fighting very close).

...and takes him down with a dynamic rush.
(Photos by Vince Volker).

Strikes with the wrist or the open glove.

Kicks to the knees unless otherwise permitted (see Allowed Techniques).

Joint locking techniques.

Holding the opponent with one hand while striking with the other.

Grabbing or holding onto the other player's foot or leg.

Stepping on the other player's foot.

Using foul or abusive language in the ring.

Maintaining a clinch to prevent fighting.

Attacking on the break from a clinch.

Attacking after the end-of-round bell has sounded.

Attacking when the opponent is out, or partially out, of the ring.

Intentionally pushing, shoving, or wrestling the other player out of the ring.

Throws or takedowns unless otherwise permitted (see Allowed Techniques).

Hitting or kicking the opponent when he is down.

Intentionally going to the mat without being hit.

Intentionally injuring the opponent.

Bill "Superfoot" Wallace, one of the greatest professional karate fighters of all time.

WINNING THE MATCH

A player shall be declared knocked down when any portion of the player's body other than the feet touch the floor, or if the player hangs helplessly over the ropes.

A player shall not be declared knocked down if he is punched toward the ground, thrown, or accidentally slips to the floor.

Contests are scored using a ten-point "must" system, meaning the winner of each round receives ten points and the opponent receives a proportionately smaller number, but under no circumstances shall a participant be awarded fewer than seven points.

If a round is judged to have been even, each player shall receive ten points. No fraction of points may be given.

Judges should base their scores on each player's relative effectiveness in a given round.

A player who wins the round and does so with exceptional above the belt kicking technique, should be given a point advantage over the other player.

TRADITIONAL KARATE SPARRING (KUMITE)

Karate-do (the Way of the Empty Hand) is one of the most popular martial arts in the world, with millions of practitioners worldwide. It was developed in Okinawa during the 17th and 18th Centuries, largely based on Kung Fu skills from China, and brought to Japan in the early Twentieth Century. Karate is a powerful art that exists both as a self-defense system and a form of martial sports. Styles of Karate include Goju-ryu, Shotokan, Isshin-ryu, Shito-ryu, Shorin-Ryu, Wado-ryu, and Uechi-Ryu.

There are three main categories of Karate sparring, which is called Kumite. Each category takes a different approach to sparring.

Freesparring using Full Contact rules.

> **POINT FIGHTING** relies on focused blows delivered with great accuracy and at high speeds to determine the outcome of a match.
>
> **FREE SPARRING** is pretty much what it sounds like: players are permitted to utilize any techniques they choose, and the degree of contact

allowed is determined either by the instructor, the host organization, or, in some cases, the players themselves.

LIMITED STEP SPARRING is a form of ritualistic drilling where pre-determined attacks and defenses are practiced at varying speeds to develop perfect form.

Kumite matches range from classmates sparring in a dojo to large, multi-school competitions. In large matches the competitors wear unmarked Karate gis (uniforms) without rank insignia. One competitor is designated "Aka" and wears a red belt; the other is called "Shiro" and wears a white belt. None of this is required in dojo sparring.

Match tournaments require participants to wear mouth guards and some even allow very thin protective mitts, but some traditionalists eschew the use of any protective gear.

As there are many hundreds of Karate organizations around the world it would be impossible to provide the rules for each. The following is a general set of rules common to most of the major Karate organizations that promote competitive matches.

KUMITE POINT FIGHTING

Formal tournaments are judged by a Refereeing Panel that consists of one Referee (named Shushin), two Judges (Fukushin), and one arbitrator (Kansa). The timing of the bout starts when the Referee gives the signal to begin, "Hajime," and stops each time he calls "Yame."

The match ends when a pre-determined number of points is reached, usually one (Ippon Kumite), three (Sanbon Kumite), or five (Gohon Kumite). Typical point sparring consists of one round of fighting.

Continuous Point Sparring is a variation that consists of multiple rounds, typically a single round of three minutes for senior male Kumite (including both teams and individuals) or two minutes for female and junior bouts.

KUMITE POINT VALUES AND AWARDS

Different techniques are awarded different point values. This means that a strike or kick can be worth half of a point, a full point, three points, or five points. An inappropriate technique can be grounds for taking a point away, requiring a contestant to forfeit the match, or disqualifying a participant. The Japanese terms for these point values are as follows:

Waza-ari:	Half Point
Ippon:	One Point
Sanbon:	Three Points
Gohon:	Five Points
Hansoku:	Foul
Kiken:	Forfeiture
Shikkaku:	Disqualification

RULES OF THE KUMITE MATCH

Depending on the form of Kumite, the winner of a match is the first person to score a total of one, three, or five points. This can be done by a combination of techniques worth different values. For example, in a three-point sparring match, the winner is the first player to score three Ippons, six Waza-ari, or any combination that totals Sanbon (three points).

A win can also be determined by a *Hasoku* (foul), *Shikaku* (disqualification), or by a *Kiken* (forfeiture) counted against the other player.

Legal target areas are strictly limited to:

The Abdomen

The Back (excluding the shoulders)

The Chest

The Face

The Head

The Neck

The Side

For a technique to be awarded an Ippon it must:

Have correct form.

Have a vigorous application.

Have a perfect finish (Zanshin).

Be executed from the correct distance.

Have correct timing.

An Ippon can also be awarded in situations where a technique lacks one of the qualities listed above but has one of these qualities:

Is performed with high kicks (*Jodan geri*).

Contains some other element of difficulty.

Parries an attack and scores a hit to the other player's unprotected back.

Uses a sweep followed by a scoring finish.

Uses a throw followed by a scoring finish.

Uses a combination technique, the individual elements of which score in their own right.

Is successfully delivered at the instant the other player attacks.

A Waza-ari is earned for any technique that falls just short of a technique that would have scored an Ippon. The referees weight the value of the technique and, if it is close enough, the player is awarded the Waza-ari.

A player wins if his opponent has been cited for a Hansoku or Shikkaku.

A player wins via a Kiken if his opponent withdraws or is withdrawn. For the purpose of keeping track of points, a Kiken is credited as a Sanbon.

If a scoring technique is delivered at the precise moment the match is ended, the point is considered valid.

No attack delivered after the match has ended will be given a score, no matter how well executed.

Techniques delivered after the match has ended are subject to being penalized.

If both players move outside of the competition area, than no scores can be awarded for either participant's techniques.

If one player is inside the competition area while his opponent is outside, his technique may be awarded a point if the referee has not stopped the match ("Yame").

Clashes, both players delivering techniques at the same time, are not valid and do not score

FREESPARRING (JIYU KUMITE)

Free-style sparring, or Jiyu Kumite, is a full speed match between two Karate-ka (practitioners of Karate). The players are required to attack and defend using correct Karate skills. The goal of the match is to score a Waza-ari (half-point), which is symbolic of the "killing blow" that might end a real fight. Naturally, in Kumite the blow is stopped short of contact or delivered lightly, but the essence of the match retains its link to actual life-or-death self-defense.

A standard Jiyu Kumite match lasts for two minutes. The winner is the player who is awarded a total of one full point (two waza-ari) before time has expired.

Kicks and strikes are often focused, meaning that they are stopped just short of contact. But if a player delivers a blow that is stopped too far from the body, even if it is in a true line to the target, the blow does not score.

RULES OF JIYU KUMITE

Matches are set for a two-minute duration.

A bell, gong, or buzzer will sound a warning 30 seconds before the end of the match and will be struck twice to signal its conclusion.

Targets are limited to the head, neck, chest, abdomen and back.

Prohibited acts include:

> Dangerous or uncontrolled techniques.

> Dangerous throws.

Being outside the fighting area too often.

Ignoring the referee's order.

Making contact with eyes, groin, and joints (such as the knee, ankle, etc.).

Purposely causing injury.

Useless grabbing.

If a point is scored on "Yame" (the command to stop) it will be counted. If a point is scored after "Yame" it will not be awarded.

A player who has scored will not be awarded the point if one of his feet was out of the competition area. Conversely, a point can be scored against a player who has one, but not both, of his feet outside the area.

The referee will break up any unnecessary grappling unless a throw is immediately made. Points will not be awarded for a throw unless it is followed up by a strong Karate technique.

When both competitors execute a blow simultaneously, no points will be awarded. However, if one participant unmistakably scores a point a moment before the other, the point will be awarded to the first man scoring.

A player may be disqualified if he deliberately fouls his opponent.

If a player avoids contact by continually moving or jumping out of the area he will first receive a warning and then will be disqualified if he continues to run from the fight.

If a game-point decision has to be made by the judges, the decision will be based on:

Fighting spirit.

A minimum of foul play.

The participants' attitudes.

Strength and skill of techniques.

Tactics.

Whether a waza-ari (half point) has been scored.

REFEREE HAND SIGNALS

No Points Scored: The referee crosses and uncrosses his hands in front of his body in a continuous motion.

Simultaneous Attack: The referee places his fists together, with the knuckles making contact and the arms forming a horizontal line.

Missed Target: The referee passes his fist over the target that was missed.

Insufficient Distance From Target: The referee's palms are placed together and then drawn apart.

Technique Is Blocked: The referee's palm is placed against the forearm.

**Traditional Shotokan Karate tournament held in
McGonigle Arena at Temple University in Philadelphia.**

Weak Technique: The referee's hand is outstretched in front of the body with the palm facing down, then gradually lowered.

Ippon: One point, or the winner, is shown by raising the arm diagonally in the direction of the winning corner.

Waza-Ari: A half-point is indicated by lowering the arm diagonally toward the direction of the scoring corner.

Draw: The arms are pointed downward in the direction of both corners.

Foul: The referee points his index finger at the face of the fighter who committed the foul.

Warning: A warning uses the same gesture as a foul, except the referee points to the chest of the fighter in question.

LIMITED STEP SPARRING

Limited Step Sparring is a vital aspect of Karate training because it is the best way for a student to learn the correct applications of blocks, body movements and counterattacks based on the skills learned in kata. The basic concept is to take specific attacks and specific responses—often directly excerpted from kata—and then perform them with a partner, first slowly and then with increasing speed and precision until they are executed at full speed. Naturally, the more speed used the more the student is require to use focus, or kime (pronounced kee-may), to prevent his blows from doing any real harm. Everything is simulated, but it is simulated at such great speeds that a mistake at full speed can be crippling or even fatal. This is one of the ways in which a karate student masters precision and control.

The "limited steps" in question are the stages of the defense, which are designed to simulate an escalating conflict. Often there are sets of skills, with One, Three, and Five steps. One student is designated the attacker (called *Uke*) and the other is the defender (*Tori*).

For example, in an *Ippon Kumite* (One Step Spar):

1. Uke throws a forward punch.

2. Tori blocks the punch.

3. Tori throws a counter punch to an opening created by the block.

This action is considered a single step, because it involves a single technique (the simultaneous block and counter strike). Ippon Kumite is often called *Kihon Ippon Kumite* (Basic Form One Step Sparring) because of its adherence to the precise base version of a skill without using variations of any kind. In this way it is very similar to Kata in that it helps the students understand the skills at a fundamental level.

Kata demonstrated by 10th dan Goju-ryu Karate Grandmaster M. Gene Holden.

A Sanbon Kumite (Three Step Spar) might expand this scenario as follows:

1. Uke throws a forward punch to Tori's face, which is blocked by Tori.

2. Uke advances and throws a second punch at Tori's face, which is blocked by Tori.

3. Uke throws a third punch, this time to Tori's solar plexus, which is parried and grabbed by Tori.

4. Tori counterattacks with a side thrust kick to Uke's knee.

This is considered a three step spar because there are three basic techniques: two blocks and then a parry and counter kick.

The variations are limited only by the number of techniques the students have learned. Limited Step Karate sparring varies from style to style, and within each style there are often many hundreds of variations, each one containing a different approach to defense and counterattack, and each offering a fresh kernel of combat wisdom.

OKINAWAN KARATE YAKUSOKU SPARRING

In Okinawan Karate styles such as Shorin-ryu and Goju-Ryu there is another traditional form-based method of sparring, called Yakusoku Sparring. *Yakusoku* translates as "promise"; therefore, *Yakusoku Kumite* means "promise-sparring."

This refers to training in which the partners agree to follow a specific set of rules and execute a specific set of movements. The purpose of this mutual

Kata demonstrated by Goju-ryu Grandmaster M. Gene Holden and Jamal El.

agreement is to cultivate a bond of trust between practitioners of Karate. The establishment of this trust allows the players to execute their most powerful techniques without worrying about unexpected contact, which would almost certainly lead to injury.

Despite the formal; acceptance of certain parameters, Yakusoku allows the players to develop reliable fighting skills because they can move with full speed and power, making minute adjustments to compensate for the size, shape, speed and proximity of their partners. This instills great battle judgment as is vital in a real fight so that a Karate-ka knows how to move in order to accomplish precisely what he needs to accomplish in order to insure victory.

Variations on this include the aforementioned Ippon, Sanbon and Gohon Kumite, but also:

KAKOMI KUMITE, which pits one player against four other players, using precisely chosen techniques but performed at very high speeds.

RENZOKU KUMITE, a form of "Continuous Sparring" where the players do not worry about points, but rather concentrate on delivering specific Karate skills with great precision and accuracy.

9.4 POINT FIGHTING

Point Fighting is a popular method of competitive sparring, used in martial arts school and in competitions. Generally favored by players with a background in Karate or a similar discipline, Point Fighting is fast-paced and exciting.

There are two basic forms of Point Fighting: traditional and non-traditional. Traditional Point Fighting, otherwise known as Jiyu kumite (Free Sparring) as discussed elsewhere in this book under "Karate Sparring Methods", is generally used for matches between players from the same system, or school, of Karate. Non-Traditional Point Fighting often involves players of different styles of Karate. Worldwide there are hundreds of different styles of Karate, including Shotokan, Chito-ryu, Uechiu-ryu, Kenpo, Shorin-ryu, Shuri-te, and Goju-ryu

The term "non-traditional" is somewhat misleading because it seems to suggest that the players do not embrace the traditional virtues, skills and practices of Karate; this could not be further from the truth. A far more accurate (though somewhat ponderous) name would be "Non Style-Specific Point Fighting."

SCORING THE MATCH

All legal hand techniques that score will be awarded 1 point.

All legal kicking techniques that score will be awarded 2 points.

All penalty points awarded will be awarded 1 point.

RULES OF THE MATCH

Point Fighting matches are generally two minutes long.

If one player scores three or more points before the allotted time has expired, he is the winner.

If neither competitor has earned three points before the match expires, then whoever is ahead at the end of the two minutes is declared the winner.

All grand championship matches are two minutes running time and five total points.

If the players are tied at the end of the allotted time, a sudden victory round is played and the first fighter to score a point wins the match.

Points are awarded by a majority vote of all judges.

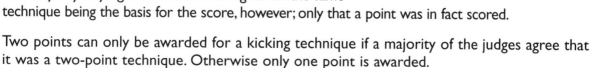

The goal of Karate sparring is the perfect Ippon - a one point win.

The majority of judges do not have to agree on the same technique being the basis for the score, however; only that a point was in fact scored.

Two points can only be awarded for a kicking technique if a majority of the judges agree that it was a two-point technique. Otherwise only one point is awarded.

TARGET AREAS

Legal Targets include the head, face ribs, chest, abdomen, collarbone, and kidneys.

Illegal Targets include the spine, back of neck, throat, side of the neck, groin, legs, knees, and back.

METHODS OF CONTACT

Sweeps may not be used to take another player down unless the match is fought on a padded surface.

On a hard surface sweeps should only be used to destabilize, in order to set up a punch or kick.

Controlled takedowns are allowed on padded surfaces.

Sweeps and controlled takedowns will only count if the move is followed by an appropriate finishing technique.

If a stomp kick is used as a finishing technique, one foot must remain on the ground at all times.

Under no circumstances may a player stomp another player on the head, throat, groin, ankle, or knee. Stomps to all other parts of the body must be light touch contact only.

Light Touch Contact is defined as contact without penetration of the body, or without visible movement of the other player as a result of the contact.

Moderate Touch Contact is defined as slight penetration of the body, or slight movement by the other player as a result of the contact. Moderate touch contact may be made to all legal target areas except the headgear and face.

CONTINUOUS POINT FIGHTING

Many different disciplines practice Continuous Point Fighting, including styles of Karate and Taekwondo. Different organizations will often have rules tailored to their own practitioners' skills and needs. The information presented herein is common to most of these organizations, but competitors should always check the rules of the hosting body of any tournament they enter.

Continuous Point Fighting matches are fought according to time limit only, rather than a point limit. Otherwise, the rules are substantially the same, including target areas and techniques that are allowed or disallowed.

The blows in most forms of Continuous Point Fighting are focused, meaning that they must be stopped approximately a hand's length from the target. Contact, no matter how light, is not permitted. It is strongly emphasized that in order for a point to be scored, the technique must be crisp, clean and controlled.

Any interpretation of the rules is done at the sole discretion of the tournament officials, judges, and referees, and all such decisions are final.

WINNING THE MATCH

The player who scores the greater amount of points (with legal techniques) within the time limit wins the fight. All decisions by the referees are final.

RULES OF CONTACT

No attacks to the groin or spine, even focused, are allowed.

No contact may be made to the face.

Contact to the body should be no more than a feather-light touch to the other player's uniform.

Grabs and holds are not permitted.

Judo/Jujutsu/Aikido throws are not permitted.

Kicks below the waist are not permitted.

Leg sweeps are not permitted.

Elbow or open hand strikes are not permitted.

Excessively going out of bounds (running out of the ring) is not permitted.

Striking an opponent when he or she is down is not permitted.

Any uncontrolled techniques to the head area (spinning hook kicks, etc.) are not permitted.

Any unsportsmanlike conduct is not permitted.

9.5 KUNG FU SPARRING

SHAOLIN FREESTYLE SPARRING

Shaolin Kung Fu was originally developed in the Shaolin Monastery in China about 1500 years ago. It has since derived into various schools such as Lohan, Bok Hok Pai, Kwang Sai Jook Lum, Hung Gar, Wing Chun, and Choy Li-Fut.

Shaolin Kung Fu sparring methods are intended to be a natural outgrowth of the complex forms (*kuen*) taught within the art. These forms are designed to simulate a series of one-on-one attack and defense encounters. They are first learned as solo exercises requiring months or even years of intense practice. Intermediate stu-

Photos of Grandmaster Chiu Chi Ling courtesy of Dr. Martin Sewer of the Martin Sewer Kung Fu School of Zurich, Switzerland, a member school of the International Chiu Chi Ling Hung Gar Kung Fu Association.

dents practice in pairs. One player will continuously act as the attacker and the other as the defender so they can move through the entire form with real blows, blocks and kicks, performed at increasing speeds.

In most traditional Shaolin schools, a student is not encouraged (or even allowed) to spar until he has developed a high degree of proficiency in his solo and paired forms. At this point he is allowed to engage in limited sparring.

The exercise is called "free sparring," but there are some restrictions. The players have to use skills learned in their forms, though they may choose which ones to use and when. Shaolin free sparring is not intended to be an opportunity for the students to engage in generic kickboxing or simply play a game of martial arts tag. Form and function, speed and grace, logic and artistry are the goals of this challenging and visually beautiful method of sparring.

Some organizations engage in school-to-school competitions and even large-scale tournaments, but the heart and soul of Shaolin sparring is the matching of one student against another, in the kwoon, using skills that showcase Kung Fu at its most refined.

SHAOLIN TIGER AND CRANE SPARRING

Hung Gar is a form of Kung Fu that originated with the "fighting monks" of the first Shaolin Temple in China's Honan province. The monks created Shaolin Kung Fu as a fitness program

As the attacker throws a punch, the defender angles to the side in Gi Ng Ma (Bow and Arrow) Stance and covers with Rising Earth.

because they had been suffering muscle atrophy from spending many hours a day in meditation. The breathing exercises they developed, combined with physical exercises based on the movements of animals (Tiger, White Crane, Dragon, Snake, and Leopard), became the basis for one of the world's most successful fighting arts.

Hung Gar incorporates external and internal methods, with a focus on the animal styles of White Crane and Tiger. It emphasizes powerful stance work, long and short hand techniques, and a blend of straight, circular, and angular movements. White Crane is known for its grace and a wide range of skills that intercept and diffuse attacking force, while the Tiger style

The attacker follows up with a left punch, and the defender intercepts it with a Crane's Beak and simultaneously counters with a Fu Jeun (Tiger Palm) to the jaw.

The defender then turns into the attacker's center line and finishes with another Tiger Palm to the sternum.

Photos on these pages are classical Hung Gar fighting techniques, courtesy of Sifu James D. Angielczyk and his Depew, New York Academy of Kung-fu.

contributes aggressive attacking skills. The combination and opposition of these two disparate styles creates a balance—a Yin and a Yang—which allow the students the chance to embrace vastly different approaches to attack and defense.

Tiger and Crane sparring is particular to the Hung Gar style of Kung Fu. It is not so much a method of sparring as a form (*kuen*) that is practiced at increasing rates of speed as the players get better and better. Though not a free-sparring method, it is similar in many respects to full-speed kata breakdown sparring (*bunkai kumite*) used in some forms of Karate. The form includes many extremely dangerous (in some cases lethal) skills, so the responsibility is on the practitioners to be faster, more accurate, and more controlled each time the form is practiced.

Tiger and Crane sparring can be played several different ways:

TIGER VS. CRANE

This is the core method of sparring. One player adopts the aggressive role of the Tiger, while the other player is the more passive Crane. The match can be done as the practice of a form at full speed, or as an actual free-form spar. In the free-form style, the players must choose techniques that are true to their animal roles.

A typical Hung style response to a sudden punch. The defender steps back into a Horse Stance and applies Gin Kiu (Threading Bridge).

As the attacker follows up with a second punch, the defender intercepts with Pak Sao while simultaneously punching to the jaw or throat.

TIGER VS. TIGER

Not for the timid, this more modern version of Hung Gar sparring is as close to full contact as the system allows. Both fighters play the role of Tiger, and attack each other with great enthusiasm and aggression. Since Tiger style has almost no blocks and is based entirely on attacking, the match is fought to a single winning point that must be symbolic of a killing blow.

This series of photos is taken from the Moon Flowing Broadsword set. The player on the left jabs with the pole, as the swordsman waits in preparatory position.

CRANE VS. CRANE

The elegant White Crane style is deceptive. It is considered a protective and defensive style, with evasion as its primary tool and counterattacking done only when violence absolutely cannot be avoided. When two Cranes battle, the match becomes one of trickery and deception. Subtle movements, traps and fakes, lures and deceptions mark this method of fighting, making it a challenge to the players as well as a great educational benefit to spectators.

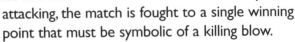

The swordsman uses the bottom front edge of the broadsword to push the pole to the side, which sets up a sword cut.

The swordsman steps in quickly into Horse Stance and executes a two-handed cut to the throat.

OTHER FORMS

Many Hung Gar forms are designed to be practiced in pairs and thereby constitute a kind of sparring. These other sets include two-person methods of sparring such as:

Eight Tri-grams Staff Sparring *

Empty Hand vs. Double Butterfly Swords

Knife vs. Stick

Trident vs. Butterfly Swords

Tiger Head Shield vs. Knife

Round Shield vs. Trident

Hung Gar polefighting forms.

---

* The 8 Trigrams, called Pa Kua or Ba Gua, are representational of different aspects of elements of nature. There are two wood, two metal, three earth, one fire, and one water elements. In martial arts, these different elements are demonstrated in different ways in fighting skills seen throughout Kung Fu.

PA-KUA SPARRING

Pa-Kua (pronounced ba-gwa, and also spelled Ba-gua and Bagua) is a Kung Fu system that (according to legend) was developed by Tung Hai Chuan around the latter Seventeenth Century. The history holds that Tung was wandering around the snowy mountains, nearly dead from cold and starvation, when he was rescued and nursed back to health by a reclusive Taoist hermit. This man then taught Tung the secrets of Pa Kua in order to preserve the health he had restored. Tung spread the art and now there are as many as twenty different sub-styles of Pa-Kau taught worldwide today.

Sifu Pete Buckman works with student Maynard Espanol on "bridging," or creating an opening for a final sparring attack.

Pa-Kua is known for its effective self-defense skills. It also teaches various methods of sparring, generally non-competitive and designed to help students learn more about their skills by applying them in a free-style match.

There are ten aspects to Pa-Kua sparring. Each must be demonstrated in every aspect of a player's performance in order for any techniques to count. Correct form, calm spirit, and presence of mind are more important than anything else in Pa-Kau sparring.

The Ten Aspects of Pa-Kua Sparring

During play, no part of the body may lose balance. If balance is even a little off, it is referred to as "focus" or "double-weight." Focus is the mental aspect of loss of balance, and double weight is the physical manifestation. They affect one another and so should be avoided. There are ten aspects to Pa-Kua sparring which are intended to show the way to avoiding loss of focus and balance.

Pa Kua students practicing palm strikes.

    1.   Fight in a way that embodies yin and yang. This refers to two separate movements that are continuous, unbroken, and derived from one root. If this is not understood, your technique will be wrong. In the martial arts sense, yin and yang are expressed as follows:

        a. Exhale and Inhale

b. Real Technique and Fake

c. Tension and Relaxation

d. Moving and Still

e. Hard and Soft

f. Fast and Slow

Coach Teresa Buckman uses a bridging Pa-Kua step and shoulder strike against Tai Chi student Luba Andreeva in a freestyle sparring exercise.

2.   An attack is considered yang (strong and aggressive); therefore the defense must be yin (yielding and deceptive).

3.   Coordinate breathing with all exertion (strikes, kicks, taking a hit, etc.)

4.   Coordinate breathing with technique.

5.   Recognize and exploit the three distances in a fight: close, medium, and long. Change distances in order to confuse the opponent.

6.   Move at speeds appropriate to the fight.   Remain still if the other player is still; but if the other play moves, then move faster in order to counterattack.

7.   Control angles of movement. When sparring, it is important to control and protect the centerline of one's own body as well as the various angles of attacking footwork.

8.   Make good use of timing to insure that the opponent is caught (and kept) off guard by assaulting him with attacks of varying speeds and from confusing angles.

9.   Move quickly, lightly, and with conviction. Do not stand flat-footed or move heavily, and always be ready to lunge inward or dodge away.

10. Develop a balance between Internal and External power. Even though it is vital to cultivate Chi, it is equally important to have a strong, healthy body.

SAN SHOU KICKBOXING

San Shou is a competitive, full contact martial art originally developed by the Chinese military. Though most often practiced as a sport, San Shou (In China, San Shou is also referred to as "San Da," an older name which refers to full contact fighting) also has a serious combat-useful aspect.

In 1924, the Chinese Nationalist Party (the Guomindang) created the Whampoa Military Academy in Guangdong, a city in Canton. The Academy was designed to train the leaders of the Party so they in turn would create an effective military force. The Academy worked in harmony with advisors from the Soviet Union, exchanging military and martial arts skills.

Because the Russians had suffered heavy losses during close-quarters combat with the Chinese during the Russo-Japanese War (1904-1905), they adopted many of the Chinese Kung Fu-based fighting skills. These skills later evolved into the Russian martial art named Sambo (see Chapter....), and became quite an effective and well-organized system of combat.

The teaching methods developed by the Soviet military forces in turn became an influence on the Chinese. In essence, Kung Fu techniques formed the basis of Sombo, and Sombo teaching methodology in turn formed the basis for teaching San Shou.

The military version of San Shou was designed to prepare soldiers for close quarters combat. It was structured as four basic categories of combat skills:

DA ("striking") includes all open and closed hand blows, as well as blows with the wrist, forearm, elbow, shoulder, and head.

NA ("seizing") includes all chokes, joint locks, pressure-point attacks, finger locks, holds, disarms, and submission techniques.

SHUAI ("throwing") includes all takedowns, throws, reaps, trips, and other similar skills.

TI ("kicking") includes all methods of kicking, sweeping, stomping, and hooking.

The sportive version of San Shou had to be adapted for safe play, so a move was made to structure it along the lines of other Asian forms of kickboxing. Unlike Muay Thai kickboxing, however, elbow and knee strikes were removed from the list of permissible skills. The sport version of San Shou debuted in 1991, and that same year World Championships were held. Since then, the number of practitioners has dramatically increased worldwide. By 1997, both the United States and China were working to establish professional-level San Shou competitions.

BASIC RULES OF PLAY

Bouts may be held in a standard boxing ring or on a raised platform without ropes.

Kicks are allowed to the inside and outside of the legs as well as the upper body.

Knee and elbow strikes are not allowed, although a minority of San Shou matches permit knee strikes.

Wrestling takedowns are legal.

Judo throws are legal.

The following are not allowed:

> biting
>
> elbow strikes
>
> head butting
>
> hitting while holding the opponent
>
> attacks to the joints
>
> blows of any kind to the back of the head
>
> attacks to the spine
>
> attacks to the groin
>
> small and medium joint-locking throws.

If the players establish a clinch, they have 5 seconds to complete a sweep, throw, or takedown or they will be separated by the referee.

San Shou allows a variety of strikes and kicks...

...as well as takedowns.

117

The referee will stop the match after each takedown and award a point, if earned, by pointing to the player who scored and emphasizing this with a verbal call.

SCORING THE MATCH

There are two basic categories of techniques that can be used in a San Shou match: Stand Up and Takedown. The scores are added together to decide the match.

COUNTING THE POINTS

One Point Techniques:

Any "clean" strike (no sloppy hits, no clashes). Slap punches delivered during a clinch do not count.

A clean kick. A kick that scores but is caught at the moment of contact by the other player and then countered is not awarded a point.

A counterattack performed while being thrown.

Reversal of a throw, with the player originally being thrown winding up in a dominant position.

Two Point Techniques:

Knockdown (from kick or punch).

Any basic takedown or throw that is not a "high altitude" throw (in which the person is thrown some height above the ground).

Any basic takedown or throw that is extremely difficult.

A sweep or shove ending in a knockdown that is not high altitude or of extreme skill/difficulty.

Three Point Techniques:

Any "high altitude" throw.

Any high speed or high difficulty throw.

Any knockdown resulting in a standing 8-count for the other player.

Any sweep that removes both of the other player's feet from the ground.

WINNING THE MATCH

The fighter who has taken (won) the most rounds wins the match.

The player who has earned a TKO (Technical Knockout) wins.

If one player is unable to continue, the other player wins.

KUOSHU SPARRING

Kuoshu ("national arts") is another name for Kung Fu. It refers to sparring methods sanctioned by various groups who hold international competitions. Over fifty countries, including the United States, have their own national Kuoshu tournaments. Kuoshu tournaments are open to all styles of Kung Fu, and these competitions have raised tremendous positive awareness and unity between practitioners of the many hundreds of styles of this ancient art. These tournaments have been gaining great popularity and notoriety over the last few decades.

There are several different types of Kuoshu competition, (The regulations of all competitions are in accordance with the International Chinese Kuoshu rules.) including Lei Tai and Weapons sparring, and forms competitions that include Tai Chi and Wu Shu.

LEI TAI (FULL CONTACT FIGHTING) RULES

The origins of Kuoshu Lei Tai fighting were in ancient China, where martial artists conducted "challenge matches" to test each others skills, because of a personal dispute, or to prove one martial system's superiority over another system.

The term "Kuoshu" came into common use in the early part of the Twentieth Century, when the Chinese government endorsed central and regional martial arts academies. The Chinese phrase kuoshu is composed of two characters, which mean "National Art" and was said to represent the unique contributions of Chinese martial arts to the culture of the Chinese people.

In 1949, the Communists won the civil war in China. Members of the Republican government, or Kuomingdang, and their allies escaped to the Island of Taiwan. In addition, many martial artist masters left mainland China for safer places such as Hong Kong, Singapore and Taiwan.

Soon after the Communists consolidated control in China, they outlawed martial arts fighting, allowing only demonstrations. Several years later, during the Cultural Revolution, the government banned all martial arts practice of any kind. Martial arts training was revived in the 1970s, initially for demonstration; fighting training was reintroduced several years later.

While mainland China curtailed martial arts training, full contact fighting training and matches continued in other Asian countries, Taiwan especially. An important tournament in Taiwan in 1955 illustrated the conditions of such matches; during this all-Island event, competitors fought without rounds or time limits, without protective gear, and without weight classes. The only restrictions were prohibited target areas, such as attacks to the groin, the eyes, the throat and the back of the head. Literally, over 100 fighters showed up; tournament organizers paired off the fighters and declared the last man standing the winner. Another tournament in 1957 introduced three weight classes: light, medium, and heavy.

In 1975, the Kuoshu Federation, Republic of China (K.F.R.O.C.), held the first World Kuoshu competition in Taiwan, R.O.C. The tournament organizers set conditions similar to those outlined above: no protective gear, limited weight categories, a few illegal strike areas, and some time limits. In 1978, a group

of martial artists formed the Chinese Kuoshu Worldwide Promotion Association (C.K.W.P.A.) to promote kuoshu on a worldwide basis; the K.F.R.O.C. became a member organization of the C.K.W.P.A.

The C.K.W.P.A., later re-named the International Chinese Kuoshu Federation (I.C.K.F.), hosted additional World Tournaments roughly every three years—1978, 1980, 1983, 1986, 1989, 1992, 1996. They conducted the 1980 tournament in Hawaii and 1989 tournament in Las Vegas; otherwise, the I.C.K.F. held these tournaments in Taiwan.

Also during this period, Kuoshu organizations affiliated with the I.C.K.F. emerged in countries in Africa, Asia, Europe, North America, and South America.

During the past decade, the United States Chinese Kuoshu Federation (U.S.C.K.F.) has become one of the principal leaders in the world for the promotion and development of Lei Tai full contact Chinese style fighting. U.S.C.K.F. President Huang Chien-Liang (who is also the 64th generation Tien Shan Pai grandmaster) revived the ancient practice of conducting fighting competitions on a raised platform in 1991 at the Pan American Cup competition that he sponsored. Grandmaster Huang also revived the phrase Lei Tai—literally a "raised platform"—and made the phrase synonymous with traditional Chinese style fighting on a raised platform.

Lei Tai Kuoshu rules have evolved considerably over the past several decades. This evolution continues today. Currently, the U.S. rules stipulate competition on a raised platform of a defined height and area without ropes or barriers on the edges. Competitors can be, and often are, chased or thrown off the platform by their opponents.

One referee stands on the platform at all times both to manage the matches and control the fighters. Five scoring judges sit at fixed positions around the Lei Tai. Each judge keeps an individual tally of the points scored and fouls accumulated by each contestant. The judges determine the winner of each round, and ultimately the match, either by the number of points awarded for valid techniques or due to the opponent's incapacity (such as knockouts, disqualification, etc.). Finally, at a head table, a chief referee presides over the conduct of the match. The head table's other duties include managing the time constraints and fight order. Disputes are managed by the Chief Arbitrator.

Each contestant may bring up to two other people into their corner (to sit near but not on the platform) during the match. These corner representatives may not provide coaching during the match (although they may coach between rounds) and may not assist the fighter with getting on or off the platform. Fighters are required to demonstrate adequate respect for their opponent, the head table and the center referee or face possible fouls and disqualification.

Tournament officials arrange the fighters in weight classes of approximately ten pounds increments. Men and women fight in separate divisions, and champions from previous years have preference for "byes" in early elimination rounds.

The following rules represent only a summary of the contest regulations; additional rules and procedures apply and are explained to the competitors in an open question and answer session held prior to the competition.

SUMMARY OF UNITED STATES CHINESE KUOSHU FEDERATION LEI TAI RULES

1. Contestants will fight on a 24-square foot, 2 1/12 foot high Lei Tai.

2. Competitors must use headgear, gloves, mouthpiece, and groin cup (Women must use chest protector).

3. Elimination rounds will be 1 1/2 minutes each. The final fight in each division will be 2 minutes each. The victor must win two of three maximum rounds.

4. Scoring:

   A. If contestant executes clear punch or kick: 1 point

   B. If contestant executes clear punch or kick that knocks opponent down: 2 points

   C. If without falling, contestant successfully throws opponent to the ground: 2 points.

   D. If contestant forces or throws opponent of the Lei Tai: 3 points.

   E. If through own error, contestant loses balance: 1 point is deducted from score.

   F. If contestant executes clear elbow/knee technique without holding: 1 point.

5. Penalties:

   A. Contact to the eyes, throat, back of head, or groin is illegal. For female competition, contact to the breasts is also illegal.

   B. Techniques using the head are illegal.

   C. Fouls (standard):

      The 1st violation of the rules is a 1 point deduction.

      The 2nd violation of the rules is a 3 point deduction.

      The 3rd violation of the rules is a disqualification.

D. Technical Fouls.

The 1st violation of the rules is a warning.

The 2nd violation of the rules is a 1 point deduction.

The 3rd violation of the rules is a disqualification.

6. Competitors who maliciously hurt their opponent will be held liable for any damages or injuries. Executive referee has full authority to stop the fight at any time for safety or other reasons.

RULES OF WEAPONS FIGHTING

Weapons Fighting matches are either one or two minutes long, or end at a preset score.

In Timed Matches, the game is won by the highest score at the end of the allotted time.

In Score Limited Matches, the game is won by the first player who reaches the prescribed number of points.

SCORING IN WEAPONS FIGHTING MATCHES

Strikes to the head and body (both front and back) count as three points.

Disarming the other opponent scores three points.

Strikes to the arms or legs are worth two points.

Protective equipment allows fighters to safely spar with weapons at full speed.

TAI CHI PUSH HANDS

Push Hands is a two-person Kung Fu exercise used to improve Tai Chi skills. The daily practice of Tai Chi solo forms helps a student learn to be balanced, focused, and relaxed while in motion; the practice of Push Hands improves these abilities by testing them against another person. Human contact makes a world of difference, and has been described by Tai Chi instructors as the difference between theoretical physics and the applications of physics to real problem-solving tasks.

To be balanced and relaxed while maintaining contact with another, moving person is not easy. It requires the refinement of basic skills learned in the solo forms. Only through this refinement is true mastery possible, so Push Hands is a vital part of Tai Chi training.

Tai Chi Push Hands performed by Sifu Stu Shames and Mike Mazzoni.

SETTING UP FOR PUSH HANDS

Two players face each other at arm's length, both placing the same foot forward.

Each player raises his forward hand to chest height with the palm turned in, facing their own chest. The back of each player's hand lightly touches the back of the other player's hand.

Each player's rearward hand (corresponding to the rear foot) is placed lightly on the other player's lead elbow.

Both players should adjust their stance so that they are comfortable and balanced.

PLAYING PUSH HANDS

To start the match, both players simultaneously move their arms, waist and legs in a circular pattern for three rotations.

After the third rotation, the match begins.

It is generally decided at the beginning of the match what constitutes a point and how many points are needed for a win.

Unbalancing the other player to make him take a step is the most common goal for a point.

Each player must maintain light contact with the other player's arms while also maintaining perfect balance.

Players are permitted to put their hands on the other's body to attempt to unbalance him.

If a player is pushed or pulled off balance, the game is paused while the players reset themselves.

No point is awarded for the following:

    Taking a step in order to unbalance the opponent.

    Using force instead of fluidity and passiveness.

    Breaking contact.

WING CHUN CHI SAO

Opinions vary as to whether Chi Sao is a method of sparring or simply a drill. Some Wing Chun purists argue that the purpose of Chi Sao is skill development and not recreation. Others hold that Chi Sao accomplishes both, and quite admirably. In either case, the exercise is an excellent one, perfect for honing close-quarters fighting skills, developing a facility for non-resistance responses, teaching traps and counters. It is also helpful for teaching courage since the participants have to maintain contact throughout (stepping out of the line of fire is not an option).

Representative of the art itself, Wing Chun's Chi Sao drills are structured to shut an opponent down before he has a chance to really get warmed up. This means immediate action and reaction, no telegraphing or hesitation, and a sensitive responsiveness to the attacker's every movement.

Sifu Stu Shames and Mike Mazzoni demonstrate the controlling skills of Wing Chun's Chi Sao.

There are several methods of practicing Chi Sao and each one takes the student further into refining his skills. The first level is Dan Chi Sao, which is Single Sticky Hands. The next level is Luk Sao, which includes various methods of rolling the hands. It is sometimes practiced with a footwork drill called Tui Ma ("Pushing Horse") which helps the student maintain proper posture during a confrontation and increases leg strength. The next stage is Jou Sao ("Running Hands"), then Jip Sao ("Capturing Hands"), and finally Gor Sao ("Bridge Crossing"). These drills are interchangeable and often mingled. For example, Luk Sao might be combined with Dan Chi Sao, so that the student needs to use rolling hand techniques while engaged in single hand fighting.

In early training a student is typically pitted against a more senior student. Facing an uphill battle pushes the student to develop greater skill, and sparring with a senior student provides an example of refined technique.

The rolling hands, traps and thrusts are attempts to "build bridges": the striking hand is one end, the body of the defender is the other end, and the interposing network of hands, wrists and forearms creates a bridge that allows the defender to trap cross his opponent's defenses, "cross over" the bridge, and strike.

The key to successful Chi Sao is to control the opponent's bridges and set him up for the next shot.

In competitive Chi Sao, many schools follow these simple scoring rules:

Both partners start with their hands lightly touching (sticking). Each player has one yang hand and one yin hand.

The referee will place his hands over the players' connected hands, feeling for tension. Play will not begin until he feels that there is no evident tension in either player's hands.

The referee uses either a whistle or voice command to start the match.

During competition, players can withdraw their hands to attack or to neutralize an attack, but contact must be restored within one second.

If contact is broken for more than one second, by either player, the match stops.

If play stops, it will resume from the position where contact was last made.

No contact may be made to the eyes, ears, mouth, nose, temples, back of the head, throat, or neck.

Points may be scored anywhere on the torso, and on the head except where restricted (see above).

Attacking the head is limited to light blows using the front section of the palm to strike the forehead or either cheek.

It is strictly prohibited to strike with the head, knee, tip of the elbow, or fingertips.

Elbows may be used for defense only, not for attack.

Players are not permitted to strike the face with the fist, root of the palm, or fingertips.

Joint locks that cause damage are prohibited.

Catches and holds that do not rotate a joint are acceptable.

Attacks to pressure points are prohibited.

POINTS ARE SCORED AS FOLLOWS:

Wins by Complete Advantage:

During competition, if one player is injured by another player having violated the rules and is unable to continue upon a doctor's recommendation, that player will be designated the winner but will not qualify for further competition.

During competition, if either participant or either coach requests to withdraw, then the other player will be designated the winner.

If a player is struck to the floor twice in one round, the other player will be designated the winner.

If a player receives up to 6 warnings and/or is cited for flaws in a round, the other player will be designated the winner.

3-Point Awards

If a player is able to strike permissible targets of the opponent cleanly, obviously, and continuously (3 times or more) and the other player is unable to adequately defend or respond, he is awarded 3 points and the match is called.

If one player is able to knock his opponent down with legal blows to legal targets, he wins 3 points.

2-Point Awards

If a player forces his opponent out of the ring using any hand technique or stepping technique, he scores 2 points.

If a player receives a warning for a severe flaw or fault, his opponent scores 2 points.

Any player who uses a hand technique to hook onto the opponent's neck without the opponent timely retaliating scores 2 points.

1-Point Awards

Any single strike, delivered cleanly, scores a single point.

If a player is penalized for being passive, his opponent scores 1 point.

If a player is advised of a fault or error (but not a severe one), the opposite player will be awarded 1 point.

Non-Scoring Actions

If both players step out of the ring at the same time, no point is scored.

If both players clash (striking at the same time), no point is scored.

If both players get into a tussle (struggling, hitting, etc.), then no point is scored and the match will be stopped and restarted.

WINNING THE MATCH

Depending on the preferences of the school or hosting event, the winner is the player who reaches the pre-determined number of points at the end of a round.

If a player knocks his opponent down twice, he wins.

If the players end with a tie score, the following factors are used to determine the winner:

(1)   The player who received the fewest warnings is the winner.

(2)   The player who received the fewest instances of advice is the winner.

(3)   The player shorter in height will be the winner because of the apparent disadvantage of mass and reach.

(4)   The player lighter in weight (according to the weight on the date of the match) will be the winner because of the apparent disadvantage of mass and muscular strength.

If the above situations are all equal then the round is designated a draw.

In a multiple round match, if a player wins the first two rounds he wins the entire match.   If both players win the same number of rounds, then the criteria for determining the winner of a round are applied.

9.6 MUAY THAI KICKBOXING

Muay Thai kickboxing is one of the oldest and most highly regarded forms of kickboxing. Like its weapons-based sister-system of Krabi Krabong (See Chapter 17: Weapons Sparring Methods), Muay Thai developed out of centuries of martial strife between Thailand and Burma.

For many years, Muay Thai techniques have been part of Thailand's military training system, a fierce and very effective collection of hard-core fighting skills. These techniques were originally influenced by Chinese Kung Fu, but over the last few centuries Muay Thai has lost much of its Chinese influence and has evolved into a uniquely Thai martial art.

Muay Thai flourished during the short reign of King Pra Chao Sua (1703 to 1709), and many sportive matches were held in villages all over the country. Though considered sports these matches were not particularly safe, however, and many a contender was crippled or killed.

King Pra Chao Sua, himself was an accomplished boxer of great reputation as a fearless and innovative fighter. He was known as the Tiger King, and legend has it that he trained with his personal guard and soldiers up to six hours a day. He would often leave the palace disguised as a peasant and enter boxing events, thus insuring that the victories he achieved were based on his own skill and not on a subject's fear of offending his king by defeating him. It is said that the Tiger King was never defeated, either fighting openly or in disguise, even when he fought regional champions. The Tiger King style of Muay Thai still exists today and is highly regarded.

Techniques demonstrated by Brad Daddis and the students of the Extreme Martial Arts and Fitness Academy of Philadelphia. http://www.extrememartialarts.tv

Muay Thai again evolved in 1930, this time moving away from the lethal skills into a more safety-conscious sport. Regulations were created, designating tournament rules, clothing, weight divisions, and time limits. Groin cups and boxing gloves were introduced as additional safety precautions.

MUAY THAI RING ATTIRE

There are a number of rules pertaining solely to the clothing that can be worn in Muay Thai competition:

> Contestants must wear only trunks (red or blue according to their corners).

> No shirt or shoes may be worn.

> Ankle covers (caps) may be worn.

> A sacred cord, known as a Mongkol, can be worn around the head only during the pre-fight ritual of paying homage to ancestral teachers of Muay Thai. It must be removed before the start of the actual fight.

> No metal objects of any kind may be brought into the ring.

> Amulets may be wrapped around biceps or waists, but only if completely covered with pieces of cloth.

> It is permitted to bind the hand with a soft surgical bandage not longer than 12 yards and not wider than 2 inches. Adhesive tape may be placed on the back of the hand or on the bandage.

> Boxing gloves must weigh at least six ounces.

WINNING THE MATCH

Knockout: A knock-down that results in a completed 10-count by the referee.

Technical Knockout (TKO): A referee's decision made when a player is visibly injured, bleeding, or otherwise deemed unfit to continue the fight. The referee will often consult with a stadium doctor before deciding the TKO.

Surrender: A decision made by one player giving up, or by his corner throwing in the towel.

Foul: Matches can be awarded to one player when the other is dismissed from the ring after committing one or more serious fouls.

Decision on Points: If both players are left standing at the end of the match, the judges must decide who has scored the most undisputed techniques. Whichever player wins a round is awarded ten points. The player who did not win will still be given anywhere from six to ten points.

Insubordination: Any player who either willfully disobeys the referee or speaks in a disrespectful manner to the referee may be dismissed from the ring. This will result in a win for the other player.

Tie Match: If the total scores are equal, the match will result in a draw.

SCORING THE MATCH

Points may be scored with punches, kicks, and strikes by the elbows and knees.

Blows must be strong, accurate, and delivered with good form in order to score points.

Points may be awarded for good defensive and evasive skills.

Points may be awarded for aggressive attacking and fighting skills.

If both boxers score an equal number of total points, the one who more clearly took the offensive in the fight will be given the advantage in scoring.

The referee is authorized to deduct only 1 point at a time as a penalty to any contestant.

9.7 PENTJAK SILAT

Pentjak Silat is a popular style of fighting originating in a vast archipelago of 13,000 islands that stretches from Malaysia to New Guinea. It is an art that has hundreds of sub-styles, 500 in Malaysia alone and another 200 in Indonesia. This powerful fighting art dates back at least to the Sixth Century in Sumatra and along the Malay Peninsula. It was instrumental in the spread of empires throughout the region. Pentjak Silat (also just called Silat) is a combination of many different influences, including grappling skills from India, weapons skills from Arabia and China, and additional technical and cultural influences from Siam (now Thailand), Nepal, and other nations.

In the Seventeenth Century, after the Dutch arrived to take control of the area's spice trade, most Silat schools went underground. They stayed out of the public (and governmental) eye until 1949, the year Indonesia gained its independence.

Since the 1970s, Silat has spread throughout the world and is studied avidly by tens of thousands of practitioners. The word Pentjak refers to the body movements when in training in

this aggressive art, and Silat refers to those same techniques as used in self-defense. Other than the name, there are few elements that are standard across the board for Silat's countless styles. Each has its own techniques, methods of practice, and technical philosophies.

Although there is no longer a need for secrecy, modern Pentjak Silat schools are still highly surreptitious and cautious. Teachers rarely accept a student unless that person has been referred by a trusted friend or relative.

For years, various Southeast Asian governments have endeavored to cultivate Pentjak Silat as a major international sport. Where once it was practiced only for defense, now competitions and tournaments are held in many towns. Some public schools in that part of the world have even accepted Silat as part of their physical education curriculum.

Silat's largest sporting competition is the Asia-Pacific Pentjak Silat Championship, held in Bedok, Singapore. These contests often draw as many as one hundred fighters, from countries such as Indonesia, the Philippines, Japan, South Korea, Myanmar, Laos, Thailand, Brunei, Viet Nam, and host Singapore.

In recent years, Viet Nam has dominated the games. Viet Nam also hosts the National Youth Pentjak Silat Tournament in its central Ha Tinh Province.

9.8 SAVATE

The martial art Savate originated in France. It was developed from street-fighting skills of the 16th and 17th centuries. Unlike most martial arts taught today, Savate is not based on any Asian fighting skills.

There are two primary styles of Savate: *Chausson Marseillais* ("Marseillais fighting"), which relies primarily on powerful kicking skills, and classic Savate, which uses many open hand blows, some fist strikes, and a lot of low kicks.

In 1845, Charles Lecour combined classic Savate with the high kicks of Chausson Marseillais and the closed hand fighting of English boxing to arrive at what is now modern Savate. Savate is also known as "*la Boxe Française,*" or French boxing.

In 1899 another Savate master, Maitre Charlemont, refined the art even further. He added influences from fencing, particularly fencing's fast attack-and-retreat footwork.

Like Taekwondo and Judo, Savate was proposed as an Olympic sport and demonstrated at the 1924 Olympics, but it was not adopted as a regular event. It is used as a regular part of the training of soldiers in the French army.

Savate matches are held in a standard boxing ring. The players wear gloves similar to regulation boxing gloves, but with longer laced cuffs. Players also wear leotards for ease of movement and special shoes with reinforced toes.

Colored rank is awarded in Savate in much the same way as in Karate, Kenpo and Taekwondo, based upon the learning of specific skills of increasing difficulty and complexity. But instead of belts, Savate players display their rank by colored gloves. The colors include blue, green, red, white, and yellow; the latter (known as "*gant de bronze*") is the highest grade

SAVATE

possible for a non-competing Savate practitioner. Players who go on to compete may earn a silver glove, or "*gant d'argent*."

THE SAVATE MATCH

Rounds may be either one minute or ninety seconds long. A one minute break is held between rounds.

Matches do not last for a specific number of rounds. Instead, a match is fought to a time limit or until there is a knockout.

Players may wear gloves, mouth guard, and a groin cup as protective equipment. No other protective padding is allowed.

Matches are supervised by referees.

Players are required to throw more kicks than punches during the match.

SCORING THE MATCH

Punches of all kinds are scored as one point.

Low kicks (below the waist) are worth one point.

Medium-height kicks (from waist height to below the head) are scored as two points.

High kicks (to the head) are awarded three points.

Three knockdowns in any single round ends the fight.

9.9 TAEKWONDO SPARRING (KYORUGI)

The Korean martial art of Taekwondo has roots reaching back to the grand Three Kingdoms: Koguryo (37 BC to 668 AD), Paekche (18 BC to 600 AD), and Silla (57 BC to 936 AD). Although it has some stylistic influences from Northern Chinese White Crane Kung Fu and Japanese Shotokan Karate, Taekwondo is a uniquely Korean art and is one of the most popular combat sports in the world.

Taekwondo is built largely around dynamic and powerful kicking techniques, many accompanied by jumps and spins that whip the practitioners through the air at incredible speeds. Since Taekwondo is the national sport of Korea, it has a long history of being used in competition. In matches it is practiced in several forms, particularly free sparring and limited step sparring.

Sparring (variously called *kyorugi*, *gyoroogi* or *Tae Ryon*) is required in order to cultivate fighting spirit, to develop the blocking and attacking tools needed for actual self-defense, to accomplish testing requirements, and to learn movements other than those found in forms and exercises.

TAEKWONDO LIMITED STEP SPARRING

Limited Step Sparring is the application of the attack and defense techniques and patterns learned in forms (*poomse*). Limited Step Sparring can be performed as One-Step (*Hanbon Kyorugi*), Two-Step Sparring (*Doe-bun Kyorugi*)or Three-Step Sparring (*Sebun Kyorugi*) matches.

In the earliest phases of Taekwondo training, students learn Three-Step Sparring sets that teach the students how to use various parts of the hand to defend against middle and high attacks, and how to use parts of the foot against low attacks. These attacks and defenses are practiced while advancing and retreating in order to teach balance and footwork.

Three-Step Sparring is done in two methods: One Way and Two Way, relating to the basic directions in which techniques can be performed. In One Way (*Han Chok*) sparring, attacks are performed only while stepping forward, and defenses only while stepping backward. In Two Way (*Yang Chok*) sparring, attacks and defenses are performed either while stepping forward or backward.

ONE-STEP SPARRING (HANBON KYORUGI)

One-Step Sparring is generally held to be the most important form of sparring because the ultimate goal of Taekwondo is victory with a single blow. In the exercise one player acts as the attacker and the other is the defender. The attacker launches a single precise and powerful attack while the defender blocks and/or evades it and delivers a counter-attack. Though the moves of both players

are predetermined, the drill allows them to strive for higher speeds, greater skill and finely tuned precision.

One-Step can be practiced at all skill levels and can be more easily applied to actual self-defense than either Three-Step or Two-Step Sparring. The key to making One-Step work is simultaneous movement: directing a counterattack at the precise moment an incoming attack is evaded or blocked.

TWO-STEP SPARRING (DOE-BUN KYORUGI)

Two-Step Sparring is practiced so that students will learn to combine hand and foot movements. One person adopts the role of attacker and the other is the defender. To ensure this progress, the attacker must use his hands and feet alternately, but whether he chooses to use his hand or foot first is optional.

The attacker generally delivers a more complex attack than used in One-Step, mixing hand and foot attacks or combination attacks of two strikes or two kicks. This forces the defender to evade smoothly and yet requires that he stay within range for a powerful combination counterattack.

THREE-STEP SPARRING (SEBUN KYORUGI)

Like Two-Step, this method of sparring involves a more complex and ornate attack and requires more sophisticated combinations of evasive footwork, blocking, striking and kicking to resolve.

FREE SPARRING (JAYU MATSOGI)

Free Sparring is an open combat where the players use controlled attacks at high speeds. They are not bound by the ritual sequences of the One-, Two- and Three-Step patterns, and are therefore able to fully express themselves, experiment, and push back the boundaries of their previous limitations.

Free Sparring, however, is not a free-for-all. Players are required to use a great degree of control. In most matches they must stop their attacks within a few inches of the target, or make only light contact, depending on the preset rules of the tournament.

Accuracy in striking is only one of the many elements considered when judges and referees award points. Consideration is also given to the quality of the focused blows, speed, power, balance, strength and accuracy of blocking, skillful dodging, and overall sportsmanlike attitude.

Many classroom (*dojang*) matches, and the majority of official tournaments, require players to wear mouth guards and chest protectors to reduce injuries.

COMPETITION DIVISIONS BY RANK

Competitions are typically divided into ranks or classes. Some tournaments further divide each class or rank into separate male and female divisions, and into different weight classes.

Novice Class: White, Yellow and Orange belts

Intermediate Class: Green, Blue and Purple belts

Advanced Class: Red and Brown belts

Black Belts

LEGAL FIGHTING TOOLS

Closed Fist (forefist and backfist).

Reverse knife-hand (ridge-hand).

Any part of the foot below the ankle.

Absolutely no other body parts may be used to deliver blows.

LEGAL TARGET AREAS

Head: Only the area of the head protected by the head-gear is a legal target area. This includes the area of the forehead covered by the gear. The face is not a legal target area.

Body: The torso, from the collarbone to the navel in the

front, and to the "posterior axillary line" on both sides (the imaginary line drawn down the side from the back crease of the armpit).

ILLEGAL TARGET AREAS

The face mask area.

The neck and throat.

The back, including the kidney area.

The groin.

The joints.

The legs.

MATCH DURATION

Colored belt matches consist of two 90-second rounds with a 30-second rest between rounds.

Black belt matches consist of two 2-minute rounds with a 30-second rest between rounds.

If Advanced Class fighters (Red/Brown belts) are combined with Black belts, then matches consist of two 90-second rounds with a 30-second rest between rounds.

SCORING POINTS IN FREE SPARRING

In order for a point to be awarded a majority of the judges and referee (three out of the five) must concur that a valid point was indeed scored.

In the case of three or five judges seeking to award different point values for a technique, the majority again applies. For example, if two call for 2 points and one calls for 1 point, 2 points shall be awarded.

In the case of four judges calling for points, if two call for 2 points and two call for 1 point, then 1 point shall be awarded.

One point is awarded for any valid hand or foot blow delivered to the legal body area.

One point is awarded for any legal hand technique delivered to the legal head area.

Two points are awarded for any legal foot technique delivered to the legal head area.

In order to be awarded a score, techniques must be executed with good balance and form, and the fighting tool (hand or foot) must touch the legal target area with sufficient firmness.

CHAPTER TEN
Grappling Sparring Methods

All martial arts can be separated into two categories: Stand-up and Scuffle. Stand-up martial arts generally use upright stances and rely on strikes, kicks and/or weapons. Stand-up arts include empty-hand systems such as Karate, Boxing, and Taekwondo. Scuffle arts are those that focus on grappling, throwing, and wrestling. Scuffle arts include Judo, Jujutsu, Aikido, Sumo, and Wrestling. Many martial arts combine both kinds of techniques, but most arts tend to favor one aspect or the other. The following pages describe forms of sparring developed primarily for the scuffle arts.

10.1 AIKIDO

Aikido, the Way of Spiritual Harmony, is a Japanese martial art. It is an offshoot of Jujutsu, developed by the legendary Morihei Uyeshiba, in the early part of the Twentieth Century. Uyeshiba developed Aikido in order to focus on spiritual values rather than battlefield aggression, and to cultivate in its practitioners a truly peaceful nature.

Aikido techniques use passive resistance instead of direct resistance, relying on circularity, subtle postural changes, lightness of foot, balance (moral and physical), and a keen understanding of the practical application of physics. Aikido styles include Aikibudo, Shin-ei Taido, Yoseikan, Yoshinkan, Tomiki-ryu, Shin-shin Toiysu, Iwama-ryu, Aikikai, and Ki Society.

Not all Aikido styles and schools engage in competition, but for those that do there are three primary types of matches:

(1) Individual Randori Competition.

(2) Embu (Kata) Competition.

(3) Kongo Dantai Sen, or Mixed Team Competition.

Aikido skills require precise form and excellent timing.

RANDORI

In Randori Competition, two Aikido players compete against each other using any of the permissible techniques listed in the competition rules. Tomiki Aikido* follows these rules:

A Randori match consists of a contest between registered competitors. At the outset of the match, one player is designated *Tanto* (meaning he is attacking with a wooden knife); and the other player is called *Toshu* (unarmed combatant).

The contest is divided into two 90-second rounds. At the midpoint between rounds, the partners change roles; the player who was Tanto becomes Toshu and vice versa. This allows for each player to have equal time attacking and defending.

There are three ways in which Toshu can score against Tanto:

TYPE 1: IPPON (FULL WIN)

Atemi waza: When Toshu throws his opponent cleanly to the mat on his back or side, using an atemi (body striking) technique.

Kansetsuwaza: When Toshu breaks his opponent's balance while maintaining a controlling hold or lock.

---

* The rules for competitive Tomiki Aikido were provided by the Board of Directors of the Japan Aikido Association, USA, Sean Flynn Marketing Director.

Ukiwaza: When Toshu throws his opponent cleanly using a "floating" technique.

TYPE 2: WAZA-ARI (HALF WIN)

When Toshu applies any technique that is almost an ippon.

TYPE 3: YUKO (NEAR HALF WIN)

When Toshu applies a technique that is almost a waza-ari.

(4) Tanto can score in two basic ways. First is by *tsuki* (a technique using his weapon): When Tanto strikes his opponent within the target area he will get *tsukiari* (a point simulating a knife thrust). Tanto can also score by a *kaeshiwaza*, a countering technique such as escaping the opponent's hold, lock or attempted throw. The criteria for judging kaeshiwaza are the same as those of judging Toshu techniques.

(5) The points scored are of three types:

Toshu points: without a tanto.

Tanto points: with a tanto.

Foul points: awarded against either player for improper behavior or dangerous conduct.

Points are awarded as follows:

Toshu/Kaeshiwaza Ippon: 4 points.

Toshu/Kaeshiwaza Waza-ari: 2 points.

Toshu/Kaeshiwaza Yuko: 1 point.

Tanto Tsukiari: 1 point.

Chui: 1 point (awarded to the other competitor).

Shido: 0 point (but 2 Shido equal 1 point).

In the event of a *Hansoku Make*, a defeat won by foul points, 8 points will be awarded.

(6) Issue of Contest (deciding a winner): The competitor scoring the highest number of points (adding up both halves of the match) is declared the winner. When both competitors score the

same number of points, the issue will be decided in the following way:

1. The number of Toshu/Kaeshiwaza Ippon.

2. The number of Toshu/Kaeshiwaza Waza-ari.

3. The number of Toshu/Kaeshiwaza Yuko.

4. The number of Tsukiari.

If the score is still tied, the match will be decided according to superiority (Kinsa) in the following way:

1. The number of near Yuko techniques.

2. The number of *Shido* (a minor violation that gives the opponent a penalty called a *Koka*, which is close to a Yuko, which in turn is close to Waza-ari).

3. General skills, techniques, attitude, etc.

In the finals, if a decision cannot be reached within the regular match time period without using Kinsa, one extension of the match is permitted. The time for this extended match is 90 seconds, and the winner must be declared according to one of the above-mentioned judgments, including Kinsa.

(7) When a contest cannot be continued due to Itami Wake (draw by injury), the judge gives the right of play (to continue to the next match in a tournament) to the competitor who is able to continue. If both competitors are injured and unable to continue, the opponent in the next match is the winner by Fusen Kachi, or victory without fighting.

(8) When a competitor who has won a match by Hansoku Machi, or victory by foul points, is unable to continue due to injury, the opponent in the next match is the winner by Fusen Kachi, or the victory without fighting. The loser by Hansoku Make is not allowed to continue in the tournament.

(9) When the margin score between the competitors reaches 8 points, the first half is over. When the total margin score of both halves reaches 12 points, the match is over.

KONGO DANTAI SEN - MIXED TEAM COMPETITION

A match is a contest between registered teams. A match lasts for two 90-second rounds.

Judging Toshu and Tsuki techniques is done under the same guidelines used for individual matches. Point scoring is also the same as in individual matches.

Winning is determined as follows:

Five teammates each compete in a match.

In each of the five matches, the competitor who scores the most points during both halves is declared the winner.

When both competitors score the same number of points, the issue will be decided the same way as in an individual tournament (as described above).

When a decision cannot be reached, neither victory by superiority nor an extension of the match is allowed, and the match will be declared a tie.

Points for the winners of each match are counted based upon the type of decision, not the number of points actually scored in the matches.

Itami Wake (Draw due to injury): 0-0

Hansoku Machi (Victory by foul points): 8-0

Fusen Kachi (Victory without fighting): 8-0

In the case of Itami Wake, the injured competitor is not allowed to continue in the competition, even if he later recovers. However, he can be replaced by a competitor who has registered beforehand.

The team having the most winners (not points) among the five matches is the winner.

If both teams have an equal number of winners, victory is decided as follows:

The team with the most points wins.

If the number of points is equal, the issue will be decided the same as in an individual tournament.

If a decision still cannot be reached, a match is played by one of the five competitors on each team. In this match, each half is 90 seconds. Superiority victory is allowed but an extended match is not permitted.

EMBU

In Embu competition two players, acting as a pair, perform a *Kata* (a series of pre-planned techniques). The score for their performance is judged against the scores of other pairs. The katas simulate various attack and defense situations.

There are two types of Embu competition:

COMPULSORY EMBU: All techniques are pre-determined.

FREE EMBU: Players are allowed to interpret defenses according to their own skill and judgment. Free Embu has two variations:

One version specifies either a particular weapon for the attacks, the number

Aikido defense against grab and punch

  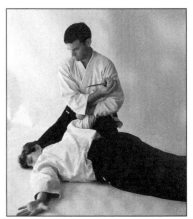

Aikido defense against knife slash.

of *Ukes* (attacking players), or the specific types of attacks the Ukes may use.

The second version gives *Tori* (the defending player) total freedom to choose the techniques that best suit him.

10.2 JUDO

Judo was developed in 1882 by Jujutsu master Dr. Jigoro Kano. Dr. Kano was a free-thinking modernist who wanted to create a version of Jujutsu that was less violent and more concerned with mental, emotional, and physical well-being.

Kano made many changes to the methods by which Judo was taught and practiced, notably changing the uniform to include long sleeves. This enabled students to accomplish throws with less stress on flesh and bone. Dr. Kano also increased the study of matwork, improved upon falling and rolling skills, and created several new throws and pins.

Kano was also a philosopher who brought many new concepts to the grappling arts. One of his most important training concepts was "jita kyoei," variously translated as "mutual welfare and benefits" or "going forward and shining together." The concept of jita kyoei is simple but elegant: when two students train together, even for competition, they are not actually competing against each other. They are training together in order for both of them to increase in skill, in understanding, and in spirit. This was a bold departure from Samurai mentality, where a person's training was solitary, no matter how many classmates shared his school.

Another concept instituted by Dr. Kano was seiryoku zenyo, the principle of achieving maximum efficiency with minimum effort. This is an ideal of both training and competition in that by learning the correct and scientific form and method for doing something, it can be accomplished with no waste of effort and energy; as a result the player will be more efficient, harder to defeat, and will not injure himself by improper form during high speed/high exertion movements.

A Judo sparring match consists of two Judo-ka (Judo practitioners or players) trying to score either (1) by throwing the other player or (2) by applying a legitimate hold that makes the opponent submit, or which immobilizes him or her for a specified time. Judo throwing skills are largely graded on accomplishing as many parts of a throw as possible; ideally all of them. The parts of a throw are:

TSUKURI: Fitting in, or positioning the body correctly, in order to perform the throw;

KUZUSHI: Taking an opponent off balance;

KAKE: The execution of the throw.

WINNING THE MATCH

Winning by a point in judo is called an Ippon. The first Judo-ka to score one full point wins the contest.

To achieve an Ippon, a throw must meet four criteria:

> The opponent must be thrown mainly onto his or her back

> The throw must be made with control

> The throw must be accomplished with force

> The throw must be accomplished at high speed.

Judo matches last five minutes for both men and women.

Judo throws are fast and powerful, requiring finely honed skills, `both in executing the throw and accomplishing the falls.

If neither person has scored a point by the end of the match, the winner is the contestant who scored a Waza-ari (half a point).

If both or neither scores a Waza-ari, the winner is determined by who has accumulated the most credits, counted in Koka and Yuko:

> A Yuko is awarded if two elements of a throw are missing, or if a Judo-ka pins an opponent for 15 to 19 seconds. A Yuko is a point, though a lesser one, awarded for the parts of the throw done correctly, not a penalty for what was missing.

> A Koka is awarded if three elements of a throw are missing or if the opponent is pinned for 10 to 14 seconds.

A match that has no other winning point may be won by immobilizing an opponent with a legal move for 25 seconds, such as with a hold that does not force a submission yet limits the other player's mobility.

If a player forces the other player to "slap out" or submit during a move such as an armlock he wins the match.

Judo grappling skills teach a great number of wrestling techniques as well as standing throws.

PENALTIES

Judo is primarily based on fair play, so penalties are taken very seriously. Penalties can lead to credits and points being awarded to the other player, and even the smallest offences lead to penalties of varying severity. More serious offences may result in Hansoku-make, which means an Ippon is awarded against the transgressor; but the referee must confer with the judges before awarding such a penalty.

If a technique is performed with some element(s) missing the player is given a reduced score (Yuko or Koko), which is still a point, though not preferred. Some competition purists regard the awarding of Yuko or Koko as penalties, but they really are not, since they recognize skills that are correct in most areas.

The various classifications of Judo penalties are:

Shido: A penalty given to any contestant who has committed a slight infringement, which includes:

Intentionally avoiding contact.

Maintaining an excessively defensive posture for more than 5 seconds.

False attacks: making an action as if attempting a throw but clearly having no intention of actually executing the throw.

Standing with both feet in the danger zone except when beginning an attack, executing an attack, countering the opponent's attack, or defending against the opponent's attack.

Continually holding the other player's sleeve in a defensive manner.

Twisting the other player's sleeve.

While standing, continually keeping the other player's fingers interlocked in order to prevent action.

Intentionally disarranging one's own *judo-gi* (uniform).

Untying or retying the belt or the trousers without the referee's permission.

Inserting a finger or fingers inside the opponent's sleeve or the bottom of his trousers.

In a standing position: taking any grip other than a "normal" grip without attacking for more than 3 to 5 seconds.

In a standing position: after kumikata (formal grasping of the other player's jacket) has been established, not making any attacking moves.

In a standing position: taking hold of the opponent's foot, leg, or trouser leg unless simultaneously attempting a throwing technique.

Wrapping or binding the end of the belt or jacket around any part of the other player's body.

Taking any part of the other player's judo-gi in the mouth.

Putting a hand, arm, foot, or leg directly into or on the other player's face.

Putting a foot or a leg in the other player's belt, collar, or lapel.

Chui: A penalty awarded to any contestant who has committed a serious infringement:

Applying a *shime-waza* (choking technique) by using the bottom of the jacket or belt, or using only the fingers.

Applying a leg scissors to the opponent's trunk (*dojime*), neck or head.

Striking or kicking in order to force the other player to release his grip.

Bending back the opponent's fingers in order to break his grip.

Intentionally leaving the contest area.

Intentionally forcing the other player outside of the contest area.

Keikoku: A penalty awarded to any contestant who has committed a grave infringement, including:

Attempting to throw the other player with a *kawazu-gake*: while facing more or less in the same direction as the other player, winding one leg around his leg and falling backwards onto him.

Applying a *kansetsu-waza* (joint lock) anywhere other than the elbow.

Lifting an opponent who is lying on the mat and then slamming him back down again.

Reaping the opponent's supporting leg from the inside while the opponent is applying a technique such as a *harai-goshi* (hip sweep throw). This kind of reap can easily break the other player's leg and is needlessly dangerous.

Disregarding the referee's instructions.

Making obscene gestures or derogatory comments to the other player or the referee.

Hansoku Make: A penalty awarded to any contestant who has committed a very grave infringement, such as:

Doing anything to intentionally endanger or injure the other player, especially his neck or spinal vertebrae.

Falling directly to the mat while applying, or attempting to apply, techniques such as *waki-gatame* (armpit armlock). Throws of this nature are exceedingly dangerous and can lead to severe injury.

Intentionally falling backwards while the opponent is clinging to the player's back when either contestant has control of the other's movement.

Bringing any metallic item into the contest area.

Judo techniques demonstrated by Sensei Art Bourgeau (4th from left) and the students of the Philadelphia Judo Dojo.

10.3 RANDORI

Randori is a grappling exercise much prized by all of the scuffle arts, particularly Judo and Jujutsu. The name breaks down in this way:

Ran: Chaotic; free; random; unplanned

Dori: Hold

In simple terms the name means "free play" or "unrestricted grappling," either of which is an apt description of the game. This exercise is the antithesis of Judo Kata, where two players perform specific throws using specific form in a specific pattern. Randori uses no patterns, no pre-chosen forms. The players choose their own techniques based on their judgment and the opportunities that are presented during play.

Most Judo Randori begins with a stand-up practice. Both partners simply try to throw each other, using only Judo throws and their variations. There are no strikes or kicks allowed, no joint locks, no attacks to pressure points, no weapons.

In some schools Randori is taught as a drill and learning exercise, where students can move past their limits and discover the methods by which opportunities may be found and exploited, and learn how to vary throws based upon changing circumstances (differences between partners in height, weight, skill, sex, age, etc.). But sometimes Randori is used as a "Shiai," or competition, either between players or between dojos.

Ideally, players should be matched for size and skill. But as this is not always possible in a dojo setting, the larger or more skillful player should reduce his intensity level to more evenly match his partner's skill.

Randori as performed by Hapkido students.

RANDORI VARIATIONS

STANDARD RANDORI: Two players, as evenly matched as possible, attempt to accomplish a clean throw. Floor pins, matwork, and chokes are not used.

SELECTED SKILL RANDORI: The Sensei, the referee, or the players themselves select a category of skills or create a short list of allowed techniques, and nothing else may be used. For example, Randori can be done using only Sutemi-waza (sacrifice techniques) or Harai-waza (sweeping techniques). This Randori helps students improve certain skill areas.

RIGHT AND LEFT RANDORI: This is a drill where the players must execute throws only on a given side (right or left), changing sides after each point is scored.

BACK AND FORTH RANDORI: In this version one person is constantly Tori and the other constantly Uke. Tori is the only one allowed to throw and Uke must allow himself to be thrown. This is a good drill for isolating throwing and breakfall skills. The partners switch roles every three or four minutes.

UKE-TORI RANDORI: This is a warm-up drill where one person executes a throw, then the other, back and forth, faster and faster. There are no points scored, but the competition comes from performing faster and better throws. Each participant is challenged to match or exceed the skill and speed used with the previous throw.

IPPON RANDORI: This is a very hard-line drill, one that is used to prepare competitors for really high-level matches. In Ippon Kumite only perfect throws are counted. A number is chosen and the match continues until the referee has decided that one player has executed that number of flawless throws. This exercise is excellent for other students to watch so they can learn what comprises a perfect throw.

NE-WAZA RANDORI: This often begins as stand-up Randori, but once a player has been thrown the real challenge begins. The throw itself does not score; the match must be won by securing a pin that lasts for at least 3 seconds or results in a slap-out, or else by securing a submission by *shime-waza* (choking technique).

Ne waza randori.

JIYU RANDORI

This is a Judo-type of exercise but is taught in many systems other than Judo, such as various styles of Jujutsu and even in some forms of Karate. Jiyu Randori (Free Continuous Throwing) is practiced by many styles of Jujutsu, some Karate styles, many Aikido schools, and quite a number of modern martial arts that combine Karate-type fighting skills with elements of grappling.

In these matches, generally held as in-school competitions, the players start by grasping their opponent's jacket (kumikata) and moving around a matted area. Like true Randori [See Judo earlier in this chapter] the goal is to use postural changes and weight shifts to position the opponent for a technique, then shoot in very fast and execute a throw or takedown.

Unlike Judo Randori, however, many schools add their own tweaks to the rules, particularly Karate-based systems that allow a wider range of kicks and even some strikes (with focused power, of course) to set up the throws. In Jujutsu-based Jiyu Randori, joint twisting locks (kansetsu-waza) are allowed, unlike in Judo.

There are few set rules except those set by individual schools. Some schools award half or quarter points for strikes and kicks with only throws receiving full points; others score it by giving a point to whomever gets the other person down by whatever means that safety and the rules allow.

WALK AND TALK

This is a grappling drill that can also be used as an in-class sparring method. Drawn out of early Judo practice, but long-since adopted by Jujutsu, Hapkido and many eclectic or combination martial arts. Walk and Talk, in the Judo sense, is a kind of non-competitive Randori where two partners grasp each other's jackets (kumikata) and then move around the floor, calling out techniques to each other and then performing them. Counter-throws are not allowed, so when one player has taken the initiative and begun the throw, the other must yield and allow himself to be thrown.

A competitive version used by other martial arts combines Walk and Talk with Randori. A third person, usually a referee, will call out the throw and the first player to perform that throw scores the point.

A second variation, much favored in Jujutsu, involves the back and forth execution of throws by partners, but the competitive edge comes in the speed of each throw. The referee gives both players a throw to perform. As they move around the matted area, clasping each other's jackets, they wait for the referee to call "Go!" The referee then starts his stopwatch. The players take turns and the player with the shortest execution time in the same throw wins the points. The match generally involves either 25 throws or the first to reach 25 points. In a tie, the throw is repeated.

COUNTER-THROW RANDORI

This is a variation of the Randori performed in Judo and Jujutsu, but with a bit of a twist. Instead of the focus being on attempting a throw, this version is based on allowing the throw and executing a counter-throw.

There are two approaches to counter-throws. The first is blocking the throw itself, actually more of a counter to a throw. The second, and the focus of this sparring drill, is to accomplish a throw while being thrown.

A person being thrown is moving with a lot of force and speed, and this momentum can either end with a thumping breakfall on the mats, or the player can use that momentum to pull his partner off balance and throw him in turn. To accomplish most throws there is a point where the thrower (*Tori*) is leaning somewhat off balance so that his weight—tilting momentarily into the pull of gravity—adds mass and impetus to the muscular power and gravity that is already working on the person being thrown (*Uke*). Normally Tori would recover his balance with a postural shift (usually tucking the sacrum in and crouching slightly,

in much the same way as a surfer regains balance on a wobbly board). However, if Uke uses his own strength to yank Tori more abruptly off balance than was intended and uses his own body as a fulcrum he can throw Tori over him and end up in the dominant position.

Furthermore, if Uke pulls on Tori's body or clothing while being thrown, the resistance acts like a speed break in much the same way as a parachute opening, so that Uke's breakfall is not as forceful, allowing him to concentrate on the counter-throw rather than his own breakfall.

10.4 JUJUTSU SPARRING

Jujutsu is an ancient Japanese battlefield art with roots deeply entrenched in the fertile soil of China and India. Originally developed by the Samurai for those times when they found themselves unarmed against enemies who still had their swords, the techniques of Jujutsu necessarily had to be efficient, subtle, and brutal.

Over the centuries Jujutsu has spawned many hundreds of sub-styles, ranging from the deeply traditional schools, or *ryu*, like Danzen-ryu, Shinowara-ryu, Sosuishi-ryu, Hakko-ryu, and Tenjin Shinyo-ryu, to modern competitive versions, like Brazilian Jiu-jitsu.

Traditional Jujutsu does not engage in competitions, but it does teach a number of combative drills that resemble sparring, such as Locked Hand Randori and Locked Arm Sparring, as well as a great number of types of weapons sparring, such as Domination and the Maze. Each of these methods has an individual listing herein.

POP AND LOCK JUJUTSU WRESTLING

Pop and Lock is a uniquely Jujutsu method of sparring that is built entirely around the first point of contact in a fight. The players have to intercept a strike or kick, deliver a quick counter-punch to stun (simulated), then effect a hold or lock. Speed and proper form are crucial. The match ends when a hold is secured and held for 3 seconds.

Variations of this skill-development sparring drill include One Point Pop and Lock and Continuous Pop and Lock.

ONE POINT POP AND LOCK

In this method the players take turns acting as attacker (Uke) and defender (Tori). In the drill, Uke has 90 seconds to strike, grab, or throw the defender. Tori has to protect himself from Uke's attack as well as manage to grab Uke and put him under control. Each bout counts as one part of a best of three points match. Scoring works as follows:

If Tori is able to successfully block and counter-punch, but does not effect a hold or lock, he scores a *Yuko* (near half-point).

If Tori lands the punch and effects a grab that he maintains for three seconds, but does not complete the lock, he scores a Yuko.

If Tori blocks, punches, and effects a lock that lasts less than three seconds' duration he scores a *Waza-ari* (half point)

If Tori blocks, punches, and effects a lock that he maintains for 3 or more seconds, or until the referee calls "Yame!" he scores *Ippon* (full point) and the round is over.

**Pop and Lock is based on immediate counterattacks,
with players taking turns as attacker and defender.**

For every strike or kick Uke lands on Tori, he scores a Yuko.

If Uke sweeps or otherwise knocks Tori down, he scores a Waza-ari

If Tori effects a hold or lock but Uke escapes within three seconds, Uke scores a Waza-ari and Tori does not score.

If Uke scores with a combination attack where both strikes make contact, he scores an Ippon and wins the round.

CONTINUOUS POP AND LOCK

In the second form of Pop and Lock, both players have equal opportunity to attack and counter, with the goal being to effect and hold a lock or pin. It is played much like competitive Jujutsu, except that the blows are focused and only a fully formed lock, hold, or pin that lasts three seconds or more can score an Ippon.

The match is set for a single three-minute round (traditional) or three two-minute rounds (non-traditional).

Strikes or kicks executed by either player and that make undisputed contact on allowed areas (torso, back, knees, collarbones, head) are considered valid points.

Strikes to the face, throat, groin, or spine are considered fouls.

Two fouls equal one "Chui", which ends the match with a forfeit to the player upon whom the fouls were made.

**In Continuous Pop and Lock both players attempt to
score strikes and holds.**

10.5 SHUAI CHIAO WRESTLING

Shuai Chiao (literally translated as "competing to throw") is a wrestling system native to China based on grappling skills used on the battlefield. The first historical mention of Shuai Chiao dates back over four thousand years, to an account of the Yellow Emperor having used it to defeat the rebel warlord Chih-yiu in 2697 B.C.E. The earliest form of Shuai Chiao was called Chiao-ti ("butting with horns") and required that practitioners wear helmets with wickedly sharp horns with which they would gore their opponents.

Shuai Chiao drawing from the Yuan Dynasty.

Over the centuries Chiao-ti was modified to include grappling and kicking skills, and during the Chou Dynasty (1122-256 B.C.E.) the system metamorphosed into Chiao-li ("contest of strength"), which included competitive wrestling as well as battlefield mayhem. Chiao-li included throws (Shuai), hand and foot strikes (Ta), joint locking (Na), attacks to vital parts (Tien), and joint-breaking skills (Tuan). The joint-locking aspect became separated from Chiao-li and, through the nurturing of Shaolin monks, evolved into Chin-na (The Art of Seizing). The remainder of the system was organized into what is now called Shuai Chiao.

Shuai Chiao painting from the Chin Dynasty.

Great Grandmaster Chang Fong-Yen was the first outstanding master of Shuai Chiao in the Twentieth Century. By this time, Chinese Shuai Chiao wrestling had evolved into four major local styles.

1. Peking

2. Paoting

3. Tienjin

4. Mongolian

Modern Shuai Chiao competitors are permitted to kick, punch and grapple. They are also permitted to strike the

Photos courtesy of The World Shuai Chiao Society, www.shuaichiao.org..

same target repeatedly (except the head) in less than one-second intervals.

Following are Rules based on Chinese Shuai Chiao commonly used in Taiwan and the U.S.A.*

1. Weight Divisions

>Feather Weight: up to 130lbs.
>
>Light Weight: 130.01 to 160 lbs
>
>Middle Weight: 160.01 to 190 lbs
>
>Heavy Weight: over 190 lbs

2. Each Shuai Chiao match consists of three rounds lasting up to 2 minutes each, with a 30 second rest between each round.

3. Winning two rounds determines the victor.

4. The winner of the round is determined when the opponent touches the ground with any part of the body, other than the feet.

5. After 3 rounds, if neither competitor wins two rounds, a fourth will be granted.

6. If after four rounds there is still no victor, the judge will determine the winner based on:

>Fighting spirit and attitude
>
>Superiority of tactics and techniques

---

* Rules generously provided by the United States Chinese Kuoshu Federation.

10.6 AMATEUR WRESTLING

Wrestling is the oldest and most widespread combative sport the world has ever known. It is certainly the oldest to be continuously practiced competitively.

Wrestling exists in a variety of forms, from Japanese Sumo to Olympic Freestyle, but the oldest documented form dates back to the Sumerian culture of 3000 B.C.E., as shown in Sumero-Akkadian cave paintings. It was also popular in ancient Egypt, and is depicted on tomb walls in the BeniGassan settlement (2600 B.C.E). These walls are covered with depictions of many different sophisticated wrestling techniques.

Wrestling as we know it today has its roots mainly in Greek wrestling, a sport introduced to the ancient Olympic Games in 708 B.C.E, only a few years after the Games were created (776 B.C.E).

There are a number of major forms of amateur wrestling practiced today (Professional Wrestling is discussed later in this chapter). These non-professional wrestling forms are marked by some of the greatest athleticism and finest sportsmanlike conduct in all of the martial arts, and are extremely exciting to both participate in or to watch.

GRECO-ROMAN WRESTLING

Greco-Roman wrestling was founded in Greece and further developed in ancient Rome (hence the name). It is especially popular in Europe, but it is widely practiced around the world.

In the Greece of three thousand years ago, wrestling was used to cultivate young men into powerful, agile, competent, and healthy specimens. Wrestling was part of a formal upbringing, as necessary as a study of language and the classics of literature. Quite a number of the most famous Greek poets, philosophers, military leaders, and statesmen were accomplished wrestlers, such as the heroic Milo (or Milon) of Crotona, the great mathematician

Pythagoras, the poet Pindar, and the great philosopher Plato.

The first Olympic Games were held in Greece in 776 B.C.E, and for 1170 years were continuously held every four years. Wars were even suspended during the Games in what was felt to be a sacred armistice, such was the universal reverence for the Olympics. The first set of rules was created by the legendary athlete Theseus, who created the three falls rule, which means that whomever earns at least two out of three falls (or pins) is the winner.

Wrestling has been an Olympic sport for thousands of years.

Greco-Roman differs from other forms of amateur wrestling in that contestants must apply all holds above the waist, and the use of the legs for attacking or defending is prohibited. A match begins with the players in a standing position, and they attempt to either throw the opponent to the mat or use holds to drop them to the mat. Trips and tackling are prohibited, as are any holds secured with the legs.

AMERICAN-COLLEGIATE WRESTLING

Collegiate-style wrestling, also known as "folkstyle" or scholastic, is a variation developed in the United States and widely practiced in high schools, colleges, and universities across the country, as well as by many wrestling clubs.

One of the major differences between American Collegiate Wrestling and Freestyle is that a player must hold the opponent's shoulders to the mat for one second to earn a fall. Collegiate-style wrestling rewards participants with "near falls," worth two or three points, for holding the other player nearly on his back.

Collegiate wrestlers also earn credit for "riding time," time during which they control their opponent on the mat but have not yet secured a pin. "Riding time" points are unique to college wrestling, and are not used in high school wrestling.

Collegiate wrestling is governed by the National Collegiate Athletic Association (NCAA).

---

* According to historians, Plato's actual name was Aristocles. His name was changed to Plato by his wrestling coach: Plato meant "broad shouldered."

NCAA Collegiate Wrestling matches are seven minutes in duration, with a 3-minute first period followed by a pair of 2-minute periods.

High school wrestling is supervised by the National Federation of State High School Athletic Associations (NFSHSAA). High school matches are six minutes long, with three 2-minute periods.

Tied matches in college and high school wrestling are decided by an overtime round.

FREESTYLE WRESTLING

Freestyle Wrestling is very similar to Collegiate Wrestling in that holds are relatively unlimited, provided they are not dangerous, and can be applied to any part of the body. Holds below the waist and the use of the legs are permitted; unlike Greco-Roman Wrestling, which limits holds to the upper body.

The United States won its first ever team title at the 1993 Freestyle World Championships and has been a power in the sport ever since. Prior to that time the sport was overwhelmingly dominated by players from the former Soviet Union.

Freestyle is the most popular form of amateur wrestling in the world, with more nations participating at the annual world championships than in Greco-Roman. In the 1980s a championship competition was established for Women's Freestyle Wrestling, and has since gained tremendous credibility and support.

10.7 PROFESSIONAL WRESTLING

Is Professional Wrestling real or is it fake?

The answer is: yes and no. It will come as no surprise to most people that Professional Wrestling is not a real competition with an uncertain outcome. The end of each match is predetermined, and the wrestlers work with each other to accomplish the amazing and out-rageous techniques that astound audiences. The personalities they adopt are roles that the wrestlers create and cultivate. So they are not in actuality a bunch of homicidal maniacs who routinely wear death masks, leather hoods, or spandex shorts.

The world of professional wrestling - the characters, the heated rivalries, the byplay between players and teams - is carefully planned by writers, organization executives, and sometimes the players themselves. Many wrestlers improvise a lot of their moves, spicing up a match with stylistic twists and turns that give the events a feeling of real spontaneity. The nickname given to this form of combat is "Sports Entertainment," a term coined by the sport's greatest promoter, Vince McMahon.

Even though the outcomes are pre-set, this does not mean that the wrestlers themselves are fakes. Across the board professional wrestlers are incredible athletes. Not only are they fit and remarkably strong, but many of them are highly accomplished in Greco-Roman and freestyle wrestling as well as martial arts and gymnastics. The moves they perform require superb timing in order to look believable and yet be executed with a high degree of safety. The slightest error could cause very real injury, and the fact that there are so few real injuries in the sport (far fewer than, say, football) is a tribute to their skill.

Some the wrestling matches are scripted from beginning to end, every move choreographed, while others are far more loosely structured. In the latter type of match (usually involving more experienced and inventive wrestlers), the outcome is predetermined, and possibly the game-winning final move, but the wrestlers themselves have to make the rest up as they go. This means that they must have very fast reflexes, quick and adaptable minds, and perfect timing for attack and response, all the while maintaining their characters, staying within the prescribed time limit, and accomplishing the correct ending at the right moment. This is not easy. It would be on a par with asking actors in a movie to improvise a knock the walls down fight scene while the cameras are rolling, and ending exactly on the right mark.

The result of this scripting and near miss ultra-realism is that the fights are not much different than the battles seen onscreen in martial arts films, only without the benefit of special effects or wires. Muscular giants of men, some over three hundred pounds, slamming into one another, leaping, throwing, falling, jumping, kicking—and all making the kind of focused contact that would impress the strictest judge in a Point Fighting tournament. That is real skill.

For the fans (nearly all of whom are in on the real/fake issue), it is the complex storylines that make Professional Wrestling so much fun. Wrestlers are "good" or "bad," with involved histories of incidents inside and out of the ring that contribute to their legends and build the tension for battles between these opposing forces. It has the intricacy of a soap opera with the excitement of a Hong Kong action flick.

10.8 ARM WRESTLING

Arm wrestling has been a popular contest of strength, endurance and technique since the earliest days of civilized man. On the surface it seems like a simple game: two players set themselves on opposite sides of a flat surface, grip hands, and then try to push each other's hands down to the board. But competitive arm wrestling and its sister art, wrist wrestling, require perfect form, finely developed muscles, good balance, great stamina, and vast determination.

Men and women, boys and girls compete in Arm Wrestling, though seldom do the sexes compete against one another. There are a number of major competitions around the world, ranging from amateur championships to big money professional matches. These bouts are organized and overseen by a number of different organizations. The following set of rules is common to most arm wrestling competitions around the world. Competitors should check with their local organization to see if there are different rules applicable to them.

RULES OF COMPETITION

The players' shoulders must be square to the table before the match will be started.

The players' shoulders may not be less than a fist's distance away from their hands at the start.

Each player's elbow (on the clasping arm) must be set into a depression, or pocket, in the table.

Each player's free hand must grasp a wooden, rubber, or plastic peg attached to the table.

The arm wrestling table.

All starts will be marked by a "Ready ... Go." The cadence will vary.

Any competitor may use a riser (a pad placed under the elbow) if their belt line is below the top of the table.

To complete a winning pin, one player must touch the other player's arm or hand to the touch pad. There will be no parallel pin calls, meaning that a player's arm must actually make contact with the surface in order to lose.

Players may touch any part of their opponent's fingers, wrist, or forearm to the pad to constitute a pin.

Players may not touch their body to their hand at any time.

If a competitor touches his body to his hand and Position is gained, there will be a foul given and the match restarted.

If a competitor touches his body to his hand and stops the opponent's momentum, there will be a foul given and the match restarted.

A player will forfeit the match with his third foul.

If a competitor intentionally opens his hand and a slip occurs, the referee will restart the match and a foul will be given.

If the grip comes apart for whatever reason, the players' hands will be strapped together.

---

* Photos of Seated Arm Wrestling provided courtesy of Bill Durant of the United Seated Armwrestling Association (USAA), http://www.geocities.com/armstrength/index.html.

The players' shoulders cannot go past the center of the table.

If the competitor is in a position that may hurt his arm, the referee will stop the match and may award a foul.

If the referee has to stop the match a second time for the "hurt arm" position, the match will be awarded to his opponent.

Players must start with at least one foot on the ground. After the "go" they may have both feet off the ground.

Players may wrap only one finger in the handgrip before the "go."

The referee must see both players' thumb knuckles at all times unless both players agree to wave the rule.

A false start is a foul.

The players must maintain a grip on the peg when the pin is made.

If a player's elbow comes out of the pocket and he gains position, there will be a foul given and the referee has the option to restart the match.

If a player's elbow comes out of the pocket and no position is gained, the referee will give a verbal warning.

If the elbow is out of the pocket when the pin is made, a foul will be given and the match will be restarted.

If the player's elbow comes out of the pocket a second time a second foul will be given, and the referee has the option to call for an additional restart.

The equal pressure rule follows the line of least resistance; both players must agree on the pressure to be applied before the start. This means that the players apply a degree of pressure before the match begins so no one is likely to use a quick snap push down to get a surprise win.

Players should not stop competing until the referee grabs their hands in the center of the table, signifying the end of the match.

The players must always conduct themselves in a sportsperson-like manner while at the tournament.

The referee has the option to give a disciplinary foul to a competitor for any un-sportsperson-like conduct.

If the players cannot get a grip the referee will give the players a "referee's grip", meaning that the referee will place and adjust the players' hands properly. After the grip is given any movement that changes this grip will result in a foul.

All decisions are final.

10.9 SUMO WRESTLING

Sumo is an ancient Japanese form of wrestling and is Japan's national sport. It originated in ancient times as both a battlefield fighting art and a religious performance to the Shinto gods. Nowadays, still performed with many formal rituals, Sumo has become a worldwide sport.

Sumo wrestlers are extremely strong men of considerable size and bulk. These mountainous men train to be as fast and as powerful as charging bulls. The size of the wrestler is based

on a diet mainly consisting of rice - the heavier the fighter, the lower his center of gravity and therefore harder to push or toss out of the ring. The Grand Champions often weigh many hundreds of pounds and eat heavily each meal while the younger and newer fighters are much slimmer in appearance.

During Feudal times, Sumo wrestlers wore ceremonial aprons embroidered with the feudal lord (Daimyo) they served. Being chosen to carry the name of a daimyo into battle gave the wrestler great fame and prestige, and many fought for the right to obtain and wear these aprons. This tradition has been handed down to the present day where at the opening ceremonies of each tournament, or "basho", the contestants parade for the audience wearing the apron that denotes their birthplace and their ranking, along with the gym (dojo) to which they belong.

The basic rules of Sumo are simple: the loser is the wrestler who touches the floor with something other than the soles of his feet, or is forced out of the ring. Matches usually last only a few seconds, and in rare cases up to one minute. Wrestlers may trip or slap with an open hand, but eye-gouging, hair-pulling, and hitting with a closed fist are not permitted and will result in forfeiting the bout.

Spectators will often see a flurry of hands as the opponents slap each other in the face, trying to break the concentration and force the other to make a bad move. Much of Sumo is mental warfare; the art of winning before the first real attacking move is even made. Wrestlers will stare at each other for long minutes to try and gain the advantage before the actual physical contact.

Six major tournaments are held every year in Japan, each one lasting fifteen days. Three of these tournaments are held in Tokyo, and one each in Fukuoka, Osaka, and Nagoya. However Sumo matches are generally broadcast every day in Japan and for many this is a staple of their daily routine.

Photos courtesy of Doreen Simmons.

At the top of the Sumo wrestler hierarchy is the Yukozuna, or grand champion, a title that, once

174

achieved, is his for life. A wrestler who has become the Yukozuna is generally expected to retire as soon as he is past his prime in wrestling skills, thereby ensuring that overall competitive standards are maintained at a high level.

10.10 CELTIC WRESTLING

Wrestling and other competitive roughhousing games have been a staple of Celtic culture for thousands of years. The oldest known mention of wrestling in Scotland was a description of the Games of Tailtinn, which dates back to 632 B.C.E. Various carvings from the 6th and 7th Centuries C.E. show sophisticated and recognizable wrestling forms such as Loose Hold and Backhold wrestling, and the legends and tall tales of folk heroes such as Cu Chulain are filled with grappling matches between heroes and giants.

There are a number of traditional wrestling forms from Scotland, Ireland and Northern England. Scottish styles include Backhold Wrestling, Loose Hold Wrestling, and Catch-as-Catch-Can. Irish wrestling styles include Collar and Elbow Wrestling, and Coraiocht. And in England there is Cumberland and Westmoreland Wrestling. The following is a brief account of each, with some notes on the various rules of play.

SCOTTISH WRESTLING METHODS

Scottish wrestling forms include Backhold Wrestling, a staple of the Highland Games, and variations thereof.

BACKHOLD WRESTLING

Scottish Backhold Wrestling is conducted in much the same way as the name suggests. Two players stand facing each other with their right arms up under the other player's left arms, hands grasping behind the other players' backs, chins resting on the opponent's left shoulder.

There is no groundwork in Backhold wrestling. The goal is to force the other player to break his hold, or to make any part of the opponent's body (except their feet) touch the ground. If both players fall down together (known as a "dog fall") they must stand, reestablish the grasp, and begin again.

In the play "As You Like It" by Shakespeare, the character Orlando was a practitioner of Backhold wrestling. Although in the play the wrestling matches were often fatal, actual Backhold wrestling, though a serious physical challenge, is a healthy and regulated sport.

The players wear kilts, often bare-chested and barefoot, and the match is fought on grass. The match is won by best two out of three falls.

LOOSE HOLD WRESTLING

This variation on Backhold Wrestling was popular for centuries but died out as recently as 1985. Unlike Backhold, Loose Hold players were not required to start with a specific grip, but were permitted to establish their own individual holds, suiting their own skills, size, and reach. The winner is the player who can force his opponent to make contact with the ground with any part of the body other than the feet.

CARACHD UIBHIST

This variation of Backhold Wrestling is played in the Hebridean islands of Uist and Benbecula. It is fought much the same way as the Highlands version, except that the form and placement of the initial hold is decided by the toss of a coin. Best two out of three falls decides the winner.

CATCH-AS-CATCH-CAN

Primarily an English form of wrestling, also known as Lancashire Wrestling and Catch Wrestling, this was also a favorite event at Scotland's Highland Games for many years. Unlike Backhold, these wrestlers go to the ground and fight it out to a pin or submission.

Catch Wrestling has received a lot of renewed interest in recent years because of the emergence of Asian-based grappling tournaments featuring Brazilian Jiu-Jitsu and Submission Wrestling.

IRISH WRESTLING METHODS

Although wrestling has been a popular sport in Ireland for many centuries, its precise origins are unknown. Some scholars claim that wrestling was first brought to Ireland by the Romans and later by the Vikings, while others insist that it developed in Ireland independent of other European influences. It is possible that all of these theories are correct, because different styles of wrestling flourished in different parts of the Emerald Isle.

COLLAR AND ELBOW WRESTLING

The existence of the Irish wrestling method called Collar and Elbow Wrestling is obscured in uncertainty, though historical records mention it as early as the Seventeenth Century.

Collar and Elbow Wrestling was fought shirtless ("Collar" referring to the bare nape of the neck rather than part of a garment), and relied on speed and subtlety. Often favoring the smaller and more nimble fighter, this was an extremely fast-paced form of wrestling. Some styles of this wrestling form permitted kicking, so players (known as "Scufflers") went bare-foot to reduce injuries.

To begin a match, the Scufflers faced each other with their left hands on the nape of the neck, and grasped the opponent's left elbow with their right hands. This is similar to the non-jacket version of kumikata (grasping form) used in Jujutsu practice. The position allowed for rushes to be easily countered, which forced players to jockey for advantage rather than barreling into each other. Kicks, sweeps, and trips were used to destabilize the other player.

The first two-thirds of a match would be fought standing as each player tried to get past the others' kicks and establish a throwing position. The last third of the match would typically involve wrestling and the pin.

CORAIOCHT

Very similar in many ways to Scottish Backhold Wrestling, Coraiocht is a stand-up grappling method found in the Western Ireland counties of Connemara, Galway, and Donegal. It has become nearly extinct, but a sports and cultural organization called the Cuman Coraiocht Cheilteach na h'Eireann is working to preserve and revive the art.

Like Backhold, this is a stand-up form of wrestling. A match is fought as a best two out of three, with a win counted when the other player touches the ground with any part of the body other than the feet.

ENGLISH WRESTLING METHODS

England has a number of wrestling styles, some shared with other countries, and others historically its own.

LANCASHIRE CATCH WRESTLING

Lancashire Wrestling, or Catch Wrestling,* is a grappling method that differs substantially from Backhold in that the players go to the floor and fight to a submission. This is a variation on Catch-As-Catch-Can, the form of grappling found throughout Northern England and Ireland.

Lancashire Wrestling is very versatile and in many ways is similar to Freestyle Wrestling, which is an Olympic event.

---

* There is also an American form of Catch Wrestling, covered in Chapter 11.

CUMBERLAND AND WESTMORELAND WRESTLING

Cumberland and Westmoreland is a tough and aggressive grappling art, believed to have been brought to Britain by the Vikings. Opponents are paired by chance: players toss their caps into the air and caps that land close to each other denote the contestants. Weight, skill, age, and experience are not factors.

A match is a best two out of three falls, and just breaking the other player's grip counts as a fall. Players can use kicks or sweeps to knock the other player to his knees or onto his back.

One of the most prestigious of the Cumberland style games is the highly respected Grassmere Games, which attracts wrestlers from all over the world.

DEVONSHIRE WRESTLING

Devonshire Wrestling has a long reputation as a fierce (some would say brutal) form of wrestling. It allows for a variety of grappling (stand-up and groundwork) as well as "showing the toe," or kicking.

Although it is often criticized for permitting kicking, Devonshire style wrestlers point out (and rightly so) that kicking was allowed in classical Greek wrestling. They feel their art is a true extension, even a preservation, of that ancient form of contest.

CORNISH WRESTLING

Wrestling has been part of Cornish history since the time of the legendary Corinaeus, the first true Chief of Cornwall (circa 1000 B.C.E.). As the story goes, Corinaeus used grappling to throw a giant named Gog Magog into the sea at a place called Plymouth Hoe. Whether this event was based on a real contest between tribal champions or a fireside tall tale doesn't really matter, because as a result of the legend a love of wrestling took hold in Cornwall and never released its grip.

Modern Cornish wrestling matches are held on a field, with a referee, rules of fair play, and plenty of spectators.

The match continues until one player has been thrown, and three points of the thrown player's body must touch the ground, (such as both knees and one hand, etc.).

10.11 GLIMA WRESTLING

Jossephson wearing the "Grettir Belt" as 1907 1908 Champion

The Vikings: massive men with long beards and horned helmets raiding the coastlines of Europe. The Norsemen were fierce fighters who craved battle and prized fighting skill - in themselves and in their enemies. Much of the Viking culture is lost these days, relegated to history books and museums, but one aspect still lives on and thrives: Viking Wrestling, or Glíma.

Glíma is a major sport in Iceland, having been brought there by the Vikings over 1100 years ago. As might be expected, it is a very tough and demanding sport. Strangely enough, the name of the art translates as "The Game of Joy," giving some insight into the love of battle so often ascribed to the Vikings. An older name for the art, "Leikfang," is often used in historical texts. The root of the word is "fang" meaning "to catch," and refers to grappling for control.

Although Icelandic weather is seldom mild, Glíma matches are generally held outdoors with the players wearing appropriate clothing. These somewhat extreme conditions of ice, snow, slush, and bitter cold contribute to the art's reputation as a tough-guy sport.

The players (called Glimumenn) stand face to face in an erect and very proud posture, each a little to the left of the other with the right foot slightly forward. They look over each other's right shoulder, but never down at the feet (the match has to be fought by feel and touch, not by sight). The participants begin moving together, circling to the right while maintaining a grip on the opponent's belt. The upright position is designed to put both players on exactly equal footing with both presenting the same vulnerabilities to attack. Starting from that kind of posture takes courage. It is regarded as cowardly for a fighter to back away or stand in a wrestling crouch of any kind.

Although the match may be fought wearing any clothing, most modern Glíma wrestlers have taken to wearing the Glimuföt, a fighting uniform with protective padding on the groin. The

---

Information on Glíma was courteously provided by Matthew Nichols.

Glimuföt also has three leather belts, one buckled around each thigh and the third girdled around the waist. There are connecting straps between the thigh belts and the waist belt. These belts are used to establish the fighting position at the beginning of a match: the right hand grips the waist belt and the left takes hold of one of the thigh belts.

Once the signal has been given to start the match, each of the Glimumenn seeks to take the other down by making him lose his balance. Leg hooks are generally used to disrupt the other player's stance. Players can even bodily pick up the other player and dash him to the floor. If any part of the fallen player's torso touches the ground, he loses.

Glíma wrestling is very quick. It requires great strength and stamina, fast reflexes, and presence of mind. With the body so exposed in the standard fighting posture, a moment's distraction could be all that the other player needs to win.

10.12 BRETON WRESTLING (GOUREN)

In the French region of Brittany there is an ancient form of wrestling that, legend has it, was practiced in the court of King Arthur. Breton Wrestling, also called Gouren, has been a popular sport since the Middle Ages and was once used to train young nobles for war.

Similar in structure and practice to Cornish Wrestling [See Celtic Wrestling], Gouren had all but faded out until 1928, when the Interceltic Tournament of Quimperlé featured the art and sparked a revival of this rough and tumble sport. Over 6,000 spectators were present at the event, which also breathed new life into other forms of Celtic wrestling, such as Backhold and Lancashire Catch Wrestling.

Gouren is a rough sport, but it is noted for its excellent sportsmanship, as well as for the participation of girls and women as well as boys and men. Gouren is fought on a padded mat called a Pallen, in either a square or circular fighting area at least 36 meters square.

PLAYING THE GAME

A bout begins with the shaking of hands and a courteous Gallic salute.

As the action gets going, the players struggle to accomplish a *Lamm*, a knockout throw accomplished by throwing the other player to the ground so both shoulders touch simultaneously before any other part of the body makes contact. If a Lamm is scored, the match ends immediately.

However, since both players are trained to counter this devastating technique, a Lamm is seldom seen. More often a throw scores a Kostin, where one shoulder touches first. If at the end of five minutes a wrestler has scored more Kostins than his opponent, he wins.

If neither player has scored a Kostin after five minutes the match goes into a two and one-half minute overtime.

A throw that makes the other player land on his lower back is called a Kein. Keins are counted in Overtime and are taken into account to decide the winner.

One Kostin will beat any number of Keins. Thus, if only Keins are scored, the player with the most wins. Otherwise, only Kostins are counted to determine the winner.

In the event of a tie, the higher quality throw always wins.

Gouren photos copyright Eric Legret and Fédération of Gouren. Additional information courteously provided by Matthew Nichols.

FAULTS AND FOULS

Diwall: This minor foul can be requested by any referee but must be given by the majority of referees. It is noted on the contest sheet. When one Diwall has been given for one kind of foul, the second warning for the same interdiction is called a Fazi.

Fazi: If a wrestler puts his hand out to foil a throw, or intentionally steps out of the ring to avoid contact, known as "fleeing the mat," a Fazi is awarded against him. This is a more serious penalty than the Diwall but it does not immediately end the game.

Poent: The Poent is a combination of two Fazi. This foul can easily make the difference at the end of a bout if the score is close or tied.

Divrud: This foul is given for very serious faults, such as hurling insults or intentionally injuring another player. The Divrud can be pronounced at any time, or is automatically awarded at the third fazi. The Divrud means either disqualification for the bout or for the entire competition.

ALLOWED AND DISALLOWED SKILLS

Matwork and groundfighting are not permitted.

If the wrestlers fall, they must stop grappling, get back to their feet, shake hands, and begin again.

If the wrestlers leave the wrestling area, they must immediately come back to the centre of the wrestling area, shake hands, and start again.

Throws do not count unless a player lands on both shoulders, one shoulder, or the small of the back.

10.13 SCHWINGEN WRESTLING

Schwingen is a grueling sport that attracts only the hardiest Swiss athletes. There have been *Schwingfests* (Swiss Wrestling matches) in the mountainous valleys of the Berner Oberland, Emmenthal, and Entlebuch, as well as in central Switzerland, for many hundreds of years.

Schwingen was started among mountain farmers, or "Sennen," who used the grappling arts to measure their strength and skill against each other. Some centuries later, the Sennen were joined by players from various wrestling clubs. The addition of loose and limber gymnastic wrestlers to ox-strong farm hands combined to make Schwingen a very exciting art to watch.

The wrestlers wear different kinds of uniforms based on their backgrounds. Players with Sennen (farming) backgrounds wear dark gray pants and light blue milk shirts. Players with a background in gymnastics (known as *Turnerschwinger*) wear white gym pants and T-shirts.

Before the matches start, judges pair off tournament entrants, roughly matching them for size and talent but not for weight. Schwingen does not recognize weight categories.

Each round is set for five minutes. Wrestlers put on their knee-long cloth trousers, tighten their belts, and roll up their trouser legs. Then together they enter a circular fighting ring that is 30 feet in diameter, called a Platz. The floor of the Platz is covered in wood shavings.

All matches start with a friendly handshake, symbolic of the general sense of good sportsmanship that has always been associated with Schwingen.

WINNING THE MATCH

A match is over when one player throws the opponent down so that his entire back touches the shavings.

A match is over when one of the wrestlers touches the shavings with the area between his shoulder blades.

A match is over when one of the wrestlers touches the shavings with the area from the neck to half of the shoulder blades.

A match is complete when a wrestler is held in a free bridge for more than three seconds.

10.14 MONGOLIAN WRESTLING

Wrestling is the most popular of all Mongol sports and is the centerpiece of the Three Games of Men, a major national competition. Historians differ on the exact age of Mongolian Wrestling, but most estimates put it somewhere near seven thousand years old, dating back to the earliest days of Asian culture.

There are no weight categories in Mongolian Wrestling, nor any age limits. The players wear heavy boots; a very small, tight-fitting loincloth; a pair of sleeves which meet across the back of the shoulders, resembling a tiny vestige of a jacket; and a pointed cap of velvet. The players enter the contest field by leaping and dancing, flapping their arms to imitate an eagle in flight.

The aim of the match is to knock the other player off balance and throw him down, making him touch the ground with his elbow and knee. Each bout is a best out of three wins, after which the loser walks under the raised arms of the winner in a sign of respect and unties his own vest, after which the victor, again leaping and dancing, takes a turn around the flag in the center of the field.

Traditionally, either one thousand and twenty-four or five hundred and twelve wrestlers participate in the contest. At the Republican Naadam, the tournament lasts nine rounds. Those who lose a round are eliminated from further rounds.

The players fight for titles of prestige. Those titles include:

Republican Falcon: A wrestler who beats five opponents in a row.

Elephant: A wrestler who beats seven opponents in a row.

Lion: A wrestler who becomes champion by beating all nine opponents in a row.

Giant: Prefix added to a wrestler who becomes champion two years in a row (Giant Lion).

Nationwide: Prefix added to a wrestler who becomes champion three years in a row (Nationwide Lion).

Invincible: Prefix added to a wrestler who becomes champion four years in a row (Invincible Lion).

10.15 TURKISH OIL WRESTLING

Turkish Oil Wrestling has been an integral part of Turkish physical culture since long before the days of the Ottoman Empire. To this day matches are held all year long throughout Turkey, culminating in the grand tournament called the Kirkpinar, held on the Sarayici peninsula in the city of Edirne. Each year up to one thousand wrestlers attend the games in Sarayici.

At Kirkpinar, the referees closely study the wrestlers (called Pehlivans), checking their records and gauging their abilities in order to categorize them appropriately for the games. Skill, rather than weight, is the deciding factor.

For the match, the Pehlivans wear leather calf-length trousers called a "Kisbet." No other garments may be worn, because true to the name of the sport, the players are slathered in oil.

In Olympic style wrestling, grabbing or holding the other player's clothing is a foul, but in Oil Wrestling the Pehlivans try to grab each other's Kisbet as much as possible in order to gain purchase on their slippery opponents. If the Kisbet is tied correctly it is almost impossible to obtain a grip.

Originally the match was fought without a time limit until a clear victory was determined, with matches sometimes lasting two days. But over the last few decades, time limits have been set. The basic match is now forty minutes long, with fifteen-minute overtimes used to keep the match from ending in a tie.

Turkish Oil Wrestling is fought for gold and cash prizes, with banks, companies, or individuals posting the prizes in return for advertising.

10.16 LOCKED BATON WRESTLING

This is a form of grappling used by some non-traditional practitioners of Escrima in the United States, especially those schools that also teach a grappling discipline like Brazilian Jiu-Jitsu or Judo. Locked Baton Wrestling was also reputedly a method of settling disputes in Tahiti and similar islands in the Seventeenth Century; alas, no documentation exists to support this.

In the modern American version of Locked Baton Wrestling, two players each hold the ends of a pair of Escrima *baston* (batons), the bars crossed, inside the circle formed by their arms.

Often the match is fought in a small, designated area, such as a square six feet each side. Sometimes it is fought in a fighting circle. Occasionally it is just fought on whatever mat space is available.

In Locked Baton Wrestling players must maintain a firm grip on the weapons...

Throwing the other player is the primary goal, but also the hardest thing to accomplish. More commonly a match is decided by accumulating points from kicks, knee thrusts, stamps, elbow strikes, head-butts, and shoulder strikes. Striking with the bar is not allowed in most cases because the blow is often much harder to control.

As this is strictly an in-school drill for improving balance, in-fighting skills, and defense, the point values needed for a win are entirely up to the drill leader. Commonly, however, scoring goes as follows:

...while working to unbalance their opponents.

Kicks score one point

Strikes with shoulder or elbow score one point

Takedowns (accomplished by balance breaking not by lifting) score two points.

Throws (lifting over thigh, hip, waist or shoulder) score three points.

The match is often set to five points.

Hits scored during a clash (simultaneous hits by both partners) do not score.

Only clean techniques score.

10.17 SOMBO

Sombo is both a fighting and competitive art that originated in the former Soviet Union (U.S.S.R.). Though the art has roots dating back many hundreds of years, both in Russia and in Asia, it was created around 1920 by Vasily Oschchepkov, Victor Spriridonov and Anatoly Kharlampief, though it was officially accepted on November 16, 1938 as a sport by the National Committee of Physical Culture of the USSR.

One of the early intentions of Sombo was to create a style of competition that would embrace stylistic elements from all of the fifteen different republics that made up the Soviet Union. Judo, the Japanese grappling art, also became a major influence on the sport's development. Sombo was also used in a somewhat modified form as a hand-to-hand fighting method taught to soldiers in the Soviet military.

In 1966 Sombo was first recognized as a sport by the The International Amateur Wrestling Federation (FILA). This occurred at the FILA Congress in Toledo, Ohio. Alongside freestyle and Greco-Roman wrestling, Sombo became the third international wrestling discipline.

The first World Sombo Championship was held in Teheran, Iran in 1973, in conjunction with the FILA World Freestyle and Greco-Roman Wrestling Championships, and the World Cup for Sombo became an annual event in 1979.

Ad for an early Sombo match in the former U.S.S.R.

In 1984 Sombo formed its own governing body, the International Amateur Sombo Federation (FIAS) and thereafter was no longer under the control of FILA. In 1985, FIAS was accepted into the General Association of International Sports Federations (GAISF), and Sombo competition was included in the World Games for the first time in London, England 1985. Because of political disagreements, FIAS split into two camps, FIAS East and FIAS West.

A second Sombo organization, Federation Mondiale de Sambo (FMS), was formed by Etienne Labrousse, former Secretary General of FIAS, in 1991. Three years later, FMS signed an agreement to join with FIAS West and the two held joint championships for three years. Six years later the FMS was completely dissolved and some of the former FMS countries broke away to join the FIAS East, and the two FIAS groups remain separate, though in 1999 a movement was made by some members of both groups to unify.

The uniform of Sombo is vital to its method of play, as evidenced by one of its nicknames: Jacket Wrestling. The uniform requirements are:

Each Sombo player must have two complete uniforms, one red and one blue, consisting of shoes, a jacket (*kuttka*), belt and shorts.

Jacket, shorts, and belt must be of matching colors (all red or all blue).

The kurtka should be made of canvas or other heavy material.

Sleeves must extend to the wrists and wide enough to allow four fingers held side by side to fit into the end of the sleeve.

The kurtka should be tight fitting and extend no more than eight inches below the belt.

The belt must be wrapped firmly around the body and must pass through belt loops on the kurtka.

Club or national patches may be attached to the left side of the chest area.

Встречу пяти городов выиграл Ленинград

The kurtka must have cuffs or epaulets (braces) sewn onto the shoulder of the jacket, perpendicular to the shoulder and the uppermost point of the arm.

A Judo jacket (*uwagi*) is not the same and is unacceptable at official competitions.

Shorts should be tight fitting and cover at least one-third of the hip.

Wrestling singlets (red or blue) may be used, although strapless trunks are preferred.

Shoes should be made of soft leather or other pliable material and should have a soft leather sole with seams inside.

Photo courtesy of the University of British Columbia.

Rubber soled wrestling shoes are acceptable, but soft-soled shoes are preferred.

THE SOMBO MATCH

The match is one period of six minutes length for seniors, five minutes for juniors, and four minutes each for masters and children.

Matches will be stopped and restarted from the center mat position for the following reasons:

Players are out of bounds.

Time out for injury or adjusting uniforms.

Time out for adjusting uniforms.

No activity by players while on the ground.

Player cautioned for illegal hold.

Total Victory or submission hold.

WINNING THE MATCH

A Sombo match may be won in one of these three ways:

Total Victory (by a perfect throw or submission hold) ends the match immediately.

Technical superiority (established by a 12 point difference in score), which ends the match immediately.

Point difference at the end of the match if there has been no total victory or technical superiority. In this case the player with the highest score wins.

Tie matches are decided by a one minute overtime period or, if there is no winner at the end of overtime, by majority decision of the officials.

ILLEGAL TECHNIQUES

Though Sombo is a grappling art, some holds are not allowed:

Twisting arm locks such as hammerlocks and chicken wings.

Submission holds on shoulder, wrist, neck, fingers or toes.

Gripping the mat or the opponent below the belt or inside the sleeve.

Twisting or squeezing the opponent's head.

Pressure point attacks to the face.

Twisting arms, legs, fingers, toes or ankles.

Punching or slapping.

Driving the opponent's head in the mat.

Gouging.

Strangling techniques or choke holds.

SCORING THE MATCH

Photo courtesy of the University of British Columbia.

Three types of technical moves will score points that count as a "Total Victory":

Pin: Similar to a Judo pin or a long wrestling near fall. One player must hold the back of the other player on the mat in a danger position (less than 90 degrees), with chest, side or back in unbroken contact with the chest of the opponent to score. A pin is "broken" when:

Contact between the players is broken when space is created between them.

The defending player turns over to the stomach or the side at an angle greater than 90 degrees.

A pin may only be scored once in a match and will earn either 2 points for a ten second hold down or 4 points for a twenty second hold down. Once a hold down is scored, a player cannot attempt another.

Submission Hold: A pressure hold (arm or leg lock), applied to the arm or leg of the opponent which makes that player surrender or submit by calling out or tapping the mat at least twice. Submission holds cannot be applied in standing position. A Submission hold ends the match by total victory.

Throw: A throw is scored anytime one player takes another to the mat in a single, continuous and uninterrupted action. A Sombo throw must:

Start with both players on the feet.

One player must unbalance the other.

The throwing player needs to take his opponent directly to the mat with one action without stopping.

A throw must knock the defender off their feet either by lifting or tripping them, not merely dragging them down.

A throw is scored based on two factors:

How the thrown player lands.

Whether the thrower remains standing (the throw scores twice as much if the thrower stays up).

A perfect throw results in total victory and stops the match when the attacker throws the defender to the back and remains standing.

Other throws will score 4 points, 2 points, or 1 point, depending on the impact point of the thrown player.

Photo courtesy of the University of British Columbia.

CHAPTER ELEVEN
Extreme Sparring Methods

Extreme Sparring methods bring together elements of different disciplines into a format that allows the players to match up using a standardized set of hard-contact rules. They often combine the strategies and tactics of stand-up percussion fighting with the scuffle techniques of the grappling arts.

Extreme Sparring methods are often very popular because they tend to be full contact matches filled with aggressive fighting and lots of action. These methods range from ancient classical systems like Greek Pankration, which has centuries of tradition behind it, to Shoot Fighting, which is barely a few decades old.

11.1 BRAZILIAN JIU-JITSU

Brazilian Jiu-Jitsu is an offshoot of Japanese Jujutsu ("The Gentle Art"), although it uses an older phonetic spelling of the name.

Made famous by Royce Gracie in the Ultimate Fighting Championships of the mid-1990s, Brazilian Jiu-jitsu specializes in submission grappling with fighters on the ground. Techniques include positional control (especially the "guard" position), and submissions such as chokes and arm locks.*

* Brazilian Jiu-jitsu skills performed by the teachers and students of Brazilian Jiu-Jitsu United of Philadelphia

In the early 1990s, Rorion Gracie moved from Brazil to Los Angeles with a desire to show-case the Gracie version of Jiu-jitsu. In Brazil, no-rules Mixed Martial Art (MMA) contests (known as "Vale Tudo") had been popular since 1925, when Rorion's grandfather, Carlos Gracie, first opened his academy.

The Ultimate Fighting Championship (U.F.C.) was devised as a series of pay-per-view television events in the United States beginning in 1993. They pitted experts of different martial arts styles against each other in an environment with very few rules. Royce Gracie entered as one of the contestants and went on to dominate the first few years of the U.F.C. against all comers, amassing eleven victories with no fighting losses.

Unlike Japanese Jujutsu, Brazilian Jiu-Jitsu is primarily a ground-fighting art and most tech-niques involve both fighters on the mat. There is a heavy emphasis on positional strategy, meaning which fighter is on top, and where each person's legs are. Positions are specific, sta-ble situations, from which a large variety of techniques are available to both fighters. The primary positions include:

Guard: The person applying the guard is on the bottom with his back on the ground. His legs are wrapped around his opponent's hips (who is said to be "in the guard").

Side Control: One player is atop the other, chest on chest, but without the legs being entangled.

Mount: One player is on top of his opponent (who "is mounted"), sitting on his chest, with one leg on either side of his torso.

Brazilian Jiu-jitsu combines stand-up fighting with intense grappling.

Back Mount: One player is behind his opponent, with his feet hooked around his opponent's hips and upper thighs.

Specific techniques are taught from these positions, some designed to improve one's position (for example: to "pass the guard" means going from being "in the guard" to getting around the opponent's legs, resulting in side control). Other techniques are finishing submissions, usually either choke techniques (cutting off the blood supply to the brain) or arm locks (hyper-extending the elbow or twisting the shoulder).

TOURNAMENT RULES OF BRAZILIAN JIU-JITSU

The following rules are for Brazilian Jiu-Jitsu point tournaments.* They are fairly common to this method of fighting worldwide, but the rules as presented here are not universal; each tournament may have some special local rules.

In a Brazilian Jiu-jitsu tournament, competitors are divided by age, belt rank, and weight class. Competitive belt ranks are white, blue, purple, brown, and black. Some tournaments do not have white belt competition. Weight categories are usually set 15 pounds apart.

Time limits are generally 5 to 10 minutes, depending on belt rank. Blue belt matches are typically 4 to 6 minutes long; higher ranks may be longer.

Matches start with both competitors standing on a floor with an open, padded mat surface. A tap-out from submission ends the match. a submission, the winner is determined on points.

SCORING THE MATCH

2 points
Takedown from standing
Knee-on-stomach position
Scissor, sweep, or flip, using legs (going from bottom position to top)

3 points
Passing the guard

* Much of the information in this section was provided by Don Geddis of www.bjj.org.

<u>4 points</u>

Mount

Mount on back (with leg hooks in)

No points are given for reversals, such as escaping from the bottom of a mount.

In addition, not all tournaments award points for sweeps. Straight ankle and knee locks are usually allowed, but twisting ones are not.

Any submission (tap-out by a competitor) ends the match.

If time expires and no submission has occurred, then the competitor who has earned the most points wins.

If time has expired and points are even, then it is a referee's decision, based on typical elements such as aggressiveness, control of the fight, minor progress, etc.

11.2 EXTREME FIGHTING

The term "Extreme Fighting" is often widely used to describe any number of similar combat methods, such as Shoot Fighting, Vale Tudo, Submission Wrestling, and King of the Cage, but it is actually the proper name for one specific style of fighting. Extreme Fighting is a roughhouse method of competitive full-contact fighting, played as a professional sport. Though it once had roots in U.F.C. and similar no-holds-barred competitions, Extreme Fighting has now become its own art with clearly defined rules, judges, referees, timed rounds, and a process for qualifying competitors so that no amateurs get into the match and sustain injury. Matches are typically fought in a roped-off ring or a cage.

RULES OF THE MATCH

No biting.

No eye gouging.

No head butting.

No fishhooking.

No kicking while either player is down. This includes an opponent being on one knee.

No kicking from the ground.

No strikes allowed to the neck, spine, or back of the head.

No small joint manipulation (twisting fingers, toes, etc.).

No groin or kidney strikes.

No attacks to the front of the throat, including gouging, pinching, or striking.

No attacks with the point of the elbow.

No use of the ropes or cage to gain an advantage.

11.3 KING OF THE CAGE

King of the Cage is a competitive sparring form based on roughhouse hand-to-hand fighting between licensed professionals. Not a style in itself, King of the Cage is a competition open to fighters of any hard contact discipline, but maintaining a specific set of rules that all players must adopt. Matches of this kind have drawn fighters from Brazilian Jiu-Jitsu, European wrestling, boxing, Muay Thai, Judo, and a number of other aggressive styles.

King of the Cage matches permit punches, kicks, elbows, knees, knockouts (percussion and choke-out), and a wide variety of throws and takedowns. During a match the fighters wear trunks (Speedo or Vale Tudo styles, etc.) and light grappling gloves. State rules vary as to whether any other protective equipment, such as a groin cup or mouth guard, may be worn.

MATCH DURATION

1. Undercard (non title) matches consist of 2 or 3 five-minute rounds.

2. Title and "Super Fight" matches consist of 3 to 5 five-minute rounds.

3. There is a one-minute break between rounds in every kind of match.

WINNING THE MATCH

1. Knock out by hits.

2. Knock out by choke (cutting off blood supply, not windpipe).

3. Tap out by player caught in an unbreakable hold.

4. A referee may stop any match if a player is injured or unable to continue.

5. Either side may end a match by having the corner man throw in the towel.

6. The ringside doctor may stop the match if any player is injured and unable to continue safely.

7. Decision, based equally on striking, grappling, and aggression.

FOULS AND ILLEGAL TECHNIQUES

No head butting, eye gouging, hair pulling, or fish-hooking.

No strikes of any kind to the back of the head or spine.

No small joint manipulation (however, control of four or more fingers/toes is necessary).

Intentionally throwing the other player out of the cage is illegal.

No chopping down on the other player with elbow strikes.

No kicking to the head when an opponent is down. An opponent is considered "down" when he has three points of contact on the mat, such as two legs and an arm.

11.4 SHOOT FIGHTING

Shoot Fighting is a hybrid sport combining elements of Muay Thai Kickboxing and Submission Wrestling (an off-shoot of Brazilian Jiu-Jitsu). Though a relatively young style of fighting, Shoot Fighting has earned an international reputation for effectiveness in both stand-up fighting and grappling.

The art developed about 30 years ago when a European-style German wrestler taught his method of grappling to two Japanese martial artists: Masami Soranaka, (a practitioner of Karate, Judo, and Sumo), and Yoshiaki Fujiwara, (a Muay Thai kickboxing champion and Judo expert). The three men combined their different interpretations of their various arts and developed what has become known as Shoot Fighting.

In Japan, Shoot Fighting has grown so much in popularity that it is now the third most popular spectator sport, behind baseball and Sumo Wrestling.

Professional Shoot Fighting currently consists only of a heavyweight division (200 lbs or more). But there are lighter divisions for amateur competitors.

Matches are fought inside a standard wrestling ring. Professional matches run 30 minutes, non-stop. Amateur matches are 10 minutes long.

RULES OF CONTEST

The players are allowed to kick, knee, or elbow any part of the body except the groin, and may use head butts.

Since no gloves are worn to facilitate wrestling, punches are only allowed to the body, not the head. Open palm blows, however, are allowed to the head.

All types of throws or takedowns are legal, and it is permitted to strike an opponent once he has been taken down.

Photos courtesy of Sensei Christopher Matthews, 1st Dan Kenpo of Jujitsu, and Tom Lancaster, Photographer. Additional materials provided courtesy of www.britishwrestling.vze.com

Joint locks of all kinds are legal.

Chokes are legal, if used against the side of the neck only.

Attacks to the windpipe are illegal.

Eye strikes and gouges are illegal.

Attacks to the groin are illegal.

WINNING THE MATCH

Knocking the opponent down for a ten-count.

Knocking the opponent down five times.

Forcing the opponent to submit.

If a player is caught in a submission hold he may grab the ropes to break the hold, but this counts as 1/3 of a knockdown.

If a player grabs the ropes 15 times he loses.

Any match that goes the full time limit is considered a draw.

11.5 CATCH WRESTLING

Catch Wrestling is an American reinterpretation of Catch-As-Catch-Can Wrestling from England and Ireland, with a bit of bare-knuckle boxing thrown in for good measure. Catch Wrestlers of the early Twentieth Century would tour the country with carnivals and town fairs, challenging all comers. Originally called "Hookers," these wrestlers earned a reputation as very tough competitors who were seldom beaten, sometimes fighting as many as thirty opponents in a single day.

Catch wrestling pictures courtesy of Tony Cecchine.

Over the last century other martial arts have influenced Catch Wrestling, and now it contains elements of Greek Pankration, Judo, Brazilian Jiu-Jitsu, Japanese Jujutsu, and other similar martial arts.

Modern Catch Wrestling is similar in many ways to Extreme Fighting and uses a very similar set of rules. Matches are fought to a submission, with a wide range of attacks being permitted to obtain that submission. A match may also be won with a standard pin determined by a 2 second slow count.

Catch Wrestling matches are either fought as one five-minute fall or the best two out of three. In cases where there is no clear winner the ringside judges must decide the outcome of the match.

11.6 SUBMISSION WRESTLING

Submission Wrestling is an outgrowth of the competition forms used by Brazilian Jiu-jitsu practitioners around the world. Unlike Greco-Roman Wrestling, Submission Wrestling allows chokes, arm locks, and leg locks of various kinds. Many of its floor holds and pins are similar to those used in Judo.

The players may wear traditional martial arts uniforms, wrestling shorts, or similar garb. Shoes are optional, but when they are worn they must be of a style used in wrestling. No street shoes or reinforced shoes are allowed.

The match is fought on a matted area that is seven meters per side with no ropes, cage, or fence around it. The players must stay within this fighting square, and the referee will stop and restart a match that has gone outside.

Different countries and even different states in the U.S.A. share many of the same rules with a few differences. The following is a set of rules common to most of the Submission Wrestling tournaments around the world.

ALLOWED TECHNIQUES

Chokes may be used, with or without the use of the uniform; however, a pinching choke that closes off the windpipe is *not* allowed.

Armbars, wristlocks, and shoulder locks are allowed.

Leg, Hip, and Ankle Locks are permitted.

DISALLOWED TECHNIQUES

No strikes of any kind are allowed.

No eye gouging or fishhooking.

No grabbing the ears.

No hair pulling.

No finger or toe holds.

No thumbing.

Techniques demonstrated by Brad Daddis and the students of the Extreme Martial Arts and Fitness Academy of Philadelphia. http://www.extrememartialarts.tv

No scratching and pinching.

No biting.

No contact with groin area.

No hands, knees or elbows on face.

No slippery substances allowed on body or clothing.

SCORING THE MATCH

Mount position: 2 points.

Back mount with hooks: 3 points.

Passing the guard: 3 points.

Knee on stomach: 2 points.

Clean Sweep: 4 points.

Sweeps: 2 points.

Clean Takedown (ends past the Guard): 4 points.

Takedown (ends Guard or Half Guard): 2 points.

PENALTIES

Go to your back (pulling opponent into Guard): minus 1 point.

Running away from other player or avoiding contact: minus 1 point.

Player and/or Coach arguing with the referee: minus 1 point.

WINNING THE MATCH

A submission instantly wins the match.

If a match ends without a submission, the player with more points is the winner.

In the event of a draw, the winner is chosen by Advantage, which is a decision by the referee or Judge, Advantages will be decided based on aggressiveness, takedown attempts, submission attempts, and overall ring generalship.

11.7 PANKRATION

Highlight of ancient stone carving.

Pankration is an ancient Greek fighting art that was also a highly dangerous sport. Pankration was featured in the original Olympic games. One early champion was Theagenes of Thasos, a boxer, Pankratiast, and runner who won the Pankration gold medal in the 76th Olympiad, 476 B.C.E.

Pankration was a grueling mix of Greek Boxing and wrestling and had two basic forms. In Kato Pankration, a contest continued after the opponents fell to the ground, a method used in the earliest Olympic Games. In Ano Pankration, the opponents had to remain standing, a safer form used for training or in preliminary matches. In ancient Pankration most of the body was open to assault, with only biting and fingernail attacks to eyes, nose, or mouth prohibited. Kicks were allowed pretty much everywhere.

Modern variations of this demanding method of sparring are still quite actively used today in Pankration schools and clubs around the world. In modern Pankration matches gloves are allowed, but individual schools vary as to whether fighters may use bare hands, boxing gloves, vinyl Karate-style chop gloves, or some version of the himantes, which are soft ox-hide tapes wrapped around the hands. World class or major competitions require open finger gloves to be worn. All competitors must wear the regulation shorts.

Modern Pankration is fought in a matted area called a Palestra, a square that measures 12 meters per side, with a circle inside it 10 meters in diameter. The Palestra is traditionally blue in color, with all necessary boundary markings taped or painted in white.

Pankration rules are established by the International Federation of Pankration Athlima. In professional Pankration, a match consists of three 15-minute matches for men, and two 10-minute rounds for women. For amateurs, the rules vary:

MEN:

World Championship: 1 round of 15 minutes.

European Championship: 1 round of 10 minutes.

National Championship: 1 round of 7 minutes.

Photos and general information courtesy of Dr. Guy Mor of the W.P.O/I.F.P.A

WOMEN:

World Championship: 1 round of 10 minutes.

European Championship: 1 round of 7 minutes.

National Championship: 1 round of 5 minutes.

There is a three-minute rest between rounds.

There are specific prohibitions about certain kinds of contact in Pankration. For example, brothers may not compete against one another; nor can parents compete against their children (even if both parties are adults). Men do not compete against women.

During a match, players may use throws and takedowns, various holds, chokes, joint locks (except to fingers and toes), strikes, and kicks. Prohibited techniques include striking an opponent who has been taken down, as well as striking or kicking to the eyes, throat, groin, or spine. Gouging the nose, eyes, mouth, and ears is strictly forbidden.

SCORING THE MATCH

Scoring targets include:

> The Head (focused contact only).
>
> Stomach.
>
> Ribs.
>
> Chest.
>
> Back (except the shoulders and spine) down to, but not below the waist.

Strikes delivered to the shoulders, thighs, calves and trunk area are out of bounds and do not score. In order for a choke to score it must be vascular (cutting off blood supply only) and not respiratory (cutting off air). The front of the throat (windpipe and hyoid bone) are decidedly off limits!

Takedowns score points as long as they are clean.

Trips and Footsweeps score 1 Point.

Trips, Reaps, and Hip Throws score 3 Points.

Lifting Throws, where the other player's feet go above the head of the thrower, score 2 Points.

Holds are scored according to the following criteria:

Any hold that immobilizes the other player for 10 to 19 seconds scores 1 Point.

A hold held for more than 20 seconds scores 2 Additional Points, and results in play being restarted with both players on their feet.

Hold held for ten seconds or less does not score.

If one player submits to the other, the match immediately ends with a 20 - 0 score (which supercedes any previous score).

If a TKO is called, the score immediately changes to a fixed 10 - 0 score for the remaining player.

If a player is disqualified, then the remaining player is given an immediate 20 - 0 winning score.

WINNING THE MATCH

The match may be won by:

The first athlete to score 20 points.

A submission.

Disqualification of the opponent.

Most points at the end of regulation time.

A player not being able to defend themselves or continue (technical knockout).

By a doctor's decision.

11.8 VARMANNIE COMBAT SPARRING

The ancient martial of Varmannie (also spelled Varamanay, Varmane, Varrmannie, and Varmany) is known for its realistic and often brutal approach to self-defense. Never considered a sportive art, this ancient Indian system does use sparring, however, to teach students how to move in harmony with an attacker and to cultivate the vital skills of reacting to random attacks.

Varmannie is different from nearly all other martial arts in that is has almost no specific set techniques. Instead students are taught concepts of movement, study the theory of combative cause and effect, then develop responses based on their own physical skills and body types.

Early stone carving of Varmannie wrestling.

Varmannie was created in the late Neolithic period of India (circa 2300 – 1750 B.C.E.).* It was taught to caravan guards for self-defense when traveling between the two principal cities in the Indus River Civilization (Harappa and Mohenjo). Varmannie was subsequently adopted by temple guards.

It was later used by the Thuggee assassins of the cult of Kâli, the wife of Si'va (also spelled Shiva). The Thugees were often called *Phansigars* ("stranglers") in the Tamil tongue, or *Aritulukar* ("noosers") in the Canarese.

---

* Some sources suggest Varmannie is older still, but this cannot be verified.

Techniques performed by Swami James Daniels and Jeff Loper-Bey.

Many scholars believe that Varmannie may be the great grandfather of Ninjutsu. The art was brought to Japan in the 1730s by an Indian tea merchant (some folktales give his name as Bashti, but this cannot be verified), and was taught to several members of the Shinowara family, a lesser Samurai Han which was involved in the importing business. It became a significant influence on Jujutsu.

Varrmanie skills appear simplistic in that they use very little movement and have no fancy flourishes. The practitioner goes for the immediate resolution of the conflict through a harsh and often lethal response. In the 1970s, one of the few American-born Varmannie teachers, Swami James Daniels, to create a less overtly destructive method of practice. He desired to keep all of the art's combat realism and practicality while at the same time introducing some safer training methods. He worked with instructors of a number of different Chinese and Japanese disciplines, and for the most part it was the teaching methods of Judo and Jujutsu that Swami Daniels used to modify the system into what he called "Varmannie-jutsu." Only a few instructors' licenses in Varmannie-jutsu were issued before Swami Daniel's death in the early 1990s.

The primary outcome of this synthesis of Indian and Japanese methodology was the introduction of focused blows during training, so that an attacker would not have to sacrifice speed and accuracy. The crushing force of any blows would be withheld at the last second in order to keep both partners safe. Swami Daniels also introduced a number of non-lethal responses to attacks, not a major part of the older system.

Varmannie's approach to sparring is very direct and not for the timid. No protective padding is worn and blows are delivered at full speed and often with considerable power. The giving and receiving of hard blows has been a traditional Varmannie "toughening" ritual for thousands of years.

Most of the sparring methods used in both Varmannie and Varmmanie-jutsu involved empty-handed defenses against weapons. Knives of various kinds were the primary threat, as well as a short club called a Bombay Truncheon. The length of the Truncheon was determined by measuring from inside of the elbow to the tip of the forefinger of the individual fighter. The ends of the Truncheon were wrapped with leather or electrical tape to give it more heft and striking power. Empty hand attacks and kicks were also used.

The players would take turns being the attacker and defender. The attacker would select a weapon (stick or knife) or opt for empty-handed attacks, and would circle the defender, attacking whenever he saw an opening. The attacker was encouraged to use as much deception and trickery as possible to create the best opening.

Once the attack was launched, the defender had to intercept, deflect the primary force and momentum of the attack, and deliver a realistic (but controlled) counterattack.

Scoring for these matches is as follows:

Three Points

Awarded for simultaneous block and strike delivered correctly.

Awarded for a weapon disarm requiring a single move.

Two Points

Awarded for parry & hits (two beats instead of simultaneous).

Awarded for a weapon disarm requiring two or more moves, including takedowns, locks or holds.

One Point

Awarded any single block unassisted by a parry or block.

Immediate Win

Awarded for any simultaneous block and counter that simulates a lethal or debilitating blow.

Varmannie uses sparring in a number of different ways, from drills based entirely on evasive footwork, such as Ghost and Guard Sparring (see Chapter 13) to a very aggressive kickfighting method known as Fighting Dragons (see Chapter 12). There are a number of other Varmannie sparring styles, involving various combinations of hands, feet, weapons, and grappling. Varmannie knife techniques are covered in Chapter 17.

CHAPTER TWELVE
Kickfighting Sparring

Used correctly, the legs are the most powerful part of the body. Unless injured or weak from infirmity, the legs are capable of generating tremendous raw power. They have greater reach than the arms, and a kicking leg is harder to deflect, evade, or injure than a punching arm.

A number of martial arts favor leg techniques over hands, such as Taekwondo, Northern Shaolin, and Capoiera. Methods of stand-up sparring that primarily rely on kicking can be found in other chapters. This chapter focuses on more unusual methods of sparring with the legs, including various kinds of leg wrestling and kick sensitivity drills.

12.1 CHI GERK (STICKY LEGS)

In the Kung Fu style of Wing Chun there is a saying: "Hands take care of the hands; feet take care of the feet." Wing Chun uses a number of different drills to develop hand sensitivity and response time, such as Chi Sao (Sticky Hands), which is explained in Chapter Nine; but Wing Chun also drills leg sensitivity and responsiveness with a similar exercise called Chi Gerk. Defined as "Sticky Legs," Chi Gerk is a difficult but excellent drill that can be done for exercise or as an in-school competition. There are a number of different interpretations of Chi Gerk, each one helping the participants develop greater skill, increased subtlety, faster reaction time, and terrific speed of movement.

HANDS FREE CHI GERK

In this style of Chi Gerk, both players stand close to each other (within easy reach), their hands clasped behind their backs. The entire exercise relies on using the legs alone, with each player attempting to hook, sweep, or deliver light but quick non-damaging kicks and stamps.

The winner is the player who either unbalances his opponent a set number of times or scores a set number of clean kicks. In the case of a tie, the match is given to the smallest person, because weight and mass are major factors in all Chi Sao and Chi Gerk drills.

LOCKED HANDS CHI GERK

For students who tend to do more evading than fighting, the Locked Hands version of Chi Gerk is very helpful. In this variation, the players grasp one or both hands so that neither can move out of range. The drill gets its structure from those situations in a fight where both parties have grabbed each other and the hands are, for all intents and purposes, no longer useful. This drill encourages students to spar much faster since the threat is constant and immediate.

CHI GERK/CHI SAO MUTUAL DRILL

One of the most demanding (and difficult) drills is combining Chi Sao (sticky hands) with Chi Gerk. That means that all four limbs are seeking to parry, trap and create combative bridges at the same time. During this kind of match the players are in constant motion, and the action is very fast and furious.

UP AND DOWN CHI GERK

This rare Wing Chun sparring method pits Chi Sao hands against Chi Gerk feet. The Chi Sao player is lying, sitting, or kneeling on the ground, while the Chi Gerk player is standing. The Chi Gerk player attempts to score a kick or leg pin, while the Chi Sao player tries to parry the kicks, trap or immobilize the legs, force a knockdown, and create openings for his own counter-strikes.

DOUBLE DOWN CHI GERK

An even more rare variation of Chi Gerk is the Double Down method, in which both players are lying on the floor, using their legs to parry, trap, and kick. Points are awarded for clean kicks or unbreakable traps. Most matches are three to five points. Kicks score one point. Immobilizing traps are worth three points, as they are far more difficult to secure.

Chi Gerk skills performed by Sifu Stu Shames and Mike Mazzoni.

213

12.2 KICKFIGHTING (NO HANDS)

Various martial arts use skill isolation drills (see Chapter 17), but a few systems (such as Tang Soo Do, Hapkido, Northern Shaolin, and Varmannie) really refine this into a serious competitive activity.

Kickfighting is a hands-free method of fighting that differs from the similarly named

Kicks Only Sparring in that the hands may not even be used to block. Defense is accomplished through evasion or parries using the defender's own legs.

Naturally this creates a very difficult drill, since each player has to really stay sharp and move very fast in order to avoid getting kicked - and at the same time has to get close enough to score.

In Tang Soo Do, a Kickfighting match is most often a three-point fight, with no points awarded for face or groin contact and no sweeps allowed. Most Hapkido schools allow sweeps but maintain the prohibition against face or groin contact.

Shaolin Kickfighting tends to be a bit more involved and allows kicks to nearly all body areas, although power and penetration are reduced to feather-light contact. Takedowns are encouraged.

In the rare Indian martial art of Varmannie, Kickfighting is done in back and forth rounds, meaning that in Round 1 one player must evade only while the other attempts to kick him; then in Round 2 the defensive player gets to kick and the other player tries to evade. This continues for five rounds, or until seven points have been scored.

The author (jumping) in a full-contact Kickfighting match in 1981.

12.3 LEG WRESTLING

Leg wrestling is a drill-based sparring method used by many of the world's martial arts, especially those based predominantly on grappling. Much like Chi Gerk, the aim of leg wrestling is to trap the opponent's legs and hold him either to a slap-out submission or until a preset time has passed. Three seconds is generally the necessary length of time for a leg hold to be awarded a winning point. The match is fought entirely by players lying down. They may not stand, though they can pivot onto a tripod formed by two palms and one knee; but the finishing hold must be accomplished while lying down.

Unlike Chi Gerk, kicking is not permitted in pure Leg Wrestling, especially as it appears in Jujutsu, Sport Krav Maga, and several Kenpo styles.

12.4 GROUNDFIGHTING

This Jujutsu-based sparring method is the most aggressive of all the leg-fighting competitions. In Groundfighting, both partners start standing upright, but at the command "Hajime!" ("Begin") they perform quick breakfalls and the match commences as soon as one or both have hit the ground.*

In Jujutsu Groundfighting, pretty much anything goes: strikes, kicks, locks, joint twisting, pinches, even attacks to pressure points. Power must be controlled and the goal is a win with only simulated injury, meaning zero damage.

Point goals are set at the beginning of a match by the sensei or exercise leader, but the

* In a few schools the players begin on the floor in Groundfighting postures similar to those used in Leg Wrestling.

matches generally follow the 1, 3, or 5 point schedule common to traditional Japanese sparring. Or matches are played until a submission via hold, lock, or pin. Submissions must end in either a slap-out or a decision by the exercise leader.

Jujutsu groundfighting can begin with the players standing or already on the floor.

Once the command to begin is given, the players go after each other.

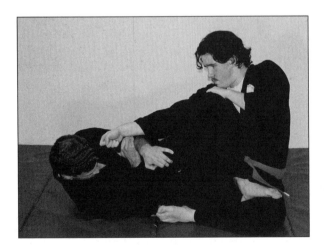

In these situations, the players will primarily rely upon leg techniques to keep the opponent at a distance or to use the strength of the legs to manipulate the opponent into a disabling hold.

12.5 HAPKIDO KICK DEFENSE SPARRING

In the Korean martial art of Hapkido (Way of Coordinated Power), developed by Young Suhl Choi as a reinterpretation of Japanese Daito-ryu Aikijutsu, there is a unique exercise involving kicks and defenses. Since many of Korea's martial arts, such as Taekwondo, Tang Soo Do, Hwarang-do, and Hapkido, favor powerful and dynamic kicks, the kick is the most feared weapon of attack in those arts.

Hapkido, an art with a focus more on defense than on sport fighting, combines kicks and strikes with grappling, and many of the defenses against kicks are grappling responses rather than counterkicks.

In the Kick Defense Sparring drill, two fighters take turns being attacker and defender. The attacker throws a series of kicks and the defender must intercept, catch and effect a takedown or controlling lock. These responses are practiced one of two ways:

LIMITED STEP KICK DEFENSE SPARRING

In this method the attack and defense are pre-arranged, based on established and very precise moves and counters. When the Hapkido-ka (practitioner of Hapkido) is just learning the art, the kicks are delivered with moderate speed and very little power, and are generally focused a few inches from the intended target. But as the student becomes more skilled and more familiar with the required patterns the speed and power of the attacks increase until the kicks are coming in at top velocity, which is a challenge for any defender, even when he knows what kick is coming.

Hapkido leg tackle. Hapkido skills demonstrated by Nick Cione and Max Schmidheiser.

RANDOM KICK DEFENSE SPARRING

The next stage in a student's development is to step outside of the shelter of foreknowledge and into the realm of true responsive skill. In this more advanced version of the drill the defender is required to defend against a preset number of kicks, but the actual types of kicks and the moment and angle of their launch is entirely up to the attacker.

The defender must be ready, sharp, aware and poised in order to evade the force of these powerful kicks and to employ a proper and efficient controlling defense.

Hapkido kick sweep.

Hapkido catch and reap.

12.6 VARMANNIE FIGHTING DRAGONS

The ancient Indian martial art of Varmannie, one of the oldest known fighting arts, has many aggressive methods of contact sparring. One of the most demanding and exciting drills is the exercise called Fighting Dragons.

The players fight in low dragon postures. They use complex close-quarters evasions, rolls and leaps to avoid contact, and a variety of kicks, sweeps, checks, and jams to defeat their opponents.

Though the exact origins of this sparring method cannot be verified, popular legend has it that a famous Varmannie warrior named Krishnamurthy, a chief of temple guards, received a tip that assassins were going to use the drainage tunnels under the palace to sneak in and

kill his master, the Maharajah. Krishnamurthy hid himself in the very low, confined tunnels and waited. When the assassins came crawling along, Krishnamurthy moved low and sinuously like a dragon, and attacked and killed the assassins.

This battle of one skilled fighter against a dozen armed killers became a staple of Varmannie's oral history, and Fighting Dragons sparring is symbolic of that great victory.

Fighting Dragons is fought by the following rules:

> The match is set for seven points, though if one player has scored five unanswered points the match is stopped and he is awarded the win.

> The starting position is a low lunge stance called the Coiled Dragon: the players each extend one foot and make contact with the blades of the extended feet, while maintaining a relaxed hand guard.

> Hands may only be used to parry and support the body during rolls or tripod kicks

(kicks performed while resting on one foot or knee and both hands).

Students may not rise to full height. They can go as high as a Low Fighting Crouch, but they are not allowed to hold this position for longer than a 2-second count.

Tumbling and rolling to escape kicks is allowed.

Acceptable targets include the groin (cups are to be worn by all players), stomach, ribs, heart and head.

Contact should be light.

Throat and eyes are the only specifically restricted targets.

PART THREE
Developmental Sparring

CHAPTER THIRTEEN
Skill Development Sparring Methods

There are skill development drills that help you to prepare for sparring methods which in turn help to improve your skills. Sometimes the distinction between drill and sparring method is impossible to decipher.

This chapter deals with methods of in-class sparring that are specifically designed to develop a variety of skills necessary to all martial artists. Some of these sparring methods require special equipment and even unique locations. As always, the sparring methods discussed herein should only be used in the presence of a qualified instructor, and while maintaining every aspect of safety and common sense. That said, these methods are excellent for building speed, skill, awareness, timing, power, and stamina.

13.1 STICK AND MOVE

The Stick and Move is a method of sparring that developed in boxing, but has since been embraced by many other martial arts that favor contact fighting. Its purpose is to develop the judgment to know when and how to close the gap between fighters, and to develop the skills to do it quickly, without telegraphing the moves.

In ring fighting there are many different interpretations of a Stick and Move. The most common interpretations are:

> A straight jab used to keep the opponent back while moving away from his line of attack, or to keep from getting backed into a corner.

A stinging jab accompanied by a sideways movement to trick the opponent into turning away from whatever posture or line of movement he had been using; essentially a disrupting move.

A jab used to stall a combination attack that also allows the defender to shift away.

A Sharpshooter's trick of performing an annoying hit and run to score points and frustrate the opponent by dancing away from whatever counterpunch he might throw.

A jab can be used to slow down or stop an attack and give you time to move.

Stick and move techniques are useful for causing damage to a much larger opponent.

In Stick and Move sparring, the players spar by whatever rules are chosen (depending on the martial art and the house rules), but all normal hits are only worth half points. A full point is scored only by throwing a jab that encourages the other player to shift and attempt a counterattack, then in turn countering that counterattack with a scoring punch.

This is a finicky method of sparring, very hard to judge; but many boxing and full-contact Karate trainers use it to hammer home the idea that Ali's old trademark phrase, "Float like a butterfly, sting like a bee" was not just cocky lip service. It was actually very sound fighting advice.

13.2 BLITZ AND DISENGAGE

Blitz and Disengage is specifically designed to teach players to be more aggressive. It can either be used to help a Blitzer refine his attack, or to teach any other kind of fighter how to use a Blitzer's driving attack to good advantage. A Sharpshooter or Road Runner,* for example, would greatly benefit from acquiring some of the Blitzer's courageous aggression. Body armor is highly recommended for all levels of practice.

In the drill the players spar by house rules, but single strikes or kicks can only score a half-point if they are worth any points at all. The real points are scored by combinations that are delivered during rushing attacks. During the rushes, the blitzing player has to accomplish the following:

> Take no serious reciprocal hits; or

> Score at least two undisputed strikes or kicks.

In forms of sparring that allow takedowns, the Blitzer should try to end each rush with a takedown and (rules allowing) a submission hold.

In boxing training, this drill helps more timid boxers learn to make the kind of move that can put them in control of a fight. It's a bit intimidating at first, but it does a world of good when that boxer eventually steps into the ring in a serious fight.

For kickboxers this sparring is used to encourage them to fight close, which reduces the odds of getting kicked.

In Muay Thai boxing, fights are usually won from close-quarters. This drill teaches students to move in and deflect an opponent's defensive hits by taking them on hip, thigh, elbow, and shoulder, so that the fighters can launch their own barrage.

For Submission Wrestling fighters, a driving blitz is just about the only way to keep from getting pounded by Sharpshooters, Road Runners, and every other style of long-distance fighter, and take definite control of the fight. It's even a good strategy against other Blitzers, because whoever can take and hold the initiative often controls and wins the fight.

---

* See Chapter 8 to read about the various types of fighters, including Blitzers, Sharpshooters, and Road Runners.

13.3 COUNTERFIGHTING

Like Blitzing, Counterfighting is a skill-specific sparring drill designed to hone a fighter's ability to strike back. In this in-class match, one player is designated as the Counterfighter and the other as the Attacker. During the spar, the Attacker can score points normally, but the Counterfighter may only score when he has performed one of the following combinations:

> Block and counter-punch.
>
> Evasion and simultaneous counterattack.
>
> Parry and hit.
>
> Parry and trap with hit.
>
> Absorb and hit.

The Counterfighter cannot score with single shots or combinations that he initiates; only in immediate response to the Attacker's moves.

13.4 LIMITED CONTACT

Limited Contact Sparring is designed to hone any fighter's accuracy in selecting and hitting specific targets. Matches of this kind are usually in-classroom bouts. The instructor will designate one or more parts of each player's body as "fair" and everything else is off limits. Choices might be: heart and right floating rib; or solar plexus only; or even as limited as left chest. The nature of the target does not matter, except that it should be moderately safe (if it is hit) and difficult to get at, which defines the nature of the drill.

Point Fighters quite often use this drill to make a student look for the perfect opening and then fire a shot into the gap without hesitation. Boxers also use this drill, modified so that not only are they given a specific target they're allowed to hit, but they have to hit it with a specific kind of punch (jab, cross, etc.)

Limited Contact Sparring can be done as a one-way drill, meaning that one player has limitations imposed on him but the other does not; or it can be done with both players having similar limitations. For the latter, the teacher may designate different targets for each player or can call out a different target every few moments during a match, changing the target when one or another player has scored a point.

13.5 FREESTYLE SPARRING

Freestyle Sparring is often confused with the similarly named Free Sparring, but the two are actually quite different. "Free Sparring" per se is a method of competitive fighting used by many of the world's traditional martial arts, such as Karate, Taekwondo, and Kung Fu. In this regard, "free" refers to sparring that is not pre-arranged or limited in specific techniques or number of steps. It is the opposite of Limited Step Sparring, which is completely pre-arranged. In Free Sparring the players get to choose their own techniques and decide whether to play for points or to a time limit, but they have to use skills and strategies that are particular to their art and their style. A Goju Karate player, for example, would fight differently than would a Uechi-ryu Karate player; just as a practitioner of Hung Gar Kung Fu would Free Spar differently than a Wing Chun practitioner.

Freestyle Sparring is completely different in that adherence to the technical philosophy and stylistic shadings of any specific art or method is not required. The "free" here is used accurately, and there are two major types of Freestyle Sparring: Tournament and Comparing.

TOURNAMENT FREESTYLE SPARRING

Tournament Freestyle Sparring is another name for Open-Style Tournaments, or tournaments where players from any martial art may participate. These are very popular around the world as they provide a great education for the players and the audience. With open tournaments, a Shorin-ryu Karate player may encounter a Northern Shaolin player in one bout and a Brazilian Jiu-Jitsu player in the next. Much of this is the pure chance of the draw, though the fighters are usually separated by weight class, sex, and, in some cases, skill level.

Whichever art is hosting the event sets the rules for the sparring competition, but they are usually fairly general. Unless a grappling art is hosting the competition, open tournaments seldom allow much in the way of takedowns (except for sweeps), locks, holds, or pins. Body targets are often limited; strikes to the eyes, throat, ears, groin, spine, kidneys, and knees are generally disallowed. Rarely are locks to small joints (fingers, toes) allowed, even when the competition is hosted by grapplers. Most of these matches are point-based, and the rounds have time limits.

In recent years, with the rising popularity of extreme grappling competitions such as Submission Wrestling, Catch Wrestling, and King of the Cage, knockouts and matwork have become more common in open tournaments than ever before.

Because of the inherent risk of injuries, there are very few Freestyle Weapons tournaments. Most weapons are fought in matches within their own, or closely related, styles.

FREESTYLE COMPARING

One of the oldest forms of communication in the martial arts has been two players of different schools, arts, or styles matching against one another in order to test themselves. In Sixth Century Chinese villages and Feudal Period Japanese town squares; in Siamese town fairs and Scottish village greens; men and women have stepped onto fighting squares to match with their peers, rivals, and colleagues. This has typically been done as a respectful meeting of like-minded martial artists, but sometimes it can end with bloodshed and tragedy.

In the Twentieth Century, when the age of dueling (as both a pastime and a way of settling disputes) had pretty much ended, fighters of different disciplines had two ways in which to test themselves against other arts and fighters. They could enter a tournament or they could compare.

Comparing is the nickname for a friendly meeting between martial artists of different arts or styles. Generally the players decide beforehand on an informal set of rules (no eyes, no forceful contact, etc.), then begin sparring. Often these matches begin slowly so that the players can get to know each other and find a level of intensity that is appropriate and comfortable to both. Speed increases as familiarity with the other player's ability grows, based largely on each person's ability to block. If a player from one style is matched with someone whose defensive skills are not as sharp, it is the better fighter's moral imperative to moderate his own intensity so that the exercise remains fair.

Comparing is not about winning, but about learning. Only the shabbiest person would use a Comparing match to inflate his own ego. Luckily, the martial arts (both Eastern and Western) stress humility and a sense of fair play.

By Comparing, each fighter gets to stretch the parameters of his own personal knowledge and experience. No art, no matter how well-rounded and developed, has all the answers; just as no art possesses every conceivable technique. There is always something wonderful to learn by looking a little farther than your own reach. There is an axiom from Kyudo, the Japanese art of archery, that observes, "Do not look to your own bow nor even your arrow, for you know what they are and what they will do. Look rather to the man who has just caught your arrow on his shield. There is something to learn in that."

Taekwondo teacher Loren Lalli executes a jump kick defense.

13.6 BLINDFOLD TOUCH SPARRING

This sparring method was mainly developed by Kung Fu practitioners to develop reaction time and sensitivity, though now many martial arts around the world use it as a skill builder.

Perceptual awareness is fundamental to a martial artist. Perception is something that must be able to function efficiently on an instinctive level, far removed from the often inefficient interference of the conscious mind. The information provided by the senses is vast, and requires the high-speed processing and analysis of the subconscious mind to make the best use of that information.

Sight is naturally the most commonly used of the five senses, but it can be relied upon too heavily. Relying too much on sight can lead to problems when involved in close-quarters grappling, fighting in the dark, taking a hit to the face that makes you see stars, having sweat or blood in the eyes, or when attacked from behind. In each of those situations, struggling to see is something of a liability because it wastes time and it tends to become more of a distraction. A person who has trained to fight with other senses, especially sound and touch, is equipped to handle those extreme situations.

Reaction time is dependent upon the time it takes for sensory information to be received and processed. This is called temporal processing. Sight has the longest temporal processing time of the five senses, because our minds tend to translate distances farther than they really are; if a punch is thrown, the body thinks it has more than enough time to react, so any reaction will naturally be delayed. Therefore, the body will not move at the highest immediate speed, though it will adjust and accelerate as the fight goes on.

Conversely, the sense of touch has an immediate temporal processing time because (obviously) at the point of contact there can be no distance between the defender and the attacker. Consider the immediate, galvanizing leap someone will make when they suddenly feel a spider touch them. If that same person watched the spider descend on a web and planned to move at the moment of contact, that deliberate movement would never be as shockingly fast or abrupt. Grapplers have known this for centuries. This is why in Olympic Judo, for example, you seldom actually see a throw completed: the players can feel the beginning of any aggressive move and immediately react to negate the throw.

All of which brings us to Blindfold Sparring. This drill is designed to help a stand-up fighter develop the same lightning fast reaction time as experienced grapplers, a skill especially useful in close-quarters fighting.

There are two approaches to Blindfold Sparring: One Man and Two Man. It is recommended that a referee or exercise leader be standing by throughout the exercise, since someone has to be an observer for safety's sake.

ONE MAN BLINDFOLD SPARRING

As the name implies, in this form of sparring only one person wears a blindfold. The other is sighted and very, very careful. Only points scored by the person with the blindfold are counted.

In the earliest stages of this drill the sighted player holds a soft object, such as a folded uniform belt, a piece of foam, or a foam-padded stick. Holding the object, he circles the other player as quietly as possible, occasionally reaching out to touch him. As soon as the blinded player either perceives the other player or feels contact, he has to deliver a quick but very light blow, simply trying to make contact. Based on the placement of the object and the angle of contact, he may be able to calculate the other player's position and aim a blow to a legitimate target. To make the exercise more difficult, it is useful to have a lot of background noise, such as music.

The next level increases the need for faster reaction time, but also increases the risk to the sighted player. In this phase the sighted player uses his own hands and feet to reach out and lightly tap the blinded player. Again, based on the type of blow and angle of hit, the blinded player may be able to correctly calculate a return blow. For example, a tap on the head would suggest that the other player is likely using his hand and standing fairly close, whereas a tap-kick to the stomach could have been delivered from extreme range. Practice helps the blinded player identify the logical angles of response, and also helps him learn to deliver fast blows. However, any counterstrikes must be done with a high degree of focused power so that making contact with the sighted player does not result in injury.

Another upgrade for this sparring form, drawn from Jujutsu and Hapkido, is for the sighted player to step in quietly and grab the blinded player's limbs or clothing. The blindfolded player has to immediately respond by striking or seizing control of the other player.

TWO MAN BLINDFOLD SPARRING

This version of Blindfold Sparring is based largely on practices from the Wing Chun and Shaolin styles of Kung Fu. In these drills both players are blindfolded and have to fight the entire match without sight, relying on touch and, to a lesser degree, sound.

In Wing Chun's Blindfold Chi Sao, the players begin by standing close with hands and wrists lightly touching (sticking). Each player has one yang hand and one yin hand*. During the match, players can withdraw their hands to attack or to neutralize an attack, but contact must be restored within one second. If contact is broken by either player for more than one second, the match stops.

No contact may be made to the eyes, ears, mouth, nose, temples, back of the head, throat, or neck. Without sight, the players have to sense where these locations are, something they can also mentally extrapolate from the body parts they touch.

Points may be scored anywhere on the torso, and on the head except where restricted. It is strictly prohibited to strike with the head, knee, tip of the elbow, or fingertips. The players' elbows may be used for defense only, not for attack.

Northern Shaolin Blindfold Sparring is a way of teaching evasiveness, immediate reaction time, and counterattack. It is used by all of the animal styles except Tiger. Tiger is omitted since it is built entirely around attack, and two players using Tiger in a blindfold drill would be very dangerous.

In other martial arts such as Taekwondo, Kenpo, and Karate, blindfold sparring has become a popular way of helping students overcome timidity, as well as for developing overall skills.

---

* This means one hand is up and the other down. See Chi Sao, Chapter 9.

BLINDFOLD GRAPPLING

Like stand-up Blindfold Sparring, the purpose of grappling while wearing a blindfold is to develop immediate reaction time. It is a very old grappling drill and one that appears in one form or another in Jujutsu, Judo, Sombo, Shuai Chiao, Hapkido, and Varmannie.

Blindfold sparring is rarely used in standup grappling practice or Randori, but is almost exclusively used in Ne-waza (matwork). Throwing while blindfolded is a needlessly dangerous exercise.

The players start out on the floor wearing blindfolds. Often they are positioned sitting back to back, or with one standing as the other kneels, or both players kneeling facing each other. Passive contact is made so that the players know where each other is situated. When the command is given to begin, both players wrestle normally, relying on what they feel rather than what they might see.

In matwork, the eyes are rarely useful and often distracting. Grappling on the floor requires spherical thinking, and many movements are so small as to be visibly imperceptible anyway. One cannot see the slight increase in the tension of an inner elbow tendon during the middle of a grapple—something that might signal an arm powered counter pull—but one can easily feel it and therefore react immediately to it.

As players practice Blindfolded Grappling they discover an important (and rather amusing) fact: the blindfold doesn't matter. It is the sense of touch all along that makes grappling work, not the sense of sight. This helps students place a higher value on their other senses.

13.7 VARMANNIE GHOST AND GUARD SPARRING

This is a method of sparring particular to the Indian martial art of Varmannie, which can be traced back to the Indus River Civilization (circa 2300 – 1750 B.C.E.). This ancient art is based more on concepts of movement rather than specific physical techniques. Those concepts are:

Evasion

Interception

Deflection

---

* See Chapter 11 for more details on the history of Varmannie.

Redirection

Simultaneous Movement

Fluidity

Ghost and Guard Sparring is most often used as a knife defense drill, but it can also be used for defense against attacks with other kinds of weapons, as well as hand and foot attacks.

PLAYING THE MATCH

One player is designated Ghost and the other is called Guard.

Guard is given a mock weapon, such as a wooden knife.

Ghost stands in the center of a large, clear space.

A third person acts as timekeeper and referee, using either an egg timer or a stopwatch.

The timekeeper calls "Now!" and the match begins.

Guard has one minute to try to deliver a simulated killing blow.

Ghost has to avoid contact completely by any means of evasion: ducking, leaping, rolling, etc.

SCORING THE MATCH

Ghost begins the match with ten points.

For matches in which Guard is using a weapon:

> Every time Ghost uses his hand or foot to block or deflect a blow he loses one point.

> For every non-lethal simulated touch managed by Guard, Ghost loses two points.

> If Guard manages a lethal simulated touch, the match ends with Ghost scoring zero points.

For matches where Guard is using hand and foot attacks instead of a weapon:

> Every hand strike to a non-crippling target deducts two points.

> Every kick scores three points.

> A simulated crippling blow ends the match.

For matches where Guard is acting as a grappler:

> Any grab that is shaken off is a one-point deduction.

> A grab resulting in a pull off balance (followed by Ghost's recovery) is a two-point deduction.

> A takedown without a finish off deducts five points.

> A takedown and finish off or pin ends with a zero score.

> Grappling rounds are ninety seconds in length.

Guard and Ghost swap roles after each round and the match is a best out of five rounds.

13.8 TETHERED SPARRING

This is a sparring exercise used by many arts to cultivate battle courage in timid students. The tether in question is usually a stout rope tied from belt to belt, or a uniform sash wrapped around each player's wrists. The tether should be long enough to allow practical evasions but short enough so that players are always within range for a hit.

Some preliminary practice is needed to learn how to maneuver with the limitations imposed by the tether. Moving combatively without getting entangled in the tether is fairly difficult. Blocking and evading attacks while unable to move completely out of range is tough as well.

Generally one of the two players is somewhat senior and plays the aggressor, controlling

One form of tethered sparring is to have the players simply hold on to the ends of a staff.

the level of intensity and making sure that the other player is given as difficult a challenge as possible while still monitoring the overall safety of the exercise.

Depending on the techniques taught in or allowed by the school which uses this method of sparring, the players have a lot of freedom in their selection of strikes, kicks, and blocks. In schools such as Kenpo and Hapkido, takedowns are allowed; in Taekwondo schools they are not.

Since the players are forced by the very nature of the exercise to stay constantly within range of each other, the match is generally very short.

Binding the other player with the tether is strictly forbidden. It would be too easy to accidentally choke or injure the other player.

13.9 WATER SPARRING

Sparring in and under water is a beneficial but highly dangerous method of non-competition sparring. Water is dense and its mass creates a great deal of resistance, which makes it far more difficult to deliver any techniques. Moving quickly through water requires a great deal of exertion, and the buoyancy of the water can easily disrupt a stance. Water changes the standard and expected effects of gravity on bodies in motion.

Regular martial arts training in water has been used as a strength-builder for centuries, by Karate masters. Gogen "the Cat" Yamaguchi, one of the earliest pioneers of Goju-ryu Karate (under system founder Chojun Miyagi), would train in the icy Sea

Karate master Yamaguchi.

of Japan and would do meditations and drills while standing or sitting beneath the heavy rush of a waterfall.

In more modern times, physical therapists have used pool training as a safe but effective way of rebuilding muscular strength and balance after injuries, strokes, or surgeries. Many martial artists have reclaimed their skills with this method following all manner of accidents.

As for sparring in water, there are two basic approaches: Partial Submersion and Aqua Fighting.

PARTIAL SUBMERSION SPARRING

In this method, the players are actually standing in water, the depth of which is their choice. For practicing hand skills, deeper water is better. For kicking skills, shallow water (no higher than waist level) provides an enormously difficult challenge. For grappling the level of water doesn't matter. In all three cases it is important that both players are competent swimmers and that there is a third person standing by to act as referee/lifeguard, preferably someone who is trained in first aid and CPR.*

Since this is a non-competitive sparring method, there are no rules for underwater sparring other than a few safety precautions and those rules set by the players, such as:

No intentional dunking of another player.

---

* It is a good idea for everyone who studies martial arts to take a licensed First Aid course and become certified in CPR. Appendix ii contains instructions on basic first aid and CPR.

No holding the other player below the surface.

No strikes at all to the face, throat, or groin.

No splashing as a distraction.

Players should agree on a hand sign for crisis situations such as injury or choking on water. A t-shaped "Time Out" is usually good.

Training in water while wearing a gi, or at least uniform pants, makes the drill even harder by adding the sodden resistance of clothing to the pull of the water.

AQUA FIGHTING

This is a sparring method used in Southern Chinese Kung Fu systems such as Chi Chi Su Gung Fu, in India's Varmannie-jutsu, and in Korea's Yu Sool Hapkido. Essentially, Aqua Fighting is underwater kickboxing.

Aqua Fighting performed by the author and Sifu Stu Shames.

The combatants wear swimsuits and diving masks. The swimsuits may either be standard trunks or tank-style body suits designed not to slip off. No fins are allowed, and aside from the mask, no protective equipment is used.

A match is fought only in a swimming pool and only with CPR-certified supervision by a third party. The length of each round is determined by the first person to come up for air. Whenever that person signals with a "Time Out" gesture, the fighting immediately stops.

PLAYING AQUA FIGHT

A match begins with the players standing up to their chests in the water.

No player may put his head below the surface until the first point is scored.

Once either player has scored a point, one or both players may go below the surface of the water and continue the match.

Contact must be fast and light, and to be scored a point must connect without interference by block or parry.

Clash points are not counted.

Kicks to the groin are not permitted.

No contact at all may be made to the facemask, head, or throat.

Grappling may be used, but the opponent may not be held for longer than five seconds.

Players may not hold onto the edge of the pool.

A tap to the upper shoulder (deltoid) counts as a face strike.

Strikes delivered out of the water do not count.

Hand strikes delivered below the water count as a single point.

Kicks delivered below the water count as two points.

The match is set for five points however many rounds it takes.

13.10 STREET CLOTHES SPARRING

This is an excellent skill building method of sparring, useful in preparing students for real-world self-defense. Training and sparring in street clothes makes sense. After all, how often is a person mugged in the middle of a dojo?

The clothing worn in martial arts training is necessarily loose and unrestrictive. Clothing worn outside of the school is often just the opposite. Suits, tight jeans, long skirts, winter coats; all of these present limitations for a person trying to use martial arts on the street. If a student has never trained in street clothes, he may not actually be able to fight in them. The distraction that comes from these unexpected limitations can create easy openings for a mugger.

There are two approaches to street clothes sparring. One is just to occasionally spar with whatever clothes one brings to class, just to get a feel for the changes in flexibility and restriction. The other is to start making clothing selections based on potential self-defense needs. High heels may be great for stamps and groin kicks, but they endanger the ankle. A tight pair of jeans may be a fashion statement, but it is nearly impossible to kick in them. A fluffy winter coat may keep out the cold but if it is too puffed up, blocking and punching may become exercises in futility.

13.11 TAG-TEAM SPARRING

Tag-Team Sparring is not like Professional Wrestling, where everyone ignores the rules and tries to see how many sucker punches they can get in before the referee notices. As used in Karate, Taekwondo, and Kenpo, Tag-Team Sparring is a controlled in-class method designed to teach speed, reaction time, courage, and above all, adaptability.

In a match, each team has two players. Size, rank, age, and sex are not considered when picking the players. The more variety the better.

Two players kneel in readiness at the outside edge of the sparring area; the other two players face each other in the center of the space. For clarity, call one team Red 1 and Red 2, and the other White 1 and White 2.

When the command is given to go, Red 1 and White 1 begin to spar.

Depending on the pre-set rules, they either fight to one or two points (or in the case of Karate, two half-points or one Ippon/full point).

If White 1 has been scored upon, he steps back and touches hands with White 2.

White 2 rises and begins sparring with Red 1.

If Red 1 scores on White 2, this time it is Red 1 who sits and Red 2 continues with White 2.

If Red 1 scores on White 2, then Red 1 sits.

After a full match has been played, the players draw lots to see which team they will be on for the next round.

Using three or more players on each team makes the drill much more challenging and unpredictable.

CHAPTER FOURTEEN
Skill Isolation and Enhancement Sparring Methods

Some of the drill-based sparring methods are used to isolate and develop specific skill areas where they have either been shown to be deficient or when simple improvement is desired. For example, a young student who has good boxing skills but is timid with his kicks may be placed in a sparring drill where he is only allowed to use his feet. Or a ring fighter experienced in kickboxing who, in entering an open tournament where grappling is allowed, may be asked to spar using grappling only so that he gets to understand the skills and mental approach of the grapplers he may soon face.

Any skill area can be isolated with the right kind of sparring drill, and this chapter includes a number of tried and true approaches from a great number of very different martial arts disciplines.

14.1 LIMITED WEAPON SPARRING

This sparring method is designed to help students improve in specific skills areas, such as kicks, blocks, hand strikes, and evasions. The "limitation" to which the name refers is the selection of tools a player will be allowed to use during the sparring match.

For example, a student who has good kicks but poor hand strikes would be required to spar using his hands. In such a drill the rules could be set in a variety of ways:

Both players fight hands only.

One player fights hands only, the other may use kicks.

One player must fight with closed fist strikes, the other must fight only with open hand blows.

One player must fight using boxing style techniques, the other may fight with any style.

One player must fight using open hands, fists, and elbows (like Muay Thai), while the other must fight using open hands only.

One player must fight using open hands, fists, and elbows (like Muay Thai), while the other fights using feet and knees only.

One player may block only but may not strike back.

Percussion vs. blocks only.

When kicks are the Limited Weapon, variations include:

A player may use only kicks to attack, and hands only to block; the other player may use any style.

Both players must use kicks only, hands may not be used to block.

One player must use snapping kicks, the other may use only hooking kicks.

One player must lie down and use kick techniques, the other player may stand.

One or both players must use jumping kicks only.

One or both players must use high kicks only (or low only).

One or both players must use spinning kicks only.

Players may only score with leg takedowns (sweeps, unassisted reaps, etc.).

These are methods that quickly work to isolate and develop specific areas of skills. They are not easy, but they are fun for students who love a challenge.

A different take on this method of sparring is Mismatched Skill Sparring, which is much the same as Mixed Style Sparring except that

Kicking vs. grappling.

it is generally used within a specific style. Mismatched Skill Sparring is used by arts such as Hapkido, Kenpo, Pankration, Krav Maga, and Jujutsu—systems that have a variety of skill areas, including kicking, striking, locking, holds, throwing, and matwork.

The idea is to give the players a specific skill area to use and then match them against players assigned other skill areas. Sparring combinations might include:

Hand fighting vs. grappling.

Hand fighting vs. kick attacks.

Grappling vs. kicking.

Grappling vs. boxing.

Medium and large joint locking vs. immobilization holds.

Sweeps and trips vs. throws.

Kickboxing (hands and feet) vs. submission grappling.

Defensive evasion and blocking (only) vs. kicking.

Defensive evasion and blocking vs. grappling.

Grappling escapes vs. throw attempts.

14.2 UP AND DOWN SPARRING

Fighting from seated and floor positions is used variously in sporting and self-defense martial arts. The seated position allows players to practice defenses from apparently vulnerable postures, to begin matches from a neutral and even meditative starting point, and to provide an interesting twist on competitive combat.

KARATE SEATED DEFENSE SPARRING

In some forms of traditional Karate there is an exercise that is used as a way of demonstrating that style's ability to go from a passive rest position into full-speed action in the blink of an eye. It has two primary variations: Ippon Kumite and Goshen-jutsu.

Ippon Kumite: In this version the players begin by sitting on chairs, facing one another. At the referee's command of "Hajime!" (Begin!), they launch themselves out of the chairs and at each other. From that point on it is a standard Ippon Kumite (One Point Sparring match), but the emphasis is more on winning quickly than merely winning.

Goshen-Jutsu: This variation is a self-defense sparring method (Goshen-jutsu means "self-defense") and is practiced either with Tori (the defender) seated and Uke (the attacker) standing; or with Tori and Uke sitting side-by-side as if on a park bench or bus seat.

In the version where only Tori is seated, Uke circles around him and selects his own moment of attack, rather than have the referee call Hajime. This means that Tori has to be constantly aware of where Uke is and be prepared for an attack from any angle. In the side-by-side version, Uke also chooses his moment of attack, but Tori knows at least where he is and from what angle he'll attack. This method is often used as a role-playing method of self-defense training for women students of Karate as it allows them to learn defense methods for attacks common in date rape situations.

Karate seated sparring skills performed by Toshiro Yamato and Andy Collins.

UP AND DOWN RANDORI

As used in Jujutsu, Up and Down Randori is a grappling exercise that allows holds, locks, pins, attacks to pressure-points, chokes (those which cut off blood, not air), as well as strikes and kicks. In short, it allows all of the techniques normally allowed in standing Jujutsu except that the sparring match begins on the floor.

Up and Down Randori is typically played in a three round match, with positions changed at the beginning of every round. In the first round, one student kneels in formal posture while the other player stands behind him. The second player's right knee and shin make light contact to the kneeling player's back, his right hand resting lightly on the kneeling player's left shoulder. This position gives the kneeling player the positional advantage because he has the lower center of gravity, but the placing of the other player behind his back is an attempt to equalize the starting advantage.

At the beginning of the second round the players swap places. For the third round both players are seated back to back on the mat with feet and palms flat on the floor before they begin.

SCORING THE MATCH

Strikes and kicks are allowed, but contact must be made very lightly.

Strikes and kicks to the torso score one point each.

Simulated (focused) strikes to the face score two points.

Chokes that cut off the blood may be used.

A choke lasting five seconds or more that does not end in a submission scores two points.

A choke that ends in a submission scores five points.

A large or medium joint lock maintained for five seconds that does not end in a submission scores two points.

A large or medium joint lock maintained that ends in a submission scores five points.

Small joint locks maintained for five seconds not ending in a submission score two points.

Small joint locks that end in a submission score five points.

Submission from a pressure point attack scores five points. Pressure points must be pressed, not struck, and may not be used on the groin, eyes, nose, kidney, throat, or liver.

The match is set for three 60-second rounds.

Winning can be accomplished either by submission or by best score.

Submissions only count in that particular round and do not end the entire match.

14.3 LOCKED HAND SPARRING

Locked Hand Sparring exists in one form or another all over the world. It has been a means to settle tribal disputes in cultures as diverse as the Vikings and the Apaches, and has been used as a test of courage for young men in countless cultures.

The fighters grip hands, usually the left hands, by circling each other's thumbs. The grip must be maintained throughout the match. Letting go results in a foul, and three fouls equal an automatic loss.

Depending on the culture, the combatants may use the other hand, heads, knees, feet, elbows, or any other part of the body they can bring to bear. Valid striking points are the face, the chest and stomach, the groin (cups are suggested), the kidneys, ribs, and instep. The throat, spine, eyes, nose, and mouth are off limits to any contact.

In European versions of the game the match is scored as follows: Valid touches (meaning not partially parried or blocked) each score a point in a five point match. Tripping the opponent is allowed, but if he hits back on the way down (or once he's on the floor) it is considered a clash and no points are awarded.

Jujutsu utilizes Locked Hand Randori, where locks, holds, and throws are attempted while keeping at least one hand clasped.

In Locked Hand Sparring anything goes... except the players must maintain a firm hand-grasp throughout.

In England and in the American West of the 18th and 19th Centuries, a form of locked hand "wrasslin'" was popular, in which players would grip with both hands and attempt to over-balance each other. This method of grappling has often been called "Indian Wrestling," especially in Twentieth Century rural America.

Among the loggers of the Pacific Northwest, a variation was played with partners gripping right hands only while balancing on a log. The person to throw the other player off would be the winner.

14.4 LOCKED ARM SPARRING

Locked Arm Sparring is similar to Locked Hand, but is almost always a grappling match devoid of any striking or kicking. This method of grappling is found in quite a few modern forms of non-traditional Jujutsu, such as Oni-Ryu and Bushi-te-Ryu.

The players stand sideways to one another with their arms hooked and fists clenched. The bout is fought in a two-ringed "fighting circle." The inner circle is about twenty inches in diameter, and the players place their right feet in this circle at the start of the match. The outer circle is about fifteen feet across, and marks the boundary for the match. Sometimes a much larger third circle surrounds both to act as a warning track.

Once the players are set and ready, the referee calls "Hajime!" (Japanese for "Begin!"), and the players immediately try to unbalance, throw, sweep, trip, or otherwise knock each other down or out of the larger fighting circle. Once the match has started they no longer need to keep their feet in the small inner circle, but they cannot leave the large circle.

SCORING THE MATCH

Trips, throws, sweeps, or takedowns earn an Ippon.

Forcing another player down to one knee scores a Waza-ari (half point). Two Waza-ari equal an Ippon.

Forcing another player out of the fighting circle scores a Waza-ari.

Most matches are Ippon Kumite (One Point Sparring), though some schools use best of three one-point rounds to decide the winner.

14.5 EVASION SPARRING

This is one of the most difficult methods of sparring to come out of Korean Hapkido, a system known for hard-core drills. The purpose here is to fight a semi-contact match (no face or throat contact; limited power contact elsewhere) where both partners may throw any kick or strike they want. But defensively, they are only allowed to evade. No blocks are permitted, though a parry while evading is often allowed by the referee as long as the evasion itself would have worked even without the parry.

The scoring is complex. Any player who scores by striking or kicking is given a full point; but at the same time the player who failed to evade is deducted a half point. The match is fought to seven points, and the scoring makes the game as much of a challenge for the scorekeeper as it is for the players.

Players may not grab or trap the opponent's arms or legs. However, sweeps are allowed.

A similar form of Evasion Sparring is used in the Brazilian art of Capoeira. Players twist and evade each other's kicks, rolling with any blows so that even if contact is made they are moving in the same direction as the blow and therefore emptying it of force. The

Capoeiristas avoid all contact, and the match ends when a simulated focused blow is executed with such precision and in the absence of an evasion that it clearly would have scored had this not been an exercise.

14.6 ONE LEG SPARRING (FIGHTING CRANES)

This sparring method is used throughout Northern Kung Fu styles, and is found in many modern and eclectic martial arts as well. Often called Fighting Cranes, the match is between two persons who adopt the one-legged posture of the White Crane. During the match they may strike with either hand and even use both legs to kick. But when kicking with the standing leg, the player must return to a one-legged stance (either leg). The challenge is to maintain balance while delivering fast, accurate, and reliable techniques.

There are no formal rules in this method of fighting, even in the traditional Kung Fu schools. Most bouts end at a time limit, with a referee (or in some cases the players themselves) keeping track of the points. Players in modern times often wear protective groin cups and shin pads.

Advanced Crane fighters can move around quite easily, hopping from foot to foot, using many aerial techniques, and attempting grabs, pulls, and reaps in order to destabilize their opponents. In Nineteenth Century Shaolin schools this exercise was sometimes practiced while standing on thick wooden poles (anywhere from four to twelve inches in diameter).*

---

* See Uneven Surface Sparring, Chapter 22, for additional information on sparring on poles.

This made the drill not only more difficult but vastly more dangerous. It is unknown whether this method of Fighting Cranes is still being used today.

This method of sparring is sometimes used by Okinawan Karate systems, such as Goju-ryu. The players start from Gankaku Dachi (Crane Stance) and then can use any skills at their disposal as long as only one foot at a time touches the floor. It is taught as a balance drill, mostly to intermediate students.

14.7 FIXED STANCE (LOCKED STANCE) SPARRING

Fixed Stance Sparring (or Locked Stance Sparring) is used by many Karate-based martial arts around the world to help timid students develop their courage. The players begin in side stances with their feet touching or hooked together. They are not allowed to move the connected feet at all, though the rear foot can be shifted slightly to maintain balance.

From this distance both players have an equal chance of scoring, and only great speed and deftly executed blocks, parries, and traps will keep the other player from scoring.

Often referred to as the Karate equivalent of Kung Fu's Chi Sao exercise, Fixed Stance Sparring helps players learn and develop trapping and counterattacking skills, and improve their precision for infighting.

Fixed Stance Sparring matches are generally fought as one, three, or five point matches, typical of most forms of Karate Kumite. Bouts can also be fought in sixty-second rounds with points accumulating in a three round bout.

CHAPTER FIFTEEN
Cross-Training Sparring Methods

Cross-Training is a very popular and useful way of increasing athletic abilities in a number of areas, as well as expanding one's overall fund of knowledge in sports. Martial arts cross-training is a little more complex, with advantages and disadvantages to be considered.

The downside to martial arts cross-training is the "jack of all trades, master of none" effect. Students who jump around too much, trying to pick a few skills from this art and a few from that one may learn a lot of exotic moves, but rarely do they obtain any real depth in martial arts knowledge. A real martial artist approaches the study of a classical fighting system with the same seriousness and completeness that a scholar approaches the learning of a science or an art form such as painting or music. It is always best to study something in great depth rather than flitting from one thing to another without lingering anywhere long enough to mature in understanding or skill.

The upside of cross-training is that for martial arts practitioners who are already solidly entrenched in one system, exploring other points of view is generally a positive thing. This is not to leave one style and go somewhere else, but to have a parent style and add at least one other art from which they can learn new skills and different perspectives. For example, practitioners of some of the sport martial arts can also cross-train in an art that specializes in self-defense. And some advanced students in one style of an art may explore another style of the same art to learn different approaches to combative problem solving.

MIXED STYLE SPARRING

This sparring method is much prized in open tournaments where players seldom know whom they'll face, or what style they'll encounter. These matches often provide wonderful insights into the methods and applications of a variety of martial arts.

The tricky part is deciding on the rules, as they are seldom the same from one art to another. For example, the tournament rules for Taekwondo and Kenpo are extremely different; as are the rules for Greco-Roman Wrestling and Judo. Naturally the advantage will rest with the art whose techniques are closest to the House Rules. For example, if a Judo player and a college wrestler spar, the wrestler will have the advantage if they fight by Olympic wrestling rules, because many of the takedowns, locks, and chokes used in Judo would be disallowed.

Kung Fu percussive forms vs. Jujutsu grappler.

In open tournaments, the hosting art usually sets the House Rules, determining which techniques may be used; which target areas are off limits; and what degrees of force and contact are allowed.

To the untrained eye, the results of such matches are often deceptive. A point fighter in a full-contact match with a boxer would probably lose, and lose quickly. Is this a deficiency in the point-fighter's Karate skills? Not at all. But as point fighting neither allows contact nor prepares a player for receiving full-power blows, the boxer would have the advantage under the rules. But if that same boxer were to enter a point-fighting tournament, he'd probably lose.

So the question is, how accurate is mixed style in terms of comparing different arts?

The answer is complex. On the surface, it is not very accurate because of the aforementioned considerations. However, in matches where both players have learned to fight by the same rules (as in Kickboxing versus full-contact Karate, or Kendo versus Naginata-do), the battles become quite interesting.

The outcome, however, does not speak to the effectiveness or apparent lack thereof of any martial art, but rather to the skills of the two individual players in the match. No single fighter is truly an accurate representative of their art, but only of the fighter's own interpretation of that art, based on how they feel that day and on the overall level of their skill. It is wrong and unfair to judge any art by a single player in a given match.

On a non-tournament level, Mixed Style Sparring is a great way for friends and colleagues in different martial arts to learn something of each other's system. This is called "Comparing" (see Chapter 13) and is a time-honored method of mutual education and experimentation. No matter what the outcome, both parties learn something. The whole Comparing experience is about mutual respect and mutual growth through exposure to new ideas.

HARD VS. SOFT

This method of sparring is very popular in both tournament level competitions and in-class sparring. In tournaments it is generally just the luck of the draw when a "hard" style player meets a "soft" style player, and the result is a fascinating look at how the two extremes match up according to House Rules. With in-class sparring, the matching of hard and soft is often the intentional choice of the players or, more often, the instructor.

A hard style relies on physical power and aggression as primary tools; a soft style focuses on passive resistance and creating power from postural changes. Neither style is better or worse, and each has its advantages. Nor is either style an absolute, much in the same way that the black area of a Yin and Yang symbol is not completely black; it has a dot of white, just as the white area has a dot of black. Balance is a key element in all martial arts.

Hard styles like Karate may rely on great muscular power when striking, but they also use many passive techniques, such as parries and evasive turns. Soft styles like Tai Chi Ch'uan may rely almost entirely on yielding and weight shifting, but the art also teaches some pretty devastating punches. It's all about balance.

In Hard vs. Soft in-class sparring, players are often asked to adopt opposing methods of fighting during the match, pitting a strong aggressive attack against a yielding defense, or a subtle and deceptive attack against a strong defense. The results are often very informative to the fighters, as well as any spectators, especially when in the next round the fighters switch roles.

This method of sparring is found most commonly in Shaolin Kung Fu schools that teach aggressive systems like Tiger and passive systems like Crane to the same body of students.

PERCUSSION VS. GRAPPLING

This is generally an in-class method of sparring, though there have been some pretty wild encounters in tournaments between grapplers and stand-up fighters. In those cases, the fighter who had the House Rules advantage generally won. Rarely are both kinds of fighters pitted against one another in a tournament match with rules that encompass both martial disciplines.

In classroom matches, however, winning is less important than learning from the experience. If one student is made to fight only as a grappler and the other only allowed to use strikes and kicks but no grappling at all, it presents intense learning challenges for each.

The grappler has to avoid blows, get in low and fast, and get his opponent to the ground before he takes a hit. If the other player is savvy, this can be quite a difficult trick, especially if the grappler is not allowed to hit back (just for the sake of perfecting certain skill areas such as closing the gap, overbalancing, evasiveness, etc.). Once down on the floor, of course, the grappler has the advantage, but that doesn't mean he can take it easy—there are many martial arts that teach how to strike and kick while supine or prostrate.

For the percussion fighter, the challenge is to keep from being taken down or grabbed. He has the advantage at the outset of the fight because he can use strikes and kicks to keep his partner at bay, but he must not allow the grappler to close. If he uses his skills correctly, theoretically he should be able to stop the grappler from closing. But as the realities of the street have proven many times, anything is possible. A grappler may be tricky and quick

enough to parry or dodge the blows while coming in; just as a percussion fighter may have enough know-how to win the fight with well-selected blows even while he's on the floor.

This is always an exciting mix, and even with the same two players the outcome is seldom the same, round after round or match after match.

Kicker vs. grappler.

256

BOXING VS. MARTIAL ARTS

One of the most commonly debated points in the martial world is whether a boxer would be able to defeat a practitioner of the (Asian) martial arts.* A simple answer is impossible because there are so many variables.

The boxer certainly has the advantage of being more used to receiving punishment than most martial arts practitioners. Boxing specializes in trading blows more than any other fighting system. Boxers are also highly trained in breath control, short-range parrying, blocking and deflecting, generating short-range power, striking in combination, and moving in a balanced and efficient way.

Now, as far as the martial artist goes, you'd first have to decide which martial art would be used against the boxer. There are hundreds of arts and tens of thousands of styles. Some are sportive, some are self-defense oriented, and some are more esoteric.

Sport fighters vary tremendously as well. Pit a Judo-ka against a boxer and you have two sets of rules with absolutely no overlapping commonalities. Each fighter would probably win on his own turf. Put a point-fighter against a boxer and you have someone trained to withhold contact pitted against someone who specializes in making full contact with full power.

There would be similar problems with putting self-defense based arts in competition with boxing since techniques that would be used in defense cannot be used at all in the ring. A Jujutsu or Hapkido fighter whose response to an aggressive hand attack on the street might be a leg-breaking kick or a knee to the crotch, certainly couldn't use them against a boxer. And if the match were fought by boxing rules, these same fighters would be denied those techniques which they trained so diligently to use.

What this leaves are the combination martial arts, such as Brazilian Jiu-Jitsu, full-contact Karate, and a few others with a competitive aspect that allows for full-contact fighting.

Full contact fighting frequently mixes martial arts disciplines.

The bottom line is this: the outcome of any match between different styles will be based on whomever's style is favored by the House Rules, and on the individual fighters themselves.

---

* Of course, boxing is a martial art, but many people for some reason consider the martial arts to be limited to those from Asia, which is not the case. This ignores the many martial arts that originated on other continents, like Europe, South America, and Africa.

ZOOMORPHIC SPARRING

Many of the world's martial arts teach fighting techniques based upon the movements of animals, birds, insects, and even mythological creatures (such as the dragon and phoenix). A great number of arts, especially those developed in China, are entirely based on animals. Shaolin Kung Fu, for example, is based on the Five Animals of Dragon, Tiger, Leopard, Snake, and White Crane; and there are animal systems based on the Monkey, Eagle, Cat, and many others.

Basing human movements on animals is intended to help the students detach themselves from the process of thinking too much during a fight, a process that generally interferes with

one's ability to fight effectively. Animals don't make mistakes based on thinking too much because they attack or defend on a level of pure instinct. The early Kung Fu masters saw in this a great lesson and developed many arts, techniques, and training methods based on zoomorphism (acting like an animal).

Sifu James Angielczyk of the Depew, NY Academy of Kung-fu demonstrates some Hung Gar zoomorphic techniques.

In many Kung Fu schools—and in some Karate systems such as Uechi-ryu and Shorin-ryu—zoomorphism is used for drills and in-class sparring. The idea is to meditate prior to a match, concentrating on a given animal or other creature, identifying its qualities, imagining its movements; essentially trying to understand it on a very deep and basic level. When the match begins, the players try to move and fight like the animal on which they've just meditated. No talking is allowed at any time because that would break the imaginative connection and bring the players back to their own personalities.

As the attacker lunges with a punch, the defender steps around it and into Rice Begging Posture, using a Tan Sao to help deflect the punch. This puts the defender in Cat Stance to the attacker's side.

The defender follows with Angry Tiger Descends Mountain to get two strong Tiger Palm hits on the attacker.

CHAPTER SIXTEEN
Uneven Skill Level Sparring Methods

In any school of martial arts it is often difficult to match students evenly for height, weight, age, reach, sex, fitness, and skill. Nor is it always a good idea to do so. But when students have to face opponents of all kinds it broadens their minds and increases the range of their skills by making them learn to vary their techniques for different partners. A leg sweep that works well against someone 5' 6" and 150 pounds will either have to be seriously adjusted or replaced against an opponent who is 6' 3" and 220.

Differences between players promote mental, physical, and tactical growth. Some sparring methods rely on these differences in order to help develop skills.

DIFFERENT RANK SPARRING

This method of training is probably the most universally employed sparring form found in the martial arts. Though obviously not a competitive form, Different Rank Sparring is excellent for helping emerging students cultivate their skills, improve confidence, develop courage, and grow as martial artists. Even with opponents as disparate as white belt and black belt there are tremendous benefits to be gained.

The challenge in this method of sparring is twofold:

For the lower-ranked player: The student or player of lower rank is forced to defend against more advanced or sophisticated attacks. The real trick is to overcome the intimidation factor of facing someone he most likely cannot defeat. That's a tough emotional problem in a match, and it forces the lower ranked player to dredge up every ounce of courage and will to do his very best.

Facing superior odds makes a person rely on the techniques he feels will work best and removes needlessly flashy or showy techniques from a fighter's repertoire. Even if the lower-ranked player is unable to defeat his higher-ranked opponent (which is generally going to be the case), the effort of simply trying refines his skills and brings him up to a higher level of capability.

For the higher-ranked player: Any person working with an opponent of lower rank has to understand that his job is not to go in there, overwhelm his partner, and leave behind a smoking pile of rubble. It is more or less a given that the higher ranked player could win if he wanted to, but he actually shouldn't be trying to win at all. Nor should he be trying to lose. What he should be doing is trying to present as tough a challenge to his partner as is safe and reasonable. He needs to raise the bar for skill, speed, endurance, technical proficiency, fighting judgment, and timing to such a degree that the lower-ranked student has to

be in a constant problem solving mode. Nothing increases ability more than facing a problem and solving it without (too much) help.

The higher-ranked player should also teach by example, using techniques the lower-ranked player doesn't know but could learn by observation. This is a great way to teach new skills or variations on known skills, with the added benefit of allowing the lower-ranked partner to see them in direct application.

A favorite sparring game used by wise higher-ranked partners is that of intentionally making positional or technical errors that would invite a counterattack. This teaches a lower-ranked student how to spot opportunities and seize the moment to go for them. Of course, it has to be made clear to the lower-ranked student that if he is being given the chance to score some points that he must use the utmost focus and control. The student should also be shown when he has missed an opportunity, in the hopes that he will recognize the same opportunity the next time it arises.

SKILL ADJUSTMENT SPARRING

Martial artists are versatile creatures. They aren't taught to do just one thing well like, say, a pole-vaulter. Martial artists are taught to do a great many things, and to strive to do each of them well: strikes, kicks, blocks, locks, holds, throws, jumps, escapes, weapons; the list goes on and on.

Selectively adjusting techniques is one method of refining each of these areas in an in-class sparring match. Chapter 13 deals with Skill Isolation methods (Hands Only, etc.) but there is another approach to this way of

**Sensei Dave Pantano of Counterstrike Kenpo
spars with a lower-ranked student.**

sparring that is more particular to Uneven Skill Level Sparring: Skill Adjustment Sparring.

A person has to bring down his skill level to just above that of his lower-ranked partner, purposely selecting techniques within that student's knowledge and experience. When a brown belt spars with a yellow belt, for example, he should endeavor to adjust his skills to a level just above yellow. This is a lot tougher than it seems, because done wrong it comes off as condescending. Done right, however, it provides clear examples of how certain techniques should work when performed with more refined skill.

It also helps higher ranked students get in touch with their own fundamentals. Re-training the basics is always a good thing.

With Skill Adjustment Sparring, the higher-ranked can also provide different types of challenges by shifting from one kind of attack mode to another, making the lower-ranked player first face a Blitzer, then a Road Runner, then a Sharpshooter.* This gives the lower-ranked student the chance to try the same kinds of attacks and defenses in a variety of ways all within the same match.

---

* See Chapter 8 for the various types of fighters.

PART FOUR
Weapons Sparring

CHAPTER SEVENTEEN
Traditional Weapons Sparring

Sparring with weapons is probably an older form of competition than sparring with hands and feet. From the sword duels of ancient Egypt, to the battles in the Roman Circus, to European Jousting, to modern stick fighting, simulated combat between armed warriors has been a constant in the martial arts.

Many of the older methods of weapons sparring and dueling have died away (such as pistol dueling) or been modified to a safer practice (such as foil fencing). There are a number of newer weapon-fighting methods used as drills for skill enhancement in the classroom. This chapter will demonstrate several competitive and drill-based weapons sparring methods.

No weapons sparring method should be undertaken without proper supervision, preparation, and protection. The risk of injury increases with any form of weapon, regardless of whether it is a blunt or bladed instrument.

17.1 STICK FIGHTING

EGYPTIAN STICK FENCING

This is probably the most ancient of weapons arts, dating back to antiquity. Descriptions and bas-reliefs of stick fencing have been found in the tombs in the Valley of Kings, such as in the tomb of Kheruef at Asasif on the West Bank at Luxor, who lived during the time of Amenhotep III in the 18th Dynasty (1539 – 1295 B.C.E.). Some of the sticks used in this method of sportive combat were short staves, while others were shaped like swords made from hardwood.

Stick fencing has been a sport that has persisted to modern times, varying in popularity over the millennia. Classical stick fencing was used not only as a sport for young warriors, but also as a part of religious ceremonies and processions. Even today ritualized stick fencing is practiced, particularly during festivals and holy days, and throughout the month of Ramadan (the Islamic fasting month).

Egyptian monument photography by Su Bayfield.
www.egyptsites.co.uk

IRISH STICK FIGHTING

Stick fighting in Ireland is an ancient and much respected sport. The weapon of choice is the cudgel or cane. It is known by many different names, including the one favored by Anglo writers, the Shillelagh. The Irish fighting stick has also been called an Alpeen, Bata, Batai, Cla'alpeen, Kippeen, Watte, Troid-da-bata, and Maidi).

The true Shillelagh got its name from fighting sticks made from wood which were gathered in the county of Wicklow in the Shillelagh Forest, but fighting cudgels of all kinds can be found throughout Ireland. A Shillelagh for combative use or even sporting play does not in

the least resemble the twisted little walking stick sold in tourist traps all over Ireland. True cudgels are often made of a hefty piece of dense blackthorn or oak, and there's nothing quaintly charming about them. It was generally about three feet in length.

For centuries, Irish lads were trained in the use of the Bata. Being old enough and sufficiently mature enough to carry one was a sign of manhood. The young men would be trained by their fathers, uncles, and older brothers in the use of the Bata, and would spar with one another constantly. Irish family clans often had a stickfighting trainer, called a Maighistir Prionnsa ("fencing master") who taught them the science and tactics of the weapon.

Most of the Bata's history is told in accounts of Faction fighting, the traditional "gang wars" among different groups of Irish folk. Since the English had out-lawed swords and other edged weapons by the middle of the Seventeenth Century, disputes had to be settled with sticks. Much of the finesse of Irish stick fencing came from sword masters who taught swordplay to recruits in the Irish Regiments of the British Army. Though the Irish regiments were used in India, Spain, and other foreign countries, fighting first the British imperial wars and then the battles against Napoleon, the skill of swordplay was eventually brought home to Ireland and translated into sophisticated stick fencing.

Other sparring weapons included various knives and swords, and the Wattle ("staff"), which was wielded in the manner of a quarterstaff. Some fighters (especially those in real battles instead of sporting matches), used a method of combat called Troid de Bata, or "two stick fight," which bears a superficial and totally coincidental resemblance to the two-stick fighting of Filipino Escrima.

At the outset of a match (as opposed to a real fight), the fighters would twirl their Bata above their heads and then set to with the initial goal of trying to remove the straw-filled hat from their opponent's head.

Faction Fights were very common in the Seventeenth Century, but by 1887 that method of dueling had come to an end. Today's stick fighting in Ireland is purely sportive, with no attempt to use sticks to settle arguments between families.

JODO

Jodo (translated as the Way of the Staff), is a stick-fighting system that is a modern interpretation of Jo-jutsu, a battlefield art of Feudal Japan. This way of using the staff was developed by master swordsman, Gonnosuke Katsukichi, specifically to defeat the legendary Samurai, Miyomoto Musashi (the author of the Book of Five Rings) in the early 1600s.

Legend has it that a famous warrior of the early Seventeenth Century, Muso Gonnosuke, fought a duel with Musashi. Muso pitted his highly praised skill with the *o-dachi* (long

Jo technique performed by Goju-ryu Karate master Kancho Robert Taiani.

sword) against Musashi's formidable two-sword style. Musashi defeated Muso but did not kill him, and the young warrior withdrew in shame to Homangu, which is part of the Kamado Shinto shrine atop Mount Homan. He meditated there for 37 days and performed various rites of humility and austerity. On the evening of the 37th day he collapsed before the altar and while in a swoon he had a vision. In one popular version of this legend, a celestial child appeared to him and said, "Holding a round log, know the suigetsu (an attack point on the body)." Inspired by his vision, Muso carved a short staff that was approximately 50 inches in length, making it shorter than a standard Bo (staff) and longer than a tachi or dachi (longsword).

The famous duel of Jo vs. two wooden swords is often played out in Jodo schools.

Exploiting the short staff's ability to shift rapidly in the hands of a skilled fighter, Muso was able to defeat Musashi in a second duel. Exactly how he did this is unclear, but it is likely he used the ends of his new weapon, the "Jo", to attack pressure-sensitive spots of Musashi's body. The juji-dome (or crossed sword block) that Musashi often used to defeat a swordsman would be a liability against a stick fighter who could use the point where the blocking weapons touched as a pivot point to swing the other end in under the block and attack the man. It's likely this happened in their duel.

Muso Gonnosuke created a school of Jo-jutsu that passed on his new techniques --and many more that he developed over time- and now Jodo (the modern version of Jo-jutsu) is a widely taught martial art. Jo versus sword is still practiced actively in many Jujutsu, Jodo and Iaido schools, an echo of the ancient duel, fought and re-fought with each new generation

There were wooden staff arts before Gonnosuke's time, such as the Tenshin Shoden Katori Shinto Ryu Bojutsu techniques using the rokushaku bo (six foot staff); as well as the Sekiguchi Ryu, Bokuden Ryu and the Takeuchi Ryu styles. Gonnosuke studied the Tenshin Shoden Katori Shinto Ryu school of Iaido under Sakurai Ohsumi No Kami Yoshikatsu, then studied the Kashima Jikishinkage Ryu. Like other Samurai of his time he engaged in various duels throughout Japan to test his skills, until he faced Miyamoto Musashi.

After defeating Musashi, Gonnosuke was summoned to the Kuroda clan where he became revered as a teacher. Out of his students, more than ten went on to become teachers of his art although the style was never taught outside of the clan. The founder of Shinto Muso Ryu Jodo became known as Muso Gonnosuke Katsuyoshi.

In 1968 the All Japan Kendo Federation recognized the importance of Jodo and felt that its study would be beneficial to the students of Kendo and Iaido. Accordingly, twelve representative Kata (forms) were taken from the Shinto Muso Ryu to form The All Japan Kendo Federation's standard Jodo forms, which were called Seitei Kata.

Photo of Ramon Lawrence and Geordie Thompson courtesy of Shingen Academy photographer Bruce Powell.

Today's Jodo techniques basically comprise three separate types of training:

1. TANDOKU DOSA (individual practice): This solo practice involves repeating one of thirteen basic techniques that teach good posture and a basic understanding of the movements of the Jo and body.

2. SOTAI DOSA (paired practice): The techniques learned in Tandoku Dosa are practiced with an opponent wielding a Bokken. This teaches an awareness of Maai (appropriate distance between attacker and defender) and Metsuke (correct vision), as well as the correct and precise places to strike an opponent's body.

3. SEITEI KATA (Twelve forms): This pits a Jodo-ka ("practitioner of Jodo) against a swordsman. The techniques (kata) in the basic forms involve a single attack from the swordsman with an avoidance Maneuver and a counter attack, either a thrust or a strike from the Jo. The more advanced techniques comprise multiple attacks and defensive moves from the sword and Jo.

Jodo is normally practiced wearing a hakama (baggy pleated trousers) and Keiko gi (training jacket). An obi (sash) is worn under the hakama cords to act as a swordbelt. There is no indication of rank of any kind on the uniform.

Though in traditional Jodo there is no free-sparring, students are trained to perform complex and difficult skills over and over against their partners, initially at slow speeds and eventually working up to full speed. Whereas this is not sparring per se, variables in size, strength, fitness, preparedness, and skill can make a drill so unpredictable as to give the sense of a match rather than an exercise.

Competitive Jodo and Iaido (a sword fighting art which uses a wooden practice sword approximating the weight and length of the Samurai's traditional steel sword, the Katana), are played by pairs of players pitted against other pairs. Both arts follow these rules:

> Players are given five techniques to exhibit.
>
> Players demonstrate their five techniques with a Bokken and then switch and demonstrate again with the Jo.
>
> The win is given to the most technically correct performance.
>
> There are no specific fouls, however if a weapon is dropped that player automatically loses.
>
> Iaido competitions are judged the same way as Jodo except the players are not paired.
>
> Players of both Jodo and Iaido must use a "Kessen Teki" (imagined opponent).

Photos courtesy Ramon Lawrence
of Shingen Academy

> Players must demonstrate zanshin ("perfect posture") throughout, showing both physical and mental perfection of form.
>
> Players must demonstrate metsuke ("gaze"), showing clarity and intensity of focus.

In non-traditional Jodo schools, meaning schools that teach the use of the Jo with modern or eclectic traditions, there are many methods of sparring. Generally it is done while wearing body armor and using either lightweight wooden sticks or foam-padded sticks. The lightweight wooden sticks allow locks and throws, but the players necessarily have to use restraint when striking; the foam sticks allow for full-speed and full-power striking against armored opponents, but are not sturdy enough for locks and throws.

In many Jujutsu schools, controlled free sparring and drilling can be done with the Jo pitted against a Bokken,. In these matches contact is allowed weapon-to-weapon, but any blow to the body must be focused (making no contact).

JOGO DO PAU

Translated as "The Game of the Wood," this European stick-fighting art was developed in the early Nineteenth Century in the North of Portugal. It was originally intended as a defense art for dealing with highwaymen and robbers and for practical use in conflicts between rival families over natural resource rights.

Jogo photos courtesy Paulo de Oliveira of Universidade de Évora

There are three distinct schools of Jogo Do Pau: Minho and Tras-os-Montes (better known as the Galician School), the Ribatejo (also called the Pataieira School), and the Lisbon School. Each school has it own style and approach to the use of this fast-moving and deadly weapon. The Galician school is known for fast blows using the tip of the stave and for repeated blows (often holding it with one hand, like a sword). The Ribatejano practitioners are close-range fighters who use the shaft of the weapon as much as the tip. The Lisbon School fights with a traditional blend of both tip and shaft, using footwork drawn from fencing.

Modern Jogo Do Pau is taught as a competitive sport, similar in many respects to Japanese Jodo (sport form of Jo-Jutsu). Matches may be structured with one opponent facing many, as well as in single combat, with the defender seated, or with both partners beginning from seated positions.

JUEGO DEL PALO

Juego del Palo ("stick play") is a stick-based martial art practiced in the Canary Islands, based largely on the fighting skills of ancient indigenous people called the Guanche. Originally these folk were the inhabitants of one of the islands, Tenerife, but the term Guanche has come to be used to identify all peoples of the Canaries. European influences over the centuries has sparked much change in these native fighting arts, bringing in various influences, including sword fighting methods and stick competition arts such as Portuguese Jogo Do Pau.

Juego del Palo photos courtesy of the Coordinadora de Colectivos Tradicionales de Juego Del Pal Canario de Tenerife.

Juego del Palo has been around for centuries but has been more popular since a resurgence that began in the early 1970s, mostly on Tenerife but spreading quickly to all islands in the chain. Many different Estilos (styles) are practiced, generally named after whichever family created them.

KALARI-PAYAT

Many martial arts scholars hold that India is the birthplace of the fighting arts. Ancient systems such as Varmannie and Vajra Musti (also spelled Vajramushti) predate the martial arts of China, Korea, and Japan by as much as one thousand years. Many of the ancient Indian arts have been lost (though Varmannie still exists in various forms), while some have evolved from violent combat systems into demanding modern sports.

Kalari-Payat (also known as Kalari-Payitt, Kalari-Payattu, and Kalari Payarchi) is one of the few Indian arts that are still practiced today. It can be traced back to the Twelfth Century C.E., though it almost certainly dates back much, much farther. The name of the art means repetitive training (*payat*) inside an arena (*kalari*), and it was originally part of the overall training that forged young men into hardened warriors.

Kalari-Payat has unarmed and armed aspects. The unarmed version looks like a combination of Karate and Aikido, or perhaps one of the older forms of Jujutsu. The armed version makes use of the otta (a hardwood bludgeon with a pointed end), the modi (a double dagger made from the horns of a gazelle), the urimi (a saber with a flexible blade and both edges sharpened), and various lances, sticks, and small shields.

In practice, the practitioners of Kalari-Payat spar and fence with their weapons at very high speeds but using great control so that no contact is made except weapon-to-weapon. All blows are focused.

The unarmed sparring of Kalari-Payat is a very rigorous grappling system that uses fierce throws and locks as well as a variety of kicks and strikes reminiscent of Muay Thai kickboxing.

LA CANNE

Near the dawn of the Twentieth Century, a variation of European fencing developed using sticks instead of swords. This new art, La Canne, developed in France. It became enormously popular and soon spread into other countries, notably Italy and England. Within just a few years there were a great number of different schools and approaches to La Canne, some very similar to the original, some vastly different. Primary variations could be seen in different approaches to blocking and striking patterns, as well as postures and movement. Some regional variations even went so far as to include hand strikes and kicks drawn from Savate (also known as La Boxe Francaise, French boxing), an aggressive unarmed fighting system (see Chapter 9).

One prominent Nineteenth Century master of La Canne was the legendary Pierre Vigny. He was a rather mysterious figure; little is known about him, other than that he gained great notoriety for the practical effectiveness of his stickfighting methods. The story has it that Vigny combined the cutting

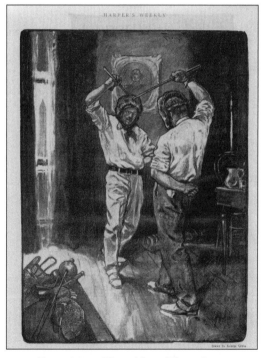

Drawing of President Theodore Roosevelt performing La Canne sparring. President Roosevelt was also a noted Judo practitioner. Picture courtesy Chris Amberger from the Amberger Collection.

and slashing techniques of broadsword and saber fencing with hand-to-hand fighting techniques he'd used when battling a vicious Parisian street gang known as the Apaches. According to some accounts, Vigny defeated several street toughs using only an umbrella, wielding it like a sword.

The rules of modern La Canne contests follow those of fencing nearly point for point.

A variation on La Canne is Le Baton, fought with a somewhat longer two-handed fighting stick. Le Baton uses many of the same rules of contest.

Early drawing of La Canne courtesy of the Amberger Collection.

SINGLESTICK FENCING

Various forms of Singlestick fighting have existed over the last couple of hundred years, ranging from crude bash-and-smash methods to the sophisticated dueling of World Singlestick Fencing.

Most Singlestick fighting uses a stick approximately the length of a fencing Saber, often sporting a similar basket hilt. The rules of play are basically those of Saber fencing, requiring players to wear an all-weapon fencing mask and a rigid shield covering the back of the head. The throat is protected by a fencing mask and bib which is reinforced by a gorget made of leather or steel. A Singlestick jacket is usually built along the lines of a fencing jacket, with reinforced areas to protect exposed bones, such as the collarbones, ribs, sternum, and xiphoid (solar plexus). Some players have even taken to wearing the shock-resistant helmets and shin pads designed for lacrosse or street hockey.

Groin cups are an absolute must, since the groin is an appropriate target. Female players wear jackets with hardshell or reinforced leather covers to protect their chests.

Many players wear a specially reinforced leather gauntlet on their fencing hand, leaving the other hand bare or wearing a lighter cotton glove.

The weapon itself is generally made of durable but flexible wood such as ash, privet, manuka, or rattan. The length can vary in length, but must be between 35 and 40 inches end to end. The basket guard covering the players' hands must be firmly braced so it does not move; the baskets on poorly made Singlesticks sometimes slide off the end or shift further up the stick. It is also important to sand the Singlestick so that it is smooth and free of any splinters.

THE SINGLESTICK MATCH

Singlestick players are known as "old gamesters" and the matches are held in a fighting square that is 14 feet per side, with a 6 foot wide warning track extending outward on all sides.

Singlesticks. Photo by Gilda Pasquil. Courtesy of Association For Historical Fencing (www.afhi.org).

The Singlesticks are dusted with colored chalk along the parts of the weapon corresponding to the point and edge of a sword. Only blows from those parts of the weapon may score. The chalk contrasts with the players' clothes, and shows where contact was made.

The Singlestick match can vary according to which rules are being used. Military Tournament and Assault at Arms rules call for the best of three successful hits. German Gymnastic Society rules call for the best of five successful hits.

Singlesticks. Photo by Gilda Pasquil. Courtesy of Association For Historical Fencing (www.afhi.org).

Many non-traditional schools set a time limit, usually two 90-second rounds, with the highest overall scoring player taking the match. In the case of a tie, a third round of 60 seconds is played to sudden death: the first player to score a point wins.

All forms of Singlestick play agree that the goal of a match is to win with finesse, not to batter each other like barbarians with cudgels. A light, deft touch is prized more than a crushing blow. In many cases a blow deemed too forceful by the referee will be disallowed and the player may be warned and even disqualified if he persists.

Wrestling, tripping, throws, hand strikes, striking the basket-hilt, and other non-weapon attacks are considered fouls. Only strikes with the Singlestick score points.

Photos of Nova Scrimia Stick Fencing courtesy of Gianluca Zanini.

ITALIAN (STICK) FENCING

Fencing has always been a part of Italian culture, from the days of the Romans with their fast short-bladed swords to the elegant rapier duels of the Renaissance to the present day, Italians have proven themselves to be among the most refined swordsmen in the world.

Though standard European fencing with the saber, foil and epee flourish in Italy, fencing in that ancient country is neither confined to those weapons or even to fencing with steel weapons at all. Rapier and dagger fencing influenced by a combination of Spanish and Filipino fighting, called *Espada y Daga*, is very popular. The term Espada y Daga comes from Filipino arts such as Kali and Escrima, where fighting with two weapons has been a staple for centuries. Also popular are fencing with a sword-length stick and Medieval sword fighting.

These weapon arts flourish under the administration of an Italian martial arts organization called Nova Scrimia,* founded in 1997.

Dueling with these weapons takes several exciting forms, influenced by the clothing and arms of earlier centuries. Sparring with a cloak, long stick, short stick, sword, knife, combinations of these are standard. The costumes give the players a theatrical look, but their fighting is in no way for show…the players are highly skilled and very dangerous fighters, capable of battling with swords, sticks and bare hands.

Though essentially a fighting art rather than a sport, the Nova Scrimia "Circolo della Tavola", or Circle of the Table (the governing body of the organization) has encouraged players to use protective padding so they can engage in full contact fighting at top speeds. For combat with the flexible swords and daggers, standard fencing helmets are used; but for the harder

---

* Information and photos of Nova Scrimia were generously supplied by Gianluca Zanini, editor of Nova Scrimia literature translations with some excerpts from "*Nova Scrimia: Arte Marziale Italiana*", "*Scherma di Bastone*" and "*Arte di Daga*", written and edited by Graziano Galvani.

contact stick fencing foam padding is used.

The stick fencing is dividing into various competitive forms:

2 Hand Stick Fencing

Stick and Buckler (a small hand-held shield)

The weapons used include:

Walking Stick: developed by Nineteenth Century Master Martinelli.

This is fought is stances similar to those used in European Sabre Fencing, with the thumb guiding the grip.

The stick is moved mostly by dexterous wrist flicks and turns while the body moves forward and back in a linear fashion.

Like Sabre fencing, the whole body is a viable target.

The match is fought to ten points.

Blows must be delivered with circular motions.

Modern Stick: This method allows for more freedom in selecting a grip, adjusting it to suit their hand size, strength and general fighting preferences.

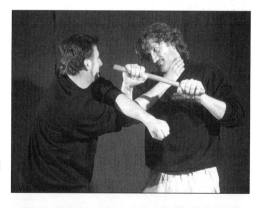

The footwork is circular rather than strictly linear.

Fighting is often long range, with large, powerful motions. more of a clubbing and hard tapping than any emulation of sword touches.

The match is fought in a square that is ten meters on each side

The match is fought in two 4-minute rounds.

Full contact is allowed.

Exceptions include no contact to the stick hand and knees.

277

MACULELE

Maculele is a fascinating blend of dance and armed martial arts that has its roots in Angola and West Africa. When these people were captured, carried to the New World, and forced into slavery, many brought with them fighting knowledge from their homelands. This was done in secret, of course. For example, armed and unarmed fighting methods were learned from tribal cultures, but out of a combination of fear and shrewdness, the slaves altered the appearance of these martial arts when they came to new lands such as Brazil. The slave owners had no idea that the slaves' exciting and dynamic dances were actually the skills that would one day liberate the slaves from captivity.

Maculele photo courtesy of the Batuque Capoeira Group of Holland.

The Maculele dance was performed with the various sticks and machetes that slaves used for chopping sugar cane on the Brazilian plantations, and any combative movements were redesigned to imitate the actions of chopping cotton. The slave owners must have found this quite amusing—at least for a while—because during times of rest, when the slavers were not present, the slaves would practice their skills over and over again, sharing the more useful applications of the cuts and strikes in their repertoire.

In 1835, the "Male Uprising" occurred, where the slaves rose up against their Brazilian enslavers. Slavery was eventually overthrown in that nation by 1850.

Today, Maculele and its companion art, the unarmed Capoeira, are practiced in similar fashion. These once lethal fighting skills are now part of stylized (but still dynamic) fighting dances.

Maculele photo courtesy of the Batuque Capoeira Group of Holland.

The players and observers form a ritual circle, spelled *rodo* but pronounced *ho-da*. Two players at a time enter the ring. The observers create and maintain a percussive rhythm by tapping their sticks or machetes together, often accompanied by one or more drummers playing the traditional Brazilian drum called an atabaque, and keeping time with a cow bell called an agogo. Taped music is also frequently used, and the kinds of music used in Maculele play are variously called afoxe, congo, and barra vento. Most of the songs are sung in the Yoruba language once spoken by the Africans who were brought to Brazil as slaves but used their martial arts skills to gain their freedom.

FILIPINO STICK AND KNIFE SPARRING

Kali, Escrima, and Arnis are the terms for the martial arts of the Philippines. The three names refer to different interpretations of the native armed and unarmed fighting skills that have developed in the islands over the centuries. Each has a different regional flavoring. Kali is a term used in the Southern Philippines, Escrima is a more Central term, and Arnis is from the North.

One of the greatest kings of the Philippines, Lapulapu, was a master of this native stick fighting art. He drilled his men intensively in stick fighting so that they could hold their own against the invading Spanish conquistadors. Lapulapu and his men fought the invaders ferociously, facing swords and bullets with sticks and spears, and overwhelmed them. Legend has it that Lapulapu and the explorer Ferdinand Magellan fought a fierce personal duel during a battle on Mactan Island on April 27, 1521. Magellan had his sword, knife, and heavy metal armor, while the Filipino king had only his sticks and a sarong. Magellan died.

Though the conquistadors eventually returned and conquered the islands, they were not able to wipe out these feared stick-fighting arts. The natives trained in secret and preserved the methods of fighting handed down by Lapulapu, methods which are enormously popular around the world today.

All three variations of the Filipino arts use weapons extensively, both in fighting and sparring. These weapons include:

* Kali/Escrima/Arnis photos courtesy of Cepeda-Abueg Martial Arts. Photos by Bryson Kim.

Baston (also called Garote or Olisi): a fighting stick made from wood or rattan, used singly, in pairs, or in conjunction with a dagger.

Dagga: a fighting dagger.

Tabak-Toyok: jointed sticks, similar to the Okinawan Nunchaku.

Tjabang: forked fighting weapon.

Sibat: a staff.

Bangkaw: spear.

Tabak Maliit (also known as Olisi Palad): "Pocket Stick," a shorter fighting stick used in similar fashion to the Japanese Yawari and Kubotan.

Sarong: a sash, used for wrapping, grappling, and defense against weapons.

Espada y Daga: a combination of sword and dagger, sometimes modified in competition to stick and dagger.

Of the three arts, Escrima and Arnis are almost entirely devoted to stick fighting, whereas Kali is a blade art.

Competition rules for all three arts are similar. The following are the rules for Escrima, which is the most commonly competed of the three arts.* For variations particular to Kali and Arnis, interested competitors should check with their local federations.

RULES FOR COMPETITIVE ESCRIMA, KALI & ARNIS

Escrima is an aggressive stickfighting art developed in the Philippines but popular around the world. Though it does have many non-stick techniques, it is best known for the use of the

---

* Information generously provided by the World Escrima Kali Arnis Forum (WEKAF.com).

Baston, a rattan fighting stick used singly or in pairs.

Escrima competition rules vary, depending on the hosting organization. Many competitions require the use of protective equipment for the players, although a few traditional federations do not permit safety equipment at all. When armor is used, players wear headgear that covers the face and has flaps to protect the back of the head and neck. Padded jackets are sometimes worn, as well as hard-shell shin and knee protectors and, of course, arm protectors. Competitors use standard rattan Baston; no padded or mock sticks are allowed.

The Escrima match consists of three one-minute rounds (though some groups use three 30-second rounds). The match is closely watched by several referees: one inside the ring and one in each corner of the ring.

SCORING THE MATCH

The match is won either by the first player to reach 10 points or the highest number of points at the end of the allotted number of rounds.

In the event of a tie, a fourth round of sixty-seconds duration will be held. The scores from the previous rounds will be discarded and the match will be given to the fighter who makes the first non-clash contact to the head.

Any player who is given three foul warnings will be disqualified and the match will be awarded to the other player.

Grappling is not allowed.

COMPETITION DIVISIONS IN ESCRIMA

Men and Women Fighting Divisions:

> Beginners
>
> Intermediate
>
> Advanced
>
> Guro level (instructor)

ALLOWED ATTACKS

1. One-Handed Attacks:

   Jab: this includes any strike that is retracted instantly after contact.

   Upper Tip Thrust: to the front of the face and stomach only.

   Lower Tip Thrust: to the front of the face only.

   Sweeps: any strike that has clear follow-through and passes to the player's opposite side.

   Hooking: performed with the upper tip.

   Punching: only with the hand holding the stick.

2. Two-Handed Attacks:

   Spearing: a thrust with the upper tip, only to the front of the face.

   Butting: a thrust with the lower tip, only to the front of the face.

   Push Hit: a blow with the shaft of the weapon, permissible only to the body.

3. Permissible Non-Weapon Techniques

   Punching with the empty hand.

   Head butting, body checking, and elbow strikes.

Kneeing to the stomach only.

Kicking and foot sweeps

Takedowns and throws. These must be executed with the stick in hand and without receiving any reciprocal contact.

DISALLOWED ATTACKS

Strikes or kicks to the groin, feet, neck, ankle, back of head, back of legs, or spine.

Thrusts of any kind to the sternum, rib cage, chest, neck, or groin.

17.2 SWORDFIGHTING

Swordfighting, as a competitive sport, has been practiced since the days of the Pharaohs (c. 1200 B.C.E.). Every country that developed swords for warfare also developed methods of drilling them through mock combat, often taking the next step to create a standardized sport form of fencing.

Though many sword-based sports have died away over the centuries, quite a few are still preserved today. Japanese Kendo, Filipino Kali, Indian Kalari-Payat, Thailand's Krabi Krabong, and many others all practice some form of sword or knife dueling. And of course there is traditional European Fencing with Epee, Foil, or Sabre.

HISTORICAL FENCING

Historical Fencing is the practice and study of Medieval and Renaissance fighting methods.* These practices are approached as a very serious study by men and women who are part combative athletes and part historians.

Historical Fencing is concerned with the realistic reconstruction and practice of historical Western sword fighting methods without any choreographed or staged elements. Though superficially similar to mock combat methods such as Stage Fighting and the jousting and

---

* Information and photos of Historical Fencing courtesy of The Western Martial Arts Workshop.

sword fighting used in events such as the Renaissance Faire, Historical Fencing is not based on entertainment or showmanship. Instead this approach to fencing is a true martial art, with masters and students, strict requirements for learning (both technical and historical) and competitions that are based on actual skill rather than theatrics.

Photo by Gilda Pasquil, taken at Western Martial Arts Workshop. Courtesy of Association For Historical Fencing.

The weapons chosen for use are beautifully made, forged for strength and fashioned for balance and speed. These swords and knives are the result of centuries of study into the swordmaker's art, not stamped-out replicas. Fencing with these swords is no joke, and only highly trained swordsmen and swordswomen are allowed to cross blades, and always under the shrewd guidance of a swordmaster called a "Maestro".

There are several organizations that oversee the development and practice of Historical Swordplay, including the The Association for Historical Fencing (A.F.H.I.). The A.F.H.I. has developed a system of classification of the eras of the history of fencing based on the various periods in the development of the art. They are:

Historical Fencing Early Period: Fourteenth and Fifteenth Centuries

Historical Fencing Middle Period: Sixteenth Century

Historical Fencing Late Period: Seventeenth and Eighteenth Centuries

Classical Fencing: Nineteenth Century

Modern Fencing: Twentieth Century

These time periods are somewhat artificial classifications used to facilitate discussion, just as we may speak of vague periods such as "the Middle Ages" and "the Modern Era." Styles and weapons did not abruptly change from one time period to the next, rather, there was always an overlap of weapons, styles, and techniques within each era. Nonetheless, the different eras of the

Poleaxe photo by Gilda Pasquil. Courtesy of Association For Historical Fencing (www.afhi.org).

development of fencing can clearly be distinguished from each other, as each era has its own distinct characteristics. Comprehension of these developments and their ramifications is necessary for the informed practice thereof.

HISTORICAL FENCING EARLY PERIOD

Though we may trace the art of defense back to the Fourteenth Century, it is difficult to talk about fencing before that time as there is simply no surviving documentation, save for anecdotal evidence. The fechtbuch (fencing book) known as I-33,* penned circa 1300, is the first known treatise on Western swordsmanship. However, specifics on styles, techniques, or methods that predate this are, due to the lack of documentation, open to speculation. Most importantly, there was no clear distinction between civilian and military use of the sword. The early treatises do, however, contain clear descriptions of timing, distance, binding, engagements, parries, feints, voiding actions, and footwork. The basics of the styles within the "middle historical" period can be traced to this time period.

The I-33 fechtbuch is also the earliest known documented evidence of the use of the sword for personal self-defense or for monomachia (that is, dueling), though the distinction between

civilian swordsmanship and military swordsmanship was just beginning to be recognized in this period. These two aims—self-defense and dueling—have guided the development of the art of fencing through the centuries. The attitude and techniques that are necessary to these ends differ in many ways from those of military swordsmanship. Thus this distinction is of no small importance.

Illustrations from the I 33 fechtbuch.

HISTORICAL FENCING MIDDLE PERIOD

The Sixteenth Century may, in fact, be considered to be a long transitional period. It is to this period that the basics of the "late historical" period can be traced, as well as the final

---

* The manuscript, simply entitled I-33, is comprised of 32 pages consisting of over a hundred ink-and-water color drawings, accompanied with Latin text describing the technique of sword and buckler combat. The original author is unknown to this day and the date of the manuscript is still in question, however, it has been dated to the late Thirteenth Century, and identified its owner as the secretary of the Bishop of Würzburg.

developments of the styles and schools of the "early historical" period. It is within this period that the use of the sword as a civilian side arm became common practice, first appearing in Fifteenth Century Spain. However, though we have texts on swordsmanship from the Fifteenth Century, it is not until the Sixteenth Century that we find numerous surviving treatises clearly documenting civilian systems of swordsmanship. In this period we find both the explication and definition of a system that already existed in the Fifteenth

Longsword vs. staff photo by Gilda Pasquil. Courtesy of Association For Historical Fencing (www.afhi.org).

Century in the work of Achille Marozzo, and, seventeen years later, the explication of a new approach and system in the writings of Camillo Aggrippa. The Sixteenth Century also saw the birth of an entirely new civilian school in Spain with the writings of Don Jeronimo de Carranza.

HISTORICAL FENCING LATE PERIOD

The late historical period may be distinguished from the early and middle periods by the fact that we may directly trace the origins of the traditional schools, styles, and techniques of the classical era to this time period. This development can be attributed to several factors: the growing influence of the printing press, the beginnings of a modern mentality that included national consciousness and a "scientific" mindset, the rise of the middle class, and the wearing of the sword as an everyday article of dress. These social changes had their affect on fencing, as they did on other areas of human endeavor. Specifically, the printing press and the

greater ease of long-distance travel helped the transmission of both first-person and vicarious knowledge, while the growth of the urban leisure class gave the fencing master a steady stream of willing patrons.

The late historical period is the era in which fencing evolved into distinct schools specifically intended for civilian use. This development resulted in schools and styles that remained intact for long

periods of time, and a direct line that may be drawn from the classical techniques to the systems already in use in this era. In short, this is the era in which a differentiation between military and civilian styles were clearly established, and national styles, such as the Spanish, Italian, and French schools, became clearly defined. Finally, the schools of thought regarding the subject, which may be documented through the printed materials left to us, can be discerned, and the origin of traditions that have come down to this very day may be positively identified.

We know, for example, that rapier technique had its birth in the late Sixteenth Century, while the Seventeenth Century was the golden age of this weapon. The Seventeenth Century also saw the development of the smallsword, but it wasn't until the Eighteenth Century that we see the full development of l'escrime français, in which, primarily under the leadership of French masters, the smallsword developed into its own distinctive system. The Italian school also developed greatly during the Eighteenth Century, but continued to adhere to the method of the striccia, or thrusting rapier, as the basis of its system.

CLASSICAL FENCING

The second half of the Nineteenth Century is historically the classical period, in which the art of fencing reached its highest development, but we may include the whole of the Nineteenth Century in this era, as this was the age when fencing was formally codified, systematized, and fully expressed in complete systems and styles. "Classical," in this sense, means "the golden age," the period when the art saw its highest peak. Clear distinctions between the French and Italian schools can be seen in this era, and national "academies" were established. A "super-national" approach established commonality in fencing language, as well as codes and rules for dueling. It is also within the classical period that the great rivalries between both schools were constantly put to the test through professional bouts and, in some cases, duels between masters of each school.

The use of the

Photo of fencing techniques with Maestro Ramon Martinez by Gilda Pasquil.
Courtesy of Association For Historical Fencing (www.afhi.org).

sword as a sidearm, for personal self-defense, was no longer a concern of fencers during this era. Rather, they focused on training in fencing for its own sake as an art form and personal accomplishment, in addition its use in personal combat. This age is distinguished by the art of the foil, which masters thought to be the fencing "weapon" par excellence. With this refined tool, the most sophisticated and artistic maneuvers are possible. However, the use of the sword as a killing weapon was always borne in mind, and the training was serious in nature.

However, earlier, more combative, techniques did not die out. In the early part of the Nineteenth Century, methods such as the use of the unarmed hand, strikes with the pommel, disarms, arm locks, and the like could be found in such works as Rosaroll and Grisetti's treatise of 1803 and Maestro Brea's book of 1805. It is also well known that methods of rapier and dagger, as well as other "historical" weapons, were practiced through the Nineteenth Century and into the Twentieth.

MODERN FENCING

This brings us to the era we term "modern." This period has seen the gradual disappearance of the duel and, with the lack of a need to prepare for mortal combat, the transformation of the discipline into a sport. Although there have been occasional duels within the Twentieth Century, modern fencing is solely concerned with the "sport" aspect. This development was aided by the inclusion of fencing into the first modern Olympic Games in 1896.

Furthermore, the founding of the Federation Internationale d'Escrime in 1913 saw a growth of "technicism" and the loss of the principles that are first and basic to the practice of fencing in a martial context. These principles are, namely, self-preservation, conservation, and defense. Fencing pedagogy has also changed with this. The fleche, the fouettee ("flick"), and similar actions, along with the use of the electrical scoring system and orthopedic grips, have no relation to preparation for lethal combat. These innovations, along with the constantly changing and subjectively reinterpreted rules, have resulted in the metamorphosis of the art and science of the sword into an athletic game. The final moments of the Twentieth Century therefore find fencing severely altered from its original form and intent from a killing art, where the stakes are life and death, into a game, where losing a bout is the worst that can happen.

TRADITIONAL FENCING

Sword styles have changed over the centuries, from the short broad-bladed swords favored by the Greeks and Romans, to the much heavier two-handed broadswords used during the Middle Ages, to the slimmer and much faster dueling swords that came into common use after gunpowder made swordplay nearly obsolete. This thinner sword became the mark of a gentleman and was one of the ways matters of honor were settled in Europe and the Americas. The French, Italians, and Spanish each make claims that modern fencing evolved in their countries, but in truth there was a parallel development in each of them.

The love of swordfighting has been perpetuated by popular culture in books and movies by Zorro, D'Artagnan, Captain Blood, and Conan, but sustained in fact by fencing academies around the world. These academies teach the formal practice of the sword, approaching it as a dignified and challenging art form that is also a deeply respected international and Olympic sport.

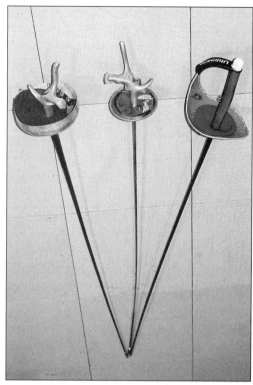

The three swords of modern fencing: Epee, Foil, and Sabre.

By the Eighteenth Century, formal rules of practice and competition were set down and are (with only minor changes) still used worldwide today. The governing body of international fencing is the F.I.E. (Federation Internationale d'Escrime). The rules set the method of scoring and prescribe the dress, masks, and sword types. Standards were also set to select specific target areas of the body and to provide for a "right of way" for attacks so that only one person could score at a time. This latter rule raised the bar for proficiency of all players since winning became substantially more difficult.

Fencing became an Olympic sport as early as 1896 and, sadly, though it gets little airtime during TV coverage of the Games, it is nevertheless a highly respected sport. Fencing stands as one of only four sports to have appeared in every modern Olympic Games.

Modern European-style fencing is conducted with the contestants standing on a long rectangular strip. The players are tethered to electronic scoring systems that track each acceptable hit. Competitions are held with three different weapons: foil, epee, and sabre.

The Foil: Descended from small dueling swords of the Eighteenth Century, the Foil has a thin and very flexible blade with a square cross-section and a guard shaped like a small bell. Points (called "Touches") are only scored with the tip of the sword on the opponent's torso, which includes the groin and back. Foil fencing stresses strong defenses and quick (simulated) "killing attacks" to the opponent's body.

Fencing with foil.

The Epee: Larger than the Foil, the Epee is adapted from Nineteenth Century dueling swords. The Epee has a stiff blade with a triangular cross section, and the bell-shaped guard is larger than that on the Foil. Touches are only scored with the point, but they can be delivered to any part of the opponent's body. Unlike both the Foil and the Sabre, there are no rules of right-of-way (discussed below) to decide which attacks have precedence, and even double hits are possible. Timing is vital in Epee fencing, and this method of swordplay places extreme emphasis on the counterattack.

Fencing with epee.

The Sabre: Adapted from naval and cavalry swords, the Sabre has a lightweight flat blade and a basket-hilted knuckle guard. Unlike the Foil or Epee, Sabre touches can be scored with either the point or the edge of the blade. Legal targets are any points above the opponent's waist. The Sabre is wielded with great speed and deceptiveness, relying on a powerful offense to command the fight from the outset.

Fencing with sabre.

RIGHT-OF-WAY

Right-of-way (or priority) is a set of rules used in competitive foil and sabre fencing to determine who is awarded the point when the opponents simultaneously make legal contact (called a double touch). The rule was established to make it easier to decide a clear win.

Right-of-way is the determination of which player was on the offensive and which was on the defensive at the moment when both touches were made. It is up to the referee to determine which player was in which mode. The player who was determined to have been on the offensive is awarded the point.

Epee fencing does not use the right-of-way method of scoring, relying instead on a determination of who scores first. If both players touch within 1/25th of a second of each other, then both earn a point. Since the entire body is fair game in Epee fencing, in the heat of a match this gets very difficult to determine. Mutual touches are common, which is why defense is such a key factor in Sabre fighting.

THE FENCING LAWS

The essence of fencing was summed up quite well in the Fencing Laws written by Matre d'Armes Iosif Vitebskiy, former coach of the USSR Silver Medalist Epee Team at the 1968 Mexico Olympics, and current Assistant Coach for the Penn State University Fencing Team. His list of "Laws" makes an excellent primer of fencing strategy.

> Don't rush; you'll always lose.

> At all times play off distance.

> Use many false motions.

> Only begin real combat after obtaining reconnaissance.

> Take stock of how your opponent moves, holds his weapon, and what his favorite actions are.

> Constantly change direction and speed of your actions.

> Your real actions must take your opponent by surprise.

> Against a false motion, answer with a false motion.

Fencing with epee.

The real attack has to be executed after several false motions.

Make parry-riposte with step back or step forward. Only rarely make it in place.

Don't often make the same actions against a strong opponent.

Always deem that your opponent is strong, but don't fear him.

If your opponent is stronger than you, strive to be more clever.

Be careful ... constantly.

Learn to relax in the bout when there is no danger.

Fence without overextension.

Learn to think fast during bouts.

Fencing with foil.

KENDO

Kendo is the Japanese "Way of the Sword," a modern sportive version of the deadly Samurai swordfighting arts. During Japan's Feudal Period (particularly the Kamakura shogunate, 1192-1333 C.E.) Samurai would spar with sharpened steel swords called Katana, relying on their great skill to prevent injury. Despite taking great care, injuries (and even deaths) did occur in training. Samurai sword masters developed a bamboo training sword, the Shinai, that approximated the length and heft of the Katana but was much safer to use.

Even so, injuries were still common, so a set of training armor was developed to allow practitioners to train at full speed and power with no risk of real harm. The armor, called Dogu, was designed to protect the head (*men*), wrists (*kote*), chest (*do*), and groin (*tare*).

In 1895, the Dai Nihon Butokukai (All-Japan Martial Virtue Society) was established to encourage Kenjutsu and other battlefield arts to become less warlike and have more of a positive focus. The various "modern" arts of Japan (those ending in "–do", such as Judo, Aikido, Karate-do, and Kendo) have become far more popular than the older battlefield arts (those ending in "–jutsu").

Techniques demonstrated by the teachers and students of the Tan Shin Kai Kendo Dojo of Philadelphia, Shoji Okutani, founder and chief instructor. www.tanshinkaidojo.org

The International Kendo Federation oversees all international tournaments and orchestrates the World Kendo Championships, held once every 3 years.

Kendo is based on a variety of attack and defense skills, known as waza, that teach various stances, stepping movements, cuts, thrusts, parries, and feints. Kendo students are called "Kendo-ka." Kendo-ka approach all aspects of their art on a very spiritual level.

To Deliver A Successful Strike In Kendo

Ki: The Kendo-ka must first become aware of the target, not only on a purely visual level but also in a visceral sense. Kendo-ka look for the right target, then quickly weigh the chances available to them at that moment. When everything "feels" right, they strike! This whole process takes a fraction of a second. Often there is a moment when mind, body, and will come together like a clenched fist, and the attack happens on a purely reflexive level. The strike is often accompanied by a piercing "Kiai!" shout.

Ken: In order for the strike to land correctly—and for it to be an artistic representation of the Kendo-ka's soul and will—the act of raising the sword and striking with it must be flawlessly coordinated. The mind guides, the body moves, the will directs, and the spirit selects the precise moment to attack, all with seamless perfection.

Tai: The will directs the body, but the body must follow. As the shinai strikes, the Kendo-ka's legs must surge forward, first to get well within striking distance and then to add power to the strike. The back must be straight throughout, and the form of the cut must be perfect. As all of this is performed, the Kendo-ka must maintain an unshakable confidence and determination in his attack. Achieving the objective is everything to him (or her!).

SCORING AND WINNING IN KENDO

The Kendo match is decided by a three-point rule called Sanbon Shobu that breaks down as follows:

> The contestant who scores two points within the given time limit wins.

> If only one competitor scores a point within the match period, then that player is the winner.

> If neither player scores a point within the match period, a match extension (*Encho*) may be allowed until a point is scored. Whoever scores this overtime point wins.

> A match may be decided by a referee's judgment (*Hantei*) by lot (*Chusen*), or can be declared a draw (*Hikiwake*). The referee's decision is based on the following criteria:

>   1. Posture and manner

>   2. Skill

>   3. Fouls

If a match is decided by a referee's decision or by lot, a single point is awarded to the winning player.

TACHIUCHI

There is another and far more rare form of Kendo sparring used by advanced Kendo-ka and practitioners of Kenjutsu (the older battlefield version of the Art of the Sword). Tachiuchi uses real, sharpened steel swords for sparring. Naturally this is something only the most advanced swordsmen should ever consider. It is not recommended for anyone else!

In some forms of Tachiuchi, swordsmen perform actual cuts on targets made from straw or rice stalks. This clearly demonstrates the reality of the danger. No body contact at all is allowed, of course. The swords are stopped short of the targets, and this requires the utmost in skill.

Kenjutsu schools often practice this with the Tori and Uke method, where

one partner is the aggressor (Uke) and the other is the defender (Tori). After each round they switch roles. Points are awarded for perfect form and control, and only for cuts that would have been fatal had they connected.

KUMDO

Kumdo means "the way of the sword." It is a Korean version of the Japanese art of Kendo.

Matches are fought with a bamboo competition sword called a *jukdo*. Players wear a set of body army, *hogoo*, that covers the head and body and offers reliable protection against sword attacks. As in Kendo, Kumdo competition swords and armor allow swordsmen to practice with greater safety. As a result, practitioners have a greater chance to experiment with tactics and techniques without risking injury or death. This has pushed many players to higher levels of skill and allowed the art to thrive.

In Kumdo, all of a swordsman's mental, physical, and spiritual energy are gathered into a single perfect moment of attack. This method of total commitment is called ki-kum-chae. In tournaments it is not the touch that scores and wins, but the evident presence of all three vital elements of ki-kum-chae. The attacking player focuses his inner energy (his *ki*), with a piercing shout. He strikes with an unrestrained swing of his sword (a *kum*), perfectly aligning his torso (*chae*) so that every element necessary to a successful attack is present.

In all other aspects, Kumdo competitions are handled the same as Kendo.

17.3 MISCELLANEOUS WEAPONS SPARRING

KRABI KRABONG

Thailand is known for many things, among them two excellent competitive fighting arts: Muay Thai and Krabi Krabong.

Krabi Krabong is primarily a fighting system that developed out of necessity during centuries of strife between Thailand and Burma. The fighting art has two aspects: empty hand combat (called Muay Thai Boran, or more commonly, Muay Thai) and weapons fighting (Krabi Krabong).

Krabi Krabong uses a great number of weapons, including two types of swords called the krabi and daab, the spear (*ngaw*), staves (*plong* or *sri-sok*), and various shields that could be used for defense as well as attack.

Krabi Krabong photos provided courtesy of the International Muay Thai Federation (IMTF).

HOW TO PLAY KRABI KRABONG

There are several different methods of practicing competitive Krabi Krabong. Practice consists of "dances" which are much like kata, and are performed with great attention to detail. Competitors also engage in freefighting, where players attempt to interpret the component moves of the dances into effective combat moves.

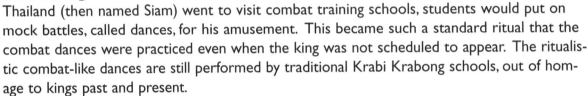

Variations of the Krabi Krabong combative dance include:

Tawai Bung Khom: In ancient times, when the king of Thailand (then named Siam) went to visit combat training schools, students would put on mock battles, called dances, for his amusement. This became such a standard ritual that the combat dances were practiced even when the king was not scheduled to appear. The ritualistic combat-like dances are still performed by traditional Krabi Krabong schools, out of homage to kings past and present.

Kuen Phrom: The Kuen Phrom is the main dance that Krabi Krabong performers must perfect. Phrom means Brahman, the name of a god who has four faces. The Kuen Phrom has two aspects: one performed from a sitting posture and the other performed while standing. During the performance, the dancer has to turn to all four directions, signifying the god after whom the dance is named, and to acknowledge Buddhism's four principles of virtuous existence which form the moral code for Krabi Krabong students.

Weapon Dancing: This solo drill is performed before an actual contest. It allows players to observe each other and assess their opponent's skills, and helps the players warm up.

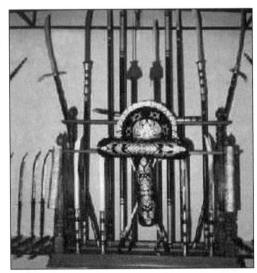

Duen Plaeng: Duen plaeng is a kind of ritualized walk used to signal the start of a contest. Each player walks boldly down to the end of the contest field and then walks back, demonstrating fearlessness and a kind of combat cool.

Fighting: During the actual contest, the players try to use the techniques they learned from their combative dances. The goal is not just to win, but to achieve a win that exemplifies their art and their skill.

A collection of Krabi Krabong weapons.

Koh Kama: When the fight finishes, both players humbly apologize to each other for any error unintentionally made. These apologies, though required by ritual, are generally heartfelt since the players pride themselves on precision in all aspects of their fighting skills. To make an error is not only a personal embarrassment but is also seen as a slight to the other player, the much respected opponent. The apology helps balance the scales and is a tacit promise that they will strive for better skill in the future. Their deep respect for each other, for their teachers and fellow students, for their king and their country, is a hallmark of the Krabi Krabong competitor.

NAGINATA-DO

The Naginata is a long spear-like weapon ending in a curved blade. Originally used by foot soldiers on the battlefields of Feudal Japan and for defense by Samurai women who had to defend themselves when their husbands were away. Much more recently the Naginata was introduced into elementary and middle schools in Japan as a physical fitness program for young women. The rigorous training and intense discipline helped Twentieth Century Japanese women emerge from centuries of gender-biased repression.

Extremely strong wrists and forearms are necessary for this sport, and a great deal of training is built around developing physical strength, balance, grace and perfect posture.

Naginata training and competition have become a worldwide sport that is completely dominated by women. It is estimated that in Japan about half a million people study the art of Naginata-do (Way of the Naginata), with the overwhelming majority of the practitioners being women.

There are two aspects of competition:

Shiai (Combat): In this form the players wear Bogu (body armor) similar to those worn in Kendo, particularly the helmet and shin pads and try to strike their opponents in certain permitted areas:

>   Shomen: Top of the head (the head is called "men").
>
>   Sokumen: Temple, side of the head.
>
>   Do: Side of the trunk.
>
>   Kote: Wrist and forearm.
>
>   Sune: Shin.
>
>   Tsuki: Throat thrust with tip of Naginata.
>
>   Tsuki: Solar plexus thrust with tip of Naginata (Not always given as a point).

Engi (Forms): In the second type of competition, players perform very precise and difficult Engi or Kata, which are pre-planned sequences that demand much of the players in terms of speed, precision, timing, balance, coordination and finesse.

Photos this page courtesy of the Southern California Naginata Federation, www.scnf.org.

The Naginata used in competition has a length between 215-225 cm (84 to 88 inches). The blade of

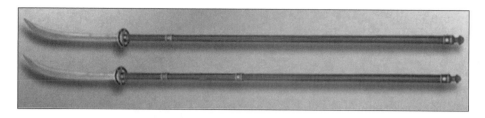

the competitive Naginata is made of two joined bamboo strips. The blade of the Naginata used in kata is wooden. Steel blades are seldom used in modern Naginata training, and even then only by the most advanced practitioners and masters.

In tournaments, women often compete with Naginata against men armed with bokken (wooden swords).

Early Japanese painting of Katana vs. Naginata.

KYUDO

The bow and arrow was the first of mankind's complex machines of warfare, surpassing the spear, club, and stone knife by a technological order of magnitude. It has been used for hunting and combat for over 10,000 years, fading from common use only in the Seventeenth Century as guns became more common and more accurate. During the decline of the bow as a major tool of combat, a movement arose in many nations to preserve it as a form of competition. Nowhere has this reached quite the artistic level as in Japan.

Japanese archery has two distinct forms: Kyujutsu and Kyudo. The former is the battlefield application of archery, used for killing. The latter is an art form used for the peaceful pursuits of self-discipline, physical culture, fitness, and meditation.

Kyudo has been used as part of religious ceremonies as early as the Nara Period of Japan (710-794). During the later Feudal Period, it was a mark of distinction for a Samurai to be a master archer as well as a swordsman of note. Archery competitions were quite often held in Imperial Court events, where the Emperor would watch and sometimes judge matches.

During the Edo Period (1603-1868), an event was held called a Toshiya (meaning "the arrow which hits its target"), in which the greatest warriors would compete to establish who had the greatest Kyudo skills. It was held at the main hall of the Rengeoin temple in Kyoto. The temple was 131 yards long, 2.4 yards wide, and five meters high, and the goal was to accurately shoot an arrow down that long, narrow length and hit a target. To make this a greater physical challenge, the competitors would continuously fire arrows throughout an entire day—while maintaining a sitting position!

Many warriors entered the contest, but only a select few managed to get through it with a distinguished record. One archer, however, gave such an outstanding performance that his name, Wasa

Photo courtesy of Miyakonojo International Kyudo Tournament Organizing Committee.

Daihachiro of the Kishu clan, is remembered today in Kyudo circles the world over. During the competitions, he launched 13,053 arrows and successfully struck the targets with 8,133 of them.

A major national Kyudo contest is still held on January 15th of every year at the Sanjusangendo in Kyoto, which is the spiritual capital of Japan. This contest celebrates what is known as the "Coming of Age Day." There are roughly one thousand competing archers, each of whom fires a number of arrows at a target placed sixty-six yards away. Typical bows are a combination of wood and bamboo, while arrows are mostly made of bamboo.

During the late Nineteenth Century, in the midst of the Meiji Restoration, Kyudo was introduced to grade schools and universities in Japan. To this day it is a major activity in hundreds of colleges and universities around the world.

The Eight Steps in the Shooting of an Arrow in *Kyudo*

(1) (2) (3) (4) (5) (6) (7) (8)

Kyudo Hassetsu

An ancient set of tenets divides the process of shooting an arrow into eight distinct and vital steps, called the Hassetsu. Each step represents a different level in the state of mind for which an archer should strive.

1. Ashibumi (footing): This is the foundation of the Kyudo Hassetsu. The feet are placed apart about an arrow's length apart, big toes in line with the center of the target and the feet at a 60° angle. The body's weight is equally distributed between both feet.

2. Dozukuri (correcting the posture): Once the feet are set, the archer turns his attention to his upper body. This is where the three-cross-relationship is first observed: the shoulders, hips, and feet are lined up with each other, parallel to the floor.

3. Yugamae (readying the bow): Yugamae consists of a series of preparatory steps known as Torikake (setting the glove), Tenouchi (gripping the bow), and Monomi (viewing the target).

4. Uchiokoshi (raising the bow): The bow is raised and an arrow nocked without any forceful jerking of the string, and the arrow is held exactly parallel to the floor. The bow should then be raised until the hands are just above the head and the arms are at a forty-five degree angle. The shoulders should remain level without being stiff. Relaxation is key in this movement.

5. Hikiwake (drawing the bow): Drawing the bow is actually a two-stage process. First, the arrow is drawn to about half its length and the archer then pauses. Next the archer begins the actual drawing of the bow.

6. Kai (completing the draw): On a physical level, Kai is the aiming process; but it is also a balancing point where all of the archer's movements, skill, concentration, serenity, and artistry are gathered together prior to the arrow's release. Ideally, an arrow is held for a full six seconds after completing the draw.

7. Hanare (the release): The rear hand releases the arrow spontaneously and without effort. The archer's goal is to allow his spirit to release the arrow rather than his hand. The arm that released the arrow moves back, parallel to the floor at all times.

8. Zanshin (continuation): After the arrow is released the archer must remain calm, dignified, and perfectly balanced. The body must be strong without being stiff, and relaxed without being weak. During the arrow's flight, the archer's spirit is given time to flow to the target and back.

There are currently two major forms of Kyudo practiced worldwide: Yabusame and Standing Competitive Kyudo.

YABUSAME

Yabusame is an exciting event, held most often in Japan, where archers dressed in the clothing and armor of Feudal Period hunters compete

Photo courtesy of Miyakonojo International Kyudo Tournament Organizing Committee.

by launching arrows while galloping on horseback. They have to steer their horses with their knees while both hands are busy drawing and fitting an arrow, aiming, and letting fly at a target not much bigger than a man's fist.

The most popular and famous of these Yabusame events takes place at the Tsurugaoka Hachiman Shrine, in Kamakura, on September 16 each year. Three square targets, made from cedar and attached to bamboo staves, are spaced about 77 yards apart

Photo courtesy of Miyakonojo International Kyudo Tournament Organizing Committee.

on the left side of a 279-yard track. Each mounted archer spurs forward and shoots at the three targets, one after another, as the horse races along the track. The whole run takes less than twenty seconds. If the archer is unable to loose an arrow at one of the targets he must discard it and ready a new arrow for the next target.

This exciting ceremony is actually part of a meditative ritual and prayer for peace. Each successful shot is held as a sign of good luck and a wish for nonviolence over the coming year.

STANDING COMPETITIVE KYUDO

In Kyudo, shooting from a standing position is practiced in two ways: using a target that is close and one that is placed much farther away.

A close target is set at a distance of 31 yards and has a diameter of 14 inches. In close target competitions, the archers kneel as they

Photo courtesy of Miyakonojo International Kyudo Tournament Organizing Committee.

draw and nock the arrow, then rise to their feet to shoot. It is important for the archer to be calm and serene, and to rise swiftly and with great composure.

In a far target match the archers remain standing throughout. The far target is set either at 98 Yards, 77 Yards, or 66 Yards, and is 1 yard in diameter.

Players compete as individuals and in team competitions. The winners have the greatest number of hits.

VARMANNIE SHADOW PASS KNIFE SPARRING

Varmannie is known as much for its knife-fighting as it is for empty-hand skills, and the Varmannie sparring game called Shadow Pass is used by most practitioners. Various knife styles are used, but over the last century the Burmese Kukri knife has become the weapon of choice

Shadow Pass sparring is a slow-motion method of mock fighting. Players use sharpened steel blades but move in a slow, sinuous way around one another, simulating attacks and defenses and sweeping knife edges mere hairsbreadths from each other's vitals. This very advanced form of fighting is used only by top Varmannie knife fighting experts.

The Kukri is also the signatures weapon of the Ghurkas of Burma, and is used in the Burmese fighting art of Bando.

Varmannie's weapon of choice, the Kukri knife.

CHAPTER EIGHTEEN
Drill-Based Weapons Sparring

Weapons training and sparring is not limited to those arts that make it their specialty. Many other martial arts, from Aikido to Kenpo, train with weapons both to learn how to use the weapons and to learn how to defend against them as well.

The sparring methods discussed in this chapter are not particular to any one system of martial arts, but rather are used by many, and with many variations.

18.1 KNIFE SPARRING

TRAINING KNIFE SPARRING (WOOD OR RUBBER)

This sparring method is used by most arts to teach knife fighting for the obvious practical purpose of keeping the students alive and uninjured. The mock knife (wooden or rubber) allows nearly every kind of knife technique to be practiced at full speed and with less need for hampering body armor.

Many arts approach Training Knife Sparring from the point of view of defense, giving the knife to the attacker and scoring the match on how well the defender defends himself and counterattacks. Aikido and Taekwondo, for example, prize this kind of drill highly as a test of timing, reflex, and correct form in the heat of a pressured attack.

Rubber knife sparring allows for full-speed, full-contact training without the risk of injury.

KNIFE SPARRING (STEEL)

This is not a recommended method of sparring for anyone but the top knife fighting experts, and even then it must be approached with a great deal of caution and common sense.

Like Tachiuchi (sword sparring with sharpened steel blades), Steel knife sparring uses real weapons. The edges are sharp, the points like needles, but the attacks are simulated. No weapon contact is allowed at all.

In Europe (Italy in particular), knife sparring is done by two players who fight stripped to the waist (women fight in t-shirts or sports bras) wearing loose trousers. They fight in a cleared area, usually fifteen feet or more to a side, with two referees watching from just outside the ring.

The Duello della Lama, or Knife Fight game, is scored by near miss cuts that referees decide could have landed in a real fight. These points are called singolo punto (one point). Three points equal Punto del Gioco, or game point.

Various forms of steel knife sparring.

In Japanese Tanto-no-jutsu ("Art of the Knife"), attack and defense situations are played out in much the same way. But in Japan one person acts as aggressor (Uke) and the other as defender (Tori), with the roles changing each round once an Ippon ("one point") has been scored.

In both cases, however, it must be stressed that sharpened knife sparring is not for beginners or even intermediate players, but only for the most highly skilled, and in this regard the highest skill area in question is the control needed to avoid cutting one's partner.

CHALKED KNIFE

Sparring with a chalked knife is a highly prized and very effective method of testing knife attack and defense skills for players of all levels. It is used both as an in-school drill and in major tournaments, by arts as diverse as Aikido and European Singlestick Fencing.

The drill is simple: the edge of a training knife, either wooden, plastic, or rubber, is dipped entirely in chalk so any "cut" will show against the defensive player's uniform. Colored chalk is used for matches where the student is wearing a white uniform; and chalk of different colors is used in matches of knife against knife.

Chalked knife sparring is useful in self-defense sparring, where both the attacker and defender may score points. In this kind of match, the player in the role of attacker has to try his level best to deliver the simulated equivalent of incapacitating, or even fatal, knife hits. In general, attacks to the eyes and throat are not allowed, even when wearing body armor, due to the obvious risks. However, this leaves much of the body open to attack and the chalk marks will show the accuracy of the attacks.

Conversely, the chalk marks, or absence thereof, will clearly show whether the player acting as defender has accomplished his goal of evading the blade.

DOMINATION

Domination is a very unusual and demanding method of Jujutsu sparring, developed by Hanshi Joshua Johnson (b. 1922 – d. 1996) and Shihan Tyrone Biswell of the Shinowara-ryu school of Jujutsu.

This sparring form is designed to teach students a number of important combative skills:

   Setting priorities in self-defense

   Weapons handling

   Psychological appraisal of the opponent

   Manipulation of the combat situation

In Domination, a training weapon is used (rubber knife, padded stick, etc.), but it is not given to the players. Usually it is placed between them or near them. In one form of Domination, two players stand

In one version of Domination, a training knife is dropped between two opponents.

309

hand-to-hand and foot-to-foot in mutual sparring readiness and a weapon is placed between the backs of their hands. Sometimes the weapon is simply dropped between the players in much the same way that a hockey referee drops the puck during a face-off. In one variation the weapon is placed between the backs of two students standing or sitting, facing away from each other. There are a great number of variations on the starting position, but in each case neither has possession and each has an equal chance of getting control of the weapon, or not.

And that is the crucial factor. Fighting for the weapon is not always the best method of winning the fight. Sometimes it is a better tactic to let the other guy scramble for it while instead deciding to attack him with hands or feet. In Domination (because it is a Jujutsu-based drill) strikes, kicks, holds, locks, and takedowns are all permitted.

The bottom line is that in Domination, just as in real self-defense, more than one fight has been won by the person who cared less about securing the weapon and more about securing the win. One of the basic lessons of weapons fighting taught in Jujutsu is that a fighter must never focus so much on a weapon that he forgets all of the other fighting abilities in his martial arts repertoire.

A variation where a rubber training knife is laid on the floor and the players must wait for the command to begin.

Most Domination matches involve grappling as both parties either fight for the knife, struggle to keep it away from the other player, or try to subdue each other by any means allowed under the rules (which are pretty liberal, though control and focus are strictly required).

Domination matches are always fought to a clear Win/Loss rather than an accumulation of points.

In this version of domination, the knife is held between the players' hands until they are given the command to begin.

18.2 STANDARD WEAPON SPARRING

Many of the world's sophisticated stick-fighting systems use rhythm drills to teach the coordination, relaxation, and timing so necessary to real and effective combat. Most notably, the Filipino systems Escrima, Arnis and Kali use complex two-man exercises to cultivate skill and to help the practitioners develop the necessary understanding that the weapon is merely an extension of the hand rather than a replacement for one's own sense of touch and control.

These sparring drills are variations on the concept of Limited Step Sparring in that the patterns are pre-set and players must maintain correct form, balance, and technique. Both players have two weapons, usually two sticks, sometimes a stick and a knife. They begin with a salute or mutual acknowledgement. The beginning patterns are often very simple, with both players doing exactly the same move. The sticks in the right hands meet and then the sticks in the left hand. What makes the drill very difficult is the increasing complexity of the patterns. A very basic pattern might be right hand high inward strike, right hand low strike, left hand high inward strike, and left hand low strike, with the sticks making contact in the middle ground between the players. More advanced drills combine mutual strikes, attacks, and defenses; advancing and yielding; turning and circling; and even traps.

Above: Two-stick rhythm-based sparring. Below: Stick and knife rhythm-based sparring.

Skills performed by Sensei Dave Pantano and Jim Winterbottom of Counterstrike Kenpo.

The contact of the sticks creates a percussive rhythm that is very musical, especially as the players influence the rhythm by subtle changes in speed and force when they move. Stepping, changing the height and angle of their stances, and altering speed all create an almost hypnotic pattern of sight and sound.

Learning these complex patterns and practicing them without missing a beat is tough enough, but as the players become advance and work out improvisations (much the same way as jazz musicians might improvise on a well-known song), the exercise crosses the line from pure drill to a form of sparring that is combative, artistic, and beautiful all at once.

18.3 ADVANCED WEAPON SPARRING

Like Tachiuchi (sparring with real steel swords) and a few forms of "live" knife sparring, standard weapons sparring is used by advanced practitioners of martial arts. Not just advanced in handling of the weapon, but in the level of control necessary to make such a sparring method relatively safe.

Sparring of this kind is not recommended for beginners or intermediate players, and is often not even suggested for advanced fighters. The risk is very high, and since very good simulated weapons exist, there is also little need for it.

However, standard weapon sparring is part of the training regimens of many martial arts around the world, both Eastern and Western.

In Kobudo (Way of Weapons), a fighting science taught both as an independent art and as a sub-system of many Okinawan and Japanese martial arts, students are often set to sparring with weapons. Three of the five primary Okinawan weapons, Tonfa, Bo, and Nunchaku are wood-based weapons. Of the other two Okinawan weapons, the Sai is entirely metal, though blunt, and the Kama has sharp sickle blades. Sparring with these weapons requires a

Okinawan weapons demonstrated by Kancho Robert Taiani.

great deal of care, because it is the intent of the drill that the weapons themselves never touch the other player. All blows are "focused," meaning that they are stopped short of the target. In the case of the Kama and the tip of the Sai, the blows are stopped well short.

When students are trained in the use of each weapon, they are introduced to the weapons' applications by different levels of sparring:

BUNKAI

Students learn their weapons through pre-set patterns or forms called Kata, which are practiced solo many hundreds of times so that each move is perfected. Once the Kata has been mastered, the student is then guided through a process where the Kata is essentially dismantled into its component moves. Those moves are practiced with a partner who adopts the role of attacker.

At first the attacks are moderately slow and obvious, allowing the student time to get used to applying the defense in actual (rather than hypothetical) terms. As the student's skill grows, the attacks become more forceful and much quicker, and this begins adding an element of uncertainty to the drill, making it feel more like sparring than drilling.

In advanced Bunkai, several student/attackers are placed at specific points around the Embusen, or pattern, that the kata in question will make on the floor (kata tend to move around a lot, simulating a series of attacks and responses). As the student who is performing the kata moves through the techniques in sequence, he encounters the student/attackers, who do, in fact, attack. Done at a brisk pace this is quite a challenge, since the student performing the kata has to be constantly ready and has to adapt to the differences in size, strength, reach, and speed of the other players.

Some tournaments use Bunkai in a competitive manner, grading the performers on accuracy, perfection of form, and overall technical ability. These team Bunkai drills are extremely difficult but also extremely exciting to watch.

SEMI-FREESTYLE SPARRING

In this more advanced version of Standard Weapons Sparring, the competitors are not restricted to specific techniques as they would be in Bunkai, but choose techniques on their own. The limitations on freedom of choice, however, come in the duration of the match, and in the choice of permissible targets: usually the torso if performed without body armor; torso, head, and arms if using body armor. Most Semi-Free Style Sparring is fought as Ippon Kumite, one point fighting. Once a single, righteous point is scored the match ends,

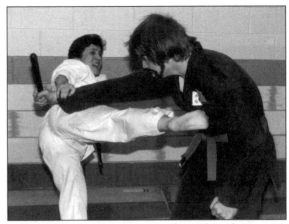

Semi-Freestyle Weapons Sparring demonstrated by Sabonim Loren Lalli.

though most organizations use Waza-ari (half points) and Yuko (near half points) to accumulate a winning score. A completely flawless and uncontested single technique scoring a true Ippon is far more rare than a collection of half-points; understandable considering each player's great motivation to avoid all attacks. In boxing you can risk taking a stomach punch in order to land a jab; when fighting with weapons you don't want to take a hit at all.

There seems to be a fairly equal division between schools and organizations that require body armor and those that don't. Both, however, maintain a very high level of caution and enforce a very strict adherence to the rules of safety and fair play. Fouls, unless completely accidental, are judged very harshly, which is appropriate to the level of real risk involved.

Non-Japanese martial arts use weapons sparring as well, such as Escrima, Hapkido, and many European stick fencing systems.

18.4 JIYU KUMITE

Weapons Free Sparring, or Jiyu Kumite, is rare and usually reserved only for the most advanced of all fighters. In this method of sparring two fighters battle with near-miss hits of their weapons until it is judged (by mutual agreement or by a referee) that one person has taken simulated injuries that add up to incapacitation or death. As with all other forms of weapons sparring, no actual contact is allowed unless the players are wearing protective equipment sufficient to the needs of the match.

In stick fighting, armor similar to that used in Kendo is quite common, as is a collection of

protective pads from sports like hockey, lacrosse, or football. Some of the foam padding common in martial arts tournaments is useful, but only in stopping a percentage of the force. Only hardshell armor will stop full-power stick blows, and even then the armor should be fully tested beforehand, and the need for such a powerful blow in a sport questioned.

In Kendo, the body armor is sufficient to stop a bamboo sword (Shinai) even at full power; but then again the Shinai is a sportive version of a real sword. Kendo armor would not stop a real sword. Perhaps this is why Tachiuchi (steel sword sparring) is practiced totally without armor, relying on the players' control as the source of protection for both.

In Escrima (as well as its sister arts, Kali and Arnis), combatants wear heavy armor similar to Kendo armor, and they do make fast and furious contact with their sticks. But attacks to the knee, throat, top of foot, and hand are illegal.

In Standard Weapons Free Sparring, the game will vary radically from school to school and organization to organization. However, there is one universal rule: Do it safely, or don't do it.

18.5 MIXED WEAPON SPARRING

Under the right circumstances, this is one of the most beneficial methods of weapons sparring in the martial arts. Generally done at moderate speeds and using many safety precautions (chief of which is that no actual physical contact is allowed), the drill allows a weapons fighter to learn the ways in which weapon handling will change when faced with different types of challenges.

For example, a spar between someone using a Japanese Hanbo (a stick about 30 inches long) and someone with a Tai Chi straight sword would present each player with certain difficulties and certain advantages. The stick fighter will have the edge in terms of versatility since he can hold every part of his weapon, creating advantages in trapping, use of leverage, and variety of blows; while the swordfighter has the edge in ... well, edge. His weapon is a big knife and any contact (simulated in practice, of course) would result in a serious wound. Plus the sword is longer, allowing that fighter to stay at a greater distance. Conversely, the stick fighter has the advantage in a close-range fight because he needs less room in which to wield his weapon.

If the Hanbo fighter were faced with an Italian dagger fighter, the tables would be turned. The dagger is a better close-range weapon than a stick. However, the stick fighter can parry more easily and can attack the hand of the knifeman at a safe distance.

By changing the mix, either by matching persons of different styles, or by matching players of the same style but with different weapons, both players get a chance to spar in a real learning atmosphere.

There are few competitions of Mixed Weapons sparring, but it is very commonly used in martial arts training around the world, from Arnis to Jujutsu.

Chinese sword vs. Japanese sais.

Japanese kama vs. Chinese three-section staff.

Chinese butterfly knives vs. Japanese sais.

PART FIVE
Sparring For Self-Defense

CHAPTER NINETEEN
Self-Defense Sparring Methods

Ordinarily, sparring and self-defense would be opposing concepts. Sparring has rules and self-defense does not. But in the martial arts there are many drills used to cultivate self-defense abilities that resemble sparring matches.

For the most part, these sparring methods are not used for competition, except in the case of Aikido and Karate. Aikido Enbu knife defense sparring is discussed in Chapter 10, and Karate Goshen-Jutsu Kumite is discussed in Chapter 17. Another exception is Self-defense Limited Step Sparring, covered in this chapter, which is common in many tournaments.

Self-defense sparring is generally a dangerous and very serious aspect of training in martial arts, especially when dealing with aspects such as rape defense and defense against lethal knife attacks. Protective equipment is a must.

19.1 ROLE-PLAYING

In real life self-defense it is almost impossible to plan what to do or how to act. A situation usually comes with little or no warning.

Or so it seems.

In fact, there are often warning signs that might tip off an experienced martial artist that a situation may turn violent. Body language, emotional reactions, placement of potential attackers in a threat situation—each of these factors (and many others) can be early tip-offs to a violent attack. The question is how to gain the experience necessary to be able to read these warning signs and take actions that might calm the whole mess down and possibly keep it from even turning violent.

The answer is role-playing.

Role-playing is one of the most useful tools in self-defense training because it allows students to relate their skills, strategies, and tactics to the real world. Instead of the situation being two guys squaring off to bash each other for sport, role-playing allows the participants to work through different methods of resolving confrontations.

In Effective Survival Methods (ESM), a self-defense system specifically tailored for women, the students do not know whether, in a role-playing situation, the people they meet will attack or not. The other players have roles assigned to them by the instructor, and only the attacker(s) and the teacher know if an attack will happen. The instructor sets the stage by describing a specific set of circumstances. For example, the student may be told:

"You're on a street corner, waiting for a bus. There are two other people with you, one of whom is a middle-aged man with a briefcase and the other a teenager with a boombox. There are only a few cars coming up and down

Role playing helps students learn how to adapt martial arts skills to real life situations.

the street, and no pedestrian traffic. There is a convenience store two blocks away. It is late afternoon, just before twilight. You are dressed for work in a skirt and blouse, but wearing sneakers for the commute. You are carrying a purse and a paperback book."

Given these circumstances, and a few props (a fake purse stuffed with foam padding, a block of foam to simulate a novel, maybe some rubber pieces sewn together to act as a ring of keys, etc.), the student has to react to anything that happens. She may be accosted by either of the other two players in this combat improv; or she may only be harassed without physical assault. If an attack happens the other players may be working together, or one of them may step in and try to assist the woman. The female student may try to talk the situation down until the bus comes; or she may try to walk away to the convenience store if one of the other players begins making uncomfortable remarks. And so on.

The variations are endless, allowing each student to face similar situations with different results. Students are graded on how well they resolve the situation, preferably with no violence; though if the situation turns violent they are required to defend themselves with a level of aggression appropriate to the level of threat. This is important because to learn real self-defense, a student has to acquire a sense of proportion: gouging the eyes of a rapist may be necessary, but the same response to a purse-snatcher is way out of bounds.

In ESM, and other top women's defense programs, the role-playing is often videotaped so the students can later review the situation and critique it. This method of using a form of sparring to teach conflict resolution is also widely used in children's self-defense programs like KidSafe and Operation Counterstrike*, all to great effect.

19.2 SELF-DEFENSE LIMITED STEP SPARRING

Self-Defense Limited Step Sparring is probably the most common method of sparring in the martial arts. It forms the technical basis for nearly all martial skills. The concept is to take specific attacks and specific responses, often excerpted from forms (kata, poomse, etc.), then perform them with as much speed, accuracy, control, and precision as possible.

The "limited steps" in question are the stages of a specific defense, which are designed to simulate an escalating conflict. For example:

Step 1: Attacker throws a forward punch.

*For information on these programs, go to: www.counterstrikekenpo.com

Step 2: Defender blocks the punch.

Step 3: Attacker throws second punch.

Step 4: Defender blocks the second punch.

Step 5: Defender throws a counter punch to an opening created when the attacker threw his second punch.

These ritual patterns are extremely useful for teaching students to neutralize an initial attack and wait for a good opening before delivering a telling counterattack. There are a few different versions of this kind of sparring, each one presenting its own unique challenges.

CONTROLLED SPEED LIMITED STEP SPARRING

In this version, the attack is delivered at some pre-determined level, generally below top speed. This is so the defender can learn to use Kata skills against a real person with minimal risk of injury.* This controlled speed version is used more often for weapon attacks and empty-hand attacks, since more caution is called for.

They are also useful in scuffle arts, such as Aikido, Jujutsu, and Hapkido, so that the attacker can learn how to perform a correct breakfall at an angle that allows the defender to accomplish as realistic a joint rotation as possible. For example, if the attack is a knife thrust and the defense is a wrist catch and wristlock rotation that would splinter a wrist if applied realistically, then the defender has to pitch into an exaggerated roll to keep his wrist from being rotated to the breaking point. This is why some wristlock throws in the scuffle arts result in dynamic and often unlikely flips into falls; it is not that the locking throw would actually cause such a fall, but if the attacker did not pitch himself over so dramatically then even a wristlock throw at a controlled speed would do severe and crippling damage to the wrist.

---

* See Chapter 23 for more on Kata Run-through Sparring.

Controlled Speed Limited Step Sparring is also sensible when practicing counterattacks that involve any kind of rotation to the elbows, fingers, shoulders, knees, ankles, toes, and, most importantly, the neck.

PRE-SET ATTACK/PRE-SET DEFENSE

In this form of Limited Step Sparring, both the attack and the defense are pre-determined. For example, a stepping front punch to the face would be countered with an outside fore-arm block and reverse punch counter.

The challenge comes when the drill is brought to full speed. Even when one knows an attack is coming, it is not necessarily easy to use a predetermined defense at top speed and in the correct form. This drill is far more challenging than it first appears because a reactive

defense, where one's ingrained combat reflexes dictate the response, is actually much easier than performing a specifically chosen movement.

It is the attacker's duty to make sure this drill is as difficult as possible. This requires the attacker to attack at his top speed, while maintaining perfect form and control.

PRE-SET ATTACK/RANDOM DEFENSE

The next stage for most martial arts that use Limited Step Sparring for teaching self-defense is to allow the defender to choose a defense he feels will work best (as well as relying partly on reflexive actions). The catch is that the chosen defense must be accomplished with perfect form and must be a technique that has been learned from one of his Kata. No techniques borrowed from other styles or made up on the spot are acceptable.

Furthermore, the entire defense must be completed in a prescribed number of steps. If it is an Ippon Kumite (one point spar), then the defender must defend and counterattack with a single powerful blow.

RANDOM ATTACK/RANDOM DEFENSE

The next stage of difficulty is allowing both attacker and defender to select their own techniques, although they must use techniques culled from their Katas.

This is a very demanding method of self-defense sparring because it requires split second timing along with a strict adherence to the correct forms. It may sound moderately easy on paper, but it is a challenge for even the most advanced practitioners.

As before, the entire defense must be accomplished in the exact number of steps dictated by the instructor or referee.

WEAPONS DEFENSE LIMITED STEP SPARRING

This is one of the safest methods of teaching defenses against armed attack, allowing the student to follow a defense from point of attack, step-by-step through the defense and the resolution.

In early stages this method of sparring is very much like Bunkai, merely a run-through of a component of a Kata, or one of the many formal Limited Step Sparring skills; but in advanced training the attacks and defenses become random rather than predetermined. This creates a far more dangerous and therefore challenging exercise.

Students are awarded points not just for successful defenses, but for employing precise and perfect traditional form.

19.3 RAPE DEFENSE SPARRING

Rape is a vicious and violent crime and the martial arts defenses against it are necessarily extreme. Shouting "No!" is seldom an effective solution, and fleeing is not always an option.

In traditional methods of sparring, women are seldom pitted against men in full-contact matches because of the safety risks that are naturally present when players of disparate sizes and strengths fight. In contact style fair fights, the stronger and larger player often wins, which is why bantamweight boxers don't climb in the ring with the heavyweight champion of the world.

Given these factors, the methods of sparring used to improve rape defense skills have to be very effective, often brutal, and immediate. There can be no play, and no extended matches based on points. The whole match has to be resolved in as short a period of time as possible because in a real attempted rape, the longer the struggle goes on the more the attacker gains the edge. Surprise is a major weapon in rape defense.

In the ESM (Effective Survival Methods) system of women's self-defense, as taught at the university level, the Final Exam is based on a sliding time scale:

> Defense in 1 - 5 seconds earns an A
>
> Defense in 6 - 10 seconds earns a B.
>
> Defense in 11 - 15 seconds earns a C.
>
> More then 15 seconds is a failing grade.

The way this exam is conducted is very much like a sparring circle, with all of the students in the class seated in a large circle. One at a time the students enter the circle and stand in the center, which is marked with a smaller "combat circle." Surrounding each student are two or more male "attackers" wearing body armor from head to toe: headgear, mouth guard, cervical collar, chest protector, arm and leg pads, and a groin cup. The heavy gear protects them but still allows them to move very fast.

The attackers move around the student, harassing her, trying to spook her, making threatening gestures, and doing everything they can to make her as jumpy as possible. This is not as cruel as it sounds, since it is more important for each woman to discover how she fights while distracted and under stress instead of during ideal conditions. Eventually one of the attackers is given a pre-arranged signal by the instructor and attacks, usually attempting to grab the woman and take her to the floor in order to pin her. In some cases the attack is done with a rubber knife.

At the first point of contact (or once the attacker has crossed the line of the combat circle in which she stands), the stopwatch begins and the student has to counterattack as quickly as possible. Defense per se is not her goal, since a defensive action favors the attacker; rather, an aggressive counterattack is required. In order to pass the test she has to neutralize the initial attack (evade, parry, etc.), and deliver as many accurate counterstrikes as she can manage, then take the attacker down and finish him off with additional blows.

The attackers, for their part, are specially coached to acknowledge only those hits that would have done real damage, and shake off anything that would have been merely painful. They are trained to make the attack as realistic as safety allows, which gives them a lot of latitude in their level of aggression.

Since the men who play the roles of attackers are martial arts students, they are trained to use simulations of non-martial arts attacks. Rapists generally don't launch in with a flying

side thrust or a spinning backfist; they use brutal grabs, shoves, pulls, takedowns, and other attacks designed to induce fear and control a woman's body.

The fighting accomplished by the women in these university level classes, as well as similar classes and workshops conducted by self-defense experts around the country, is often sloppy, off balance, rife with poor technique—and thoroughly effective. In desperate fights of this kind it is the goal of survival that matters, not aesthetics. A martial artist who has trained for years is expected to be an example of correct form and proper effect, but a woman taking a limited-week self-defense program merely has to be able to defend herself.

Another valuable and commonly used tool of Rape Defense Sparring is Role-Playing, discussed earlier in this chapter. The difference in this exercise as applied to Rape Defense is the choice of situations: they are tailored to suit a woman's defensive needs, such as a date rape, home intrusion, purse-snatching, or physical abuse. These situational role-playing matches allow the women to practice strategies and tactics for diffusing a potentially violent situation as well as practicing the actions needed to follow up any crisis or near-crisis situation.

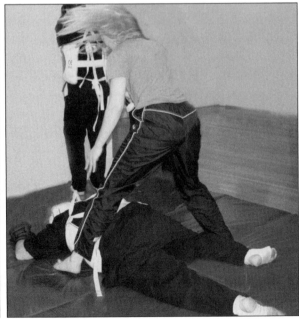

CHAPTER TWENTY
Multiple Opponent Sparring Methods

A primary purpose of studying martial arts is to teach people how to defend themselves. A typical self-defense encounter is thought of as a one-on-one fight. However, on the mean streets of the modern world it's just as likely that a person will be attacked by two or more people. Predators tend to hunt in packs.

Many Kata (forms) teach techniques for defending against a series of different attackers, but this is not the same thing as actually fighting more than one opponent. In the movies, attackers form a circle and rush in one at a time so the hero can dispatch them with quick, clean techniques. On the street that never happens. Generally, attackers close like a fist around the defender then beat and stomp him in chorus.

Teaching realistic self-defense against multiple attacks is never easy, and many martial arts approach the problem by creating as real and serious a situation as possible. Though such sparring methods are seldom found in tournaments, they offer as dynamic and energetic a challenge as any full-contact title match.

This chapter presents self-defense sparring methods that concentrate on developing the skills necessary to defeat multiple opponents.

20.1 MODES OF ATTACK

To understand how to defend against multiple attackers, the first thing to do is to identify the different Modes of Attack:

Converging V   Close V   Skirmish line

Trap   Pinch   Box

The Converging V: Sometimes the situation starts with the attackers at a greater distance, but the closer they get the easier it is for them to use both sets of hands. This is the easiest (relatively speaking) type of multiple attacker situation to defend against because the initial position of the attackers makes it easy for a quick-witted and light-footed defender to engage one opponent at a time.

The Close V: In this classic confrontation situation the attackers come in from two sides, their positions limiting the avenues of escape. This allows both attackers to strike at once and is extremely dangerous.

The Skirmish Line: If the attackers are allowed to close ranks they can create a wall of threat, often set up so that the defender does not have the option to turn and flee.

The Trap: This is where one attacker confronts the defender while his partner comes up quietly from behind. Being blindsided is a fast way to lose right at the beginning of a fight. Though this attack is cowardly, it is no less dangerous.

The Pinch: A step up in threat from the Trap, in this variation the second attacker has already secured a restraining hold. This is the worst-case scenario for self-defense.

The Box: One of the most dangerous of all self-defense positions, this one combines the threat of the Close V with the dire limitation of having no chance of flight. The defender is surrounded on all sides by attackers and walls or other objects making it impossible to retreat.

There are a number of basic strategies the defending player can follow when dealing with multiple attackers:

Move: The defender's primary consideration is movement: he has to get in motion and stay in motion throughout the fight. Letting the attackers close at their own pace and in their own way is suicidal, so the fight must be carried to them.

As the attackers approach, the defender shifts his weight slightly backward to get out of the way, then slams the attackers into each other.

Shift: Shifting abruptly to use one attacker as a temporary barrier is wise because it creates a one-on-one fight and at the same time presents an obstacle for the other attacker to negotiate. When making such a movement, the defender must be very harsh in his selection of (simulated) techniques. A punch is seldom enough. He should use multiple hits or kicks, takedowns, redirections, or any combination of the above permitted by house rules.

Circle Beats A Straight Line: A counterattack that uses circular footwork to grab the attacker and pull him off balance is always a good start because it uses one attacker against the other, or at very least reduces their overall efficiency. The more confusion, the better for the defender. Circular movements also help with quick close-quarters evasions and the generation of power for kicks, blocks, and strikes.

When the two attackers rush head on, the defender moves around one of them, in a circular direction.

Straight Line Cuts A Circle: When the attackers circle like a pack of wolves, a good tip for the defender is to go straight at one and engage him quickly and decisively.

Fight Small: Bigger movements take more time; smaller ones take less. Time is crucial, so don't waste it.

Speed: Speed is the most essential element of good fighting. It is more important than power, accuracy, or form.

Accuracy: A fast strike is good, but a fast and accurate strike is best.

Fighting small: the defender uses a tight, fast double-kick to slow down his opponents.

20.2 MULTIPLE ATTACKER SPARRING TECHNIQUES

THE MAZE

The Maze is used by countless martial arts, including Kenpo, Jujutsu, Hapkido, Karate, and Aikido, for both unarmed and armed self-defense. The premise is simple: all of the students in the class form a large circle, then one at a time each student enters the circle and waits in a defensive posture. Eventually each member of the circle will attack and the student will be graded on how many successful defenses he accomplishes.

For training against multiple attackers, the instructor or drill leader will signal to two or more of the people in the circle and they will move forward to attack. The person in the center will not know which players will attack, or by what specific means. This requires extreme preparedness and great skill, though the drill's intensity can be modified to allow beginners a chance to get used to the rigors of the Maze.

It is very important for all of the attackers to have protective padding because the focus and control of a person defending against multiple sparring partners is seldom as finely tuned as everyone would like it to be. The nature of the exercise makes it difficult to use sufficient control, which is enough of a challenge when it's a one-on-one match. But when attackers are closing in from all sides, the defender has more things to worry about than control.

Scoring the match is difficult, but there are guidelines:

> Number of attackers

> Skill level of the defending player

> Method of attack (see below for Modes of Attack)

> Time needed to complete the defense

The Maze is a powerful exercise, and one to be taken seriously. All available safety precautions should be used throughout.

THE GAUNTLET

This is a variation of the Maze used by many Kenpo schools, as well as a number of non-traditional Karate dojos. The Gauntlet is as forbidding as it sounds: students form two lines down the center of a sparring area (a matted area is suggested), spaced so that they won't collide with any other players. A single player the (Primary Player) stands at the head of the line, ready in a fighting stance.

At the instructor's command the Primary Player steps forward, and as soon as he reaches a certain spot one of the fighters on either side will attack. The instructor has a stopwatch and gives the Primary Player 15 seconds to defend against the attack (including takedown and finish-off). Regardless of whether the Primary Player successfully completes the defense, as soon as the instructor calls "Stop!" the attacking player steps or rolls out of the way and the Primary Player takes another step, at which point the next attacker launches at him.

He proceeds in this fashion, making his way through the Gauntlet without knowing from which side the next attack will come. The players take turns as Primary Player, and whoever runs the Gauntlet in the lowest total time is the winner.

Although only one opposing player will attack at a time, this is by no means an easy drill. It is very fast, demanding and brutal, but it is superb for developing reaction time and simplified, practical defenses.

SWITCH-UP MAZE

This is a highly demanding and very intense sparring exercise involving multiple attackers. This in-school drill works best with five or more players, each of them wearing (at the very least) mouth guards and groin protectors, as well as whatever additional padding is suggested by the instructor.

In the Switch-Up Maze, all of the players are given a number which they must remember. They form a circle and stand ready to fight throughout the duration of the exercise. The instructor or referee stands just outside the circle and calls out three numbers in this fashion: "Three and five on two!"

**The defender does not know which
of the three might attack.**

**Only One and Two attack,
while Three looks on.**

This means that the player designated Two is the defender and as he steps into the circle he is immediately attacked by Players Three and Five. A stopwatch keeps the time, which is recorded on a clipboard.

A somewhat more difficult version, used in Jujutsu, has a Primary Player step into the circle first. The instructor then calls out numbers, like "Four and Six!" and those players immediately launch in. This gives the player in the center almost no preparation time, which in turn forces the development of reaction time and skill.

Another variation has three players enter the ring, numbered One, Two, and Three, and the instructor will call something like, "Two and Three!" which means they are instantly designated the attackers and have to turn on Player One. After a few seconds, the instructor says, "Stop!" and then calls different numbers: "One and Three!" This means Player Two is now the defender.

This is no game for the unwary, because the abrupt change-up is jarring. Only very sharp-witted players can manage this extremely advanced version of the Switch-Up Maze.

MULTIPLE MAZE

In this variation of the other Maze forms, it is not one against two or more, but two against three or more. This requires a fairly large sparring area and plenty of protective padding for all players.

Two players are teamed as defenders while three, four, or even five other students are designated as attackers. There are several different versions of this sparring method:

HIGH ODDS SPEED MATCH

This version is basically a straight fight with disparate odds. The defending pair is graded on a pass/fail basis. Ten seconds is usually the maximum amount of time allotted to complete the defense, and many schools shave that number in half to make it really challenging.

THROUGH THE FIRE

In this version, also called "Cut and Run," the goal is not simply winning by points. Two players have to break through a line of three or more attacking players. The match is given no more than five seconds, but those seconds can feel like hours to the players trying to force their way through a wall of fists and feet.

The purpose of this drill is purely practical in terms of self-defense. When attacked by a gang, sometimes the best defense is flight. But if there is no opening through which to flee, one must be created.

Buddy Defense

Along similar lines, the Buddy Defense method of Multiple Attacker Sparring presents a survival problem, but this one is much harder to solve. In this drill, which is generally a two-on-two situation, one of the two defensive players is designated a "non-fighter" (some systems use the term "civilian") who has to be protected by the Primary Player.

Defending against multiple attackers is tough enough, but doing it while protecting another person is very, very difficult. It requires stepping up to a level of toughness, presence of mind, and combat efficiency that is well above regular defense scenarios.

This sparring method, graded on a pass/fail rating, is fairly realistic. After all, how often are two martial artists mugged together? But muggers can attack someone walking with boyfriend or girlfriend, or a parent walking with a child. In those situations a person can find reserves of strength, courage, and resourcefulness they hadn't known they possessed.

**A variation of Buddy Defense sparring, where the
defender must protect herself as well as a small child
(real child not recommended).**

**It is much more difficult to fight while protecting a defenseless child rather than an adult.
For that reason, this version of Buddy Defense sparring is excellent self-defense
practice for martial artists with children.**

Stand-up version of a combat circle.

COMBAT CIRCLES

The Combat Circle is similar in many respects to the Maze, except that the circle is very confined. In the martial art of Capoeira, for example, the players sit in a close circle called a roda, leaving only a small gap for the fighters to enter. Though the movements of Capoeira are highly gymnastic, with many spinning and jumping techniques, cartwheels, and movements similar in appearance to break-dancing,* the players seldom leave the roda because they've been taught to use their space very well.

In the ancient Indian martial art of Varmannie there is a sparring exercise called the Council of Peers, which is essentially the same set-up as a roda, except all of the people in the circle are seated in chairs. In pairs, selected by mutual agreement and given an assenting nod by the teacher, players stand up, salute, and begin fighting within the circle. Varmannie uses many turning and evading techniques as well as takedowns, so keeping the fights confined within the Council of Peer's circle is very tough.

---

* Many martial arts scholars hold that Capoeira, which is centuries old, influenced the development of break-dancing, which has been at the forefront of the hip-hop scene for the last three decades.

** See Chapters 11, 12, 13 and 17 for more details on Varmannie.

CHAPTER TWENTY-ONE
Situational Sparring Methods

Thinking outside the box is one of the most important survival skills in any aspect of life, from sparring to business. Conventional thinking is excellent as a base or starting point, but imaginative thinking lifts your mind and takes you farther.

This chapter discusses several sparring methods, each one very different from the others, and each one requiring that the players think not only outside the box, but outside the dojo as well.

21.1 LIMITED SPACE

Sparring usually happens in nice (relatively) wide-open spaces: a fighting circle, a ring, a combat square. Fighting as a rule does not. Sparring methods that are designed to develop and enhance self-defense skills are often tailored to address real-life situations, one of which is limited space.

In Limited Space Sparring, players are given a confined space in which to fight and they lose points for straying out of it. In the basic version, the space is just a taped out area on the floor with a definite and obvious warning track. But as the fighters

The defender disables one attacker while keeping the other at bay ...	**... then takes advantage of the limited space by slamming the first attacker into the wall.**

become more expert at close-quarters sparring, the space is either made smaller or redefined by actual barriers. A stack of folded mats, for example, will work well, as will a corner of a room that has padded walls. This can simulate an elevator or a narrow alley.

Training in confined areas is a quick reality check for students who tend to chew up a lot of real estate with big techniques when smaller ones might be more sensible. It's also a good way to introduce new students to efficiency in fighting from the beginning.

21.2 AVAILABLE RESOURCE SPARRING

For schools that have a large training space with lots of padding, there is a fascinating sparring drill from the Yu Sool style of Hapkido.* In this match the room is set with "props" which are available for either player to use. The props in question are usually made from foam or padding, but are designated as other objects - telephone, book, umbrella - objects that a person might encounter in real life.

Two players are introduced into this environment, given a time limit and a point goal, and the match is begun. During the ensuing match they may use anything they find in their controlled environment. They can pick up objects and use them for defense or attack, they can shield themselves behind obstacles, they can even pick things up and throw them (providing

---

*Yu Sool ("Soft Style") Hapkido is influenced primarily by Jujutsu. Kuk Sool ("Hard Style") Hapkido favors Taekwondo-style techniques.

they are made of foam) as a distraction to set up a hand or foot follow-up attack.

The game is entertaining and exciting, especially if the class puts some real thought into filling the space with soft and safe objects; but it is also very useful in terms of developing reliable self-defense skills. In a real fight, any object at hand can be used as a weapon if the players can locate it in the heat of battle and discover its uses in the very short time available to them.**

21.3 WORST CASE SCENARIO

This exercise is intended both for the development of self-defense-based sparring skills and for the cultivation of problem solving abilities. As the name suggests, the match starts from a position of severe threat and the defenders have to fight their way out and secure a win against extreme odds.

There are hundreds of variations of this sparring drill, but some of the more common ones include:

Seated against standing multiple attackers.

Supine (face up on the ground) against standing multiple attackers.

Prostrate (face down on the ground) against standing multiple attackers.

Starting in a corner.***

** For further information on this style of fighting, refer to the Japanese art of Hadaka Korosu ("Naked Kill"), the use of everyday objects as weapons, a technique taught by traditional Jujutsu schools. See <u>Ultimate Jujutsu: Principles and Practice</u> by Shihan Maberry for further details. The use of environmental factors as offensive and defensive weapons is also a staple of Kung Fu movies by stars such as Jackie Chan, Sammo Hung, and Jet Li.

*** When there are multiple attackers, this situation is the Box, described in Chapter 20. This variation of Worst Case Scenario is only to be used in gyms and dojos with padded walls.

Multiple armed attackers (using padded or mock weapons).

Starting with a simulated injury to an arm or leg.

Starting by allowing the attackers to secure a hold or pin.

Wearing restrictive garments (bulky coats, mittens, etc.).

Each variation allows all of the players involved to gain great insight into real-world applications of fighting skills.

Worst case scenarios: starting from a choke (left) and seated against standing attackers (right).

CHAPTER TWENTY-TWO
Conditions Sparring

Conditions Sparring, as the name implies, involves sparring methods built around unique environmental conditions, such as uneven surfaces, slippery surfaces, and confined spaces. The sparring methods in this chapter are generally non-competitive and are used primarily for developing skills in specific areas such as self-defense, balance, and situational control.

Many of these exercises are very advanced and should only be practiced by the most skilled players, and even then great care should be taken to maintain a high standard of safety.

22.1 UNEVEN SURFACE SPARRING

This sparring method is both difficult and dangerous, but it is also one that has a long history in real combat. Seizing and maintaining the higher ground has always been a smart tactical move. The higher ground allows for better visibility and it increases the ability to use gravity as a weapon.

Fighting uphill requires more physical exertion because weight and mass is being pushed upward against gravity's pull, and the more effort needed to move upward, the less strength can be applied to whatever blows and blocks are needed to continue the fight. Fighting a downhill battle has just the opposite effect. Gravity aids in the physical movement of advancing downhill, and since gravity is a constant downward pull, it makes descending blows far more powerful than upward rising blows. This fact of physics has played a part in many a sword battle over the centuries, and the uphill advantage holds true in any kind of fighting, from gunnery (shooting upward creates aiming problems that are not involved in shooting downward), to boxing (again, descending blows hit harder).

In unarmed martial arts, sparring on a ramp or slope is a great way of presenting additional challenges to the players that level ground matches cannot provide. Each player is presented with different problems to solve, and each actually has some advantages:

ADVANTAGES ON HIGHER GROUND

Less fatigue.

Easier reach to opponent's upper torso and head.

Can use legs to block.

Less likely to be kicked.

ADVANTAGES ON LOWER GROUND

Can duck or evade more easily.

Can more easily attack feet, legs, and groin.

Can grapple more easily.

One of the hardest parts about ramp or slope sparring is actually finding an incline on which two people may safely spar. Since covering such a slope with mats would be difficult, takedowns should not be used.

To make the matches fair, the players should switch position at the end of every round.

Another approach to uneven ground sparring is the Uneven Posts Method used in Shaolin training, where players fight atop a series of wide posts, ranging in thickness from just a few inches across to the width of a telephone pole. The poles are also different heights, making the players have to constantly change angle to each other and be extremely careful of their footwork.

Shaolin Uneven Posts Method of Sparring.

22.2 STAIRWELL SPARRING

This method of sparring should only be practiced by the most advanced practitioners, because the risk of injury is high. As discussed in Uneven Surface Sparring, holding the higher ground in a fight creates certain advantages, just as fighting uphill creates problems. Sparring on stairs allows fighters to take that conceptual ball and run with it by making the incline far more steep (stairwells are generally steeper than ramps or other inclines).

There is another reason some of the hard-core fighting schools teach sparring drills in stairwells: practical self-defense. The often-deserted stairwells of buildings, schools, parking garages, and hospitals are familiar hunting grounds for muggers and rapists. Stairs make flight difficult. The turnings of each landing reduce visibility and make surprise attacks easier to initiate.

The structure of stairs presents a serious danger for footwork. If the defender is below the level of the attacker then kicking skills won't work, and turning, shuffling, and sliding are out of the question. Plus there is the very real danger of being knocked backward down the stairs.

If standing above the attacker, then the defender has the option of using low-power speed kicks (high power kicks on stairs create too great a danger of overbalancing), as well as their hands. But for women there is the risk of the attacker rushing upward and pressing her down on the stairs, using the stairs as a sharp-edged slanting bed for a sexual assault.

With these risks and vulnerabilities in mind, some schools have taken to practicing controlled and limited sparring in stairwells. Players take turns as attacker and defender, and whoever plays the attacker must wear headgear that protects all sides of the head, a cervical collar, a chest protector, and other padding in case of falls.

However, falls are not encouraged. The sparring should go up to the point where a throw or knockdown might be used and then stop, it being understood that the attacker could have been tossed down the steps.

It needs to be stressed again that this is a self-defense sparring method used by some schools, and only under very strict and careful supervision. It is not recommended for anyone to try this method without proper supervision.

22.3 OUTDOOR SPARRING

Nearly everyone spars outdoors, and for several good reasons: more room, fresh air, sunshine, and beauty. Official tournaments are held outdoors in many disciplines. In some competitive forms, outdoor sparring is a regular part of the rules, such as in Celtic wrestling, sportive Jogo Do Pau, or Irish Stick Fencing. Many Aikido and Tai Chi Push Hands matches are held outdoors for the express purpose of making use of the serene power of nature.

On a grass-roots level, martial artists and their classmates will get together on any clear stretch of ground, from back yard to sandy beach, to compare, spar, and train.

Sparring in specific outdoor areas is also useful for certain aspects of skill development, and different locations come with their own advantages and cautions.

BEACH SPARRING

Sparring on the beach is a favorite of classical Karate practitioners, not surprising since both Okinawa and Japan are islands. The variety of footings, from loose dry sand to hard-packed wet sand to frothing surf, allows the players to learn quite a lot about maintaining balance, adapting footwork, and choosing (or discarding) techniques based on the surety of a surface.

Naturally the area chosen for sparring should be policed of all shells, driftwood, and other debris before any match is started.

On loose sand, footwork is clumsier and simple moves like pivots and turns become problematic. The sand that is literally "kicked up" is a consideration that must be dealt with. Even when not intentionally directed at the eyes, loose dry sand will fill the air

during an active spar, and the players have to protect their eyes while they fight. Adjustments in evasion and blocking are required to keep away from flying sand while still paying attention to incoming punches and kicks. This increased demand on the senses and reflexes makes for wonderful growth because it forces the players to think outside the box.

Wetter, firmer sand is much closer to the slight yield of sparring mats. But seastrand is often gently sloping, so again there is a challenge for footwork and balance.

Training in the surf is very difficult, far more so than in a pool or pond. The constant movement of tons of water and shifting sand seems specifically designed to disrupt footwork. Salt water, clouded by sea foam and billowing sand, is generally opaque, disguising the other player's footwork until it is felt.

Grappling on soft sand is common practice in many Judo and Jujutsu schools, but dry sand is not the soft, comfortable cushion that one would expect. Granted, it is less dense than wet sand, but it is by no means an easy fall. Only grapplers who are well trained in Ukemi (breakfalls) should even consider it, and even then only with supervision.

One of the great advantages to beach sparring is the freedom of movement, with wide open spaces available. This encourages weapons practitioners to train and spar with everything from swords to staffs to nunchaku on the beach.

SPARRING ON GRASS

Grass makes a soft but slippery surface for sparring. The springiness of the grass and the soil beneath help to reduce jarring to the leg joints, and make tumbling and rolling fairly comfortable.

However, the slickness of fresh grass can make for an uncertain surface, and sparring partners have to be very careful not to slip and slide. Practicing turning,

sliding, and jumping kicks prior to sparring will help the players get a sense of what they can and cannot do.

SPARRING IN THE WOODS

In Kung Fu, being near to nature is a meditative tool that is vital to a serious student's growth. Training outdoors is not just a way of acquiring skills and testing one's abilities, but a way to calm the soul and expand the consciousness. Outdoor training is often done following a long and deep meditation, and as the players begin sparring they carry with them tranquility and enlightenment.

In Ch'uan Chi Tao Kung Fu, sparring is almost always practiced outside, using the roughest landscape possible in order to simulate the rocky terrain of Southern China. Stone walls, rock-strewn slopes, and stream beds are the battleground of choice for this style of Kung Fu, which is known for its extremely intense training practices.

PART SIX
Non~Contact Sparring

CHAPTER TWENTY-THREE
Form Sparring Methods

Forms are basically a collection of many different encounters between the performer and a series of imaginary opponents. They are not, as a rule, based on simulated encounters with actual opponents, but rather a series of related skills performed with simulated opponents.

There are a number of sparring methods and sparring drills that are designed to accomplish two things: to increase students' ability to perform their forms with greater skill, speed, and efficiency, and to develop a deeper understanding of the moves which make up each form so that these techniques can be put to better use.

23.1 KATA SPARRING

KATA RUN-THROUGH SPARRING (JIYU-BUNKAI)

Bunkai is a Japanese term referring to an analytical dissection of a Kata (form) so each individual move or defense can be practiced as a complete skill, independent of the larger set of techniques.

Kata Run-Through Sparring, also called Jiyu-Bunkai, is not performed solo; rather, the entire kata is performed by two or more players. As the Primary Player moves through the techniques of the kata, other players are positioned at key points on the Embusen, or pattern, formed by the kata. As the Primary Player goes through his moves, he faces one after another player. This is a challenge even when practiced slowly, since form and precision are crucial. As speed increases, so does ability.

The match is judged by having each player in turn take the primary role, and the instructor watches and awards points for each encounter as follows:

Yuko (near half-point): Awarded for a performance that is just barely effective or which contains some flaws.

Waza-ari (half-point): Awarded for a performance that is technically accurate but deficient in only one element (form, preferred speed, balance, completeness).

Ippon (full point): Awarded when the techniques are performed without flaw and at the assigned speed.

Since most Kata are comprised of many techniques, the player who has performed the greatest number of techniques correctly is the winner.

Kata form the basis for most promotions in the martial arts, and are also a featured event in tournaments. This controlled sparring dill, done at a speed where all participating parties can closely analyze the nuances of each movement, does wonders for improving the knowledge and abilities of everyone involved.

SLOW MOTION WEAPONS SPARRING

Slow Motion Weapons Sparring helps beginning and intermediate students perfect their forms. A strictly in-school method of sparring, these matches are staged between players who have already learned at least one complete form (kata, kuen, poomse, etc.) with a given weapon.

This method of sparring is an outgrowth of the standard

Kata demonstrated by Goju-ryu Grandmaster M. Gene Holden and Jamal El.

Jiyu-Bunkai, except that the form in question is a weapons pattern. Whether the item is a staff, spear, sword, or other traditional weapon, the method of practice is pretty much the same: the Primary Player begins slowly moving through the form and other players wait at crucial points around the pattern, armed in whatever manner is required by the form. They attack with the prescribed moves and the Primary Player defends appropriately.

The drill's slow speed allows all of the players to concentrate on proper form, balance, stance, timing, and movement while maintaining a very high degree of safe control. It also allows the rest of the class to observe and learn from the match.

As with non-weapons Kata Run-Through Sparring, the players are graded on how each component of the Kata is performed. Players rotate positions so that every person has a chance to be the Primary and to deliver each different attack.

PERFECTION

Perfection is a drill much prized and practiced in Shaolin Kung Fu. Many of the forms (*kuen*) of Kung Fu are intricate and lengthy two-person sets. Though students are eventually taught to do these sets at great speed, they first learn them using the Perfection Drill.

Perfection is an exercise where both partners, right from the beginning, endeavor to perform each move as exactly as possible, beginning very slowly so they can really learn the mechanics of each skill and focus on developing perfect posture, balance, coordination, and more.

As all of the students learn the form in this manner, they are set in pairs to compete against others, generally with the whole class watching. The added pressure of competition and spectators teaches the students to cope with pressure and to ignore distractions in the heat of a fight.

CLASSICAL FORM SPARRING

Classical Form Sparring is different from Bunkai in that students do not follow the pattern of a kata, nor do they encounter a series of opponents positioned at various points around the floor. In Classical Form Sparring, the students spar freely, selecting techniques according to need and choice. However, in order to score points, each technique of attack or defense must be executed with the structure and precision of a kata. This is very, very difficult.

In sparring and fighting, exact form tends to go out the window in favor of immediate reaction time, and is affected by nervousness and the overall speed of the match. This is not to say that empty-hand fighters are sloppy, that is certainly not the case. But in the heat of a full-speed match, players tend to modify moves to suit their physical abilities (size, strength, reach, speed, etc.) and to suit the moment. In Classical Form Sparring, the players are required to use correct form or none of their techniques will be awarded any points. The goal is to develop each player's ability to use correct form even at top speed and in the uncertainty of a competitive match. This is very difficult, but it is possible with hard work and lots of practice. The weapons art of Kendo maintains this requirement even in competition.

23.2 SHADOWBOXING

Former top amateur boxer Tyrone "Tiger" Selles once said: "Shadowboxing is the hardest thing to do, 'cause the person you're fighting is yourself."

For centuries, Shadowboxing of one kind or another has been used as a training method by boxers, fencers, and kickboxers. Shadowboxing provides fighters with a variety of benefits, such as increased endurance, refined form, great speed, finesse in footwork, and improved timing.

Some fighters groan when their trainers suggest they Shadowbox, and just go through the motions of stabbing the air with simulated hits. As a result they lose out on some pretty amazing benefits. Fighters who approach Shadowboxing as a valuable training tool will strike gold every time they do the drill.

Shadowboxing is a much more advanced exercise that it would appear. It cultivates visualization, which is the active aspect of imagination. When sparring with a partner there is little room for imagination and almost no place for visualization, leaving the player with nothing but execution. The less pressured atmosphere of Shadowboxing gives a fighter a chance to focus on his own needs, and on his own skills.

Shadowboxing has many benefits:

It allows the player to practice punch combinations.

It allows the player to work out new footwork patterns.

It allows the player to ponder different attack and counterattack scenarios, over and over again, with infinite variations.

It allows the player to imagine different reactions and practice footwork and striking moves to counter those reactions.

It allows the player to feel how to throw specific strikes with perfection—hooks, jabs, crosses, and uppercuts, for example.

It allows the player to practice a variety of defensive moves, like ducking, slipping, parrying, covering, and shifting.

The value of contemplating and practicing strategies and their variations over and over again before a match is invaluable. In the ring there is time only to act and react, rarely to invent. If scenarios are drilled repeatedly with Shadowboxing then they will be there when needed in the ring. Repetition creates new combat reflexes; this is the basis for all martial arts, and boxing is a martial art.

The combination punch has far more value than the single shot, and in Shadowboxing the player gets to learn new combinations and drill them so they are second nature to him. It also lets him know which combinations will work for him in terms of comfort. Differences in size, weight, reach, and musculature will make each separate combination feel different. A fighter can learn which ones feel best for him in full speed Shadowboxing.

Shadowboxing also teaches a player to be economical and meaningful with his punches, rather than just paw and slap. This economy of motion burns less energy and helps a fighter last longer in the ring.

Shadowboxing can be practiced so that the fighter varies speed and force, changes his intensity, switches from offense to defense to counterattack with ease, and essentially conditions himself for the changes that happen in the ring. Boxing isn't just hitting: it's moving, adapting, yielding, aggressing, being ready, and being in charge.

In Shaolin Kung Fu and Southern Praying Mantis, Shadowboxing has a more literal interpretation: the player actually moves and responds to his own shadow. Practiced with a light (sunlight or lamplight) behind him and a while wall (stucco, paint, or rice paper) in front of him, the player begins by going through the opening moves of a form. But as soon as the "shadow" self throws a punch or kick, the player tries to move to simulate a block and counter, and then a counter to the counter, and so on. Of course it isn't possible to outmaneuver one's shadow, but the drill allows the player to both study his form via the pattern of the shadow, and to push for faster and faster movements until everything is a shadowy blur. In this way astounding whipping speed is learned.

CHAPTER TWENTY-FOUR
Mock Combat Sparring Methods

To a great degree, fighting is a spectator sport. From the earliest days of gladiatorial combat to the latest Hong Kong action flick, people have always loved to watch a good fight. It is the thrill of seeing competent warriors using their wits, courage, and superb technique.

Some methods of competitive fighting, such as medieval jousting, are no longer practiced in their original form; yet jousts still exist and even draw great crowds in events such as Renaissance Faires.

Sword dueling exists in two forms today: competitive fencing (foil, epee, and sabre) and stage fighting, which adds excitement to performances of Shakespeare and other classic plays. On TV and in the movies, fight choreography can lift even a formulaic action flick to great heights.

This Chapter discusses these "Mock Combat" methods used in various aspects of the entertainment industry. Take note: although the combat is simulated, the choreographers are generally highly trained athletes who are masters of various fighting disciplines; and the actors performing these choreographed moves have to be very talented in order to be believable.

24.1 JOUSTING

These early tournaments were often conducted like war games, with groups of knights and soldiers practicing skirmishing tactics and other skills to locate and defeat their opponents in forested areas. Though

Photo courtesy of Pennsylvania Renaissance Faire.

357

the intent was not to do any real harm, many accidents happened, and a few private scores were settled under cover of the alarms and excursions.

During the Twelfth Century these tournaments became more organized and less overtly violent. The focus also changed from the group melee to man-to-man combat. The "lance charger," originally a staple of the melee clashes, became the highlight of these matches. Men on horseback who would slam into each other, often resulting in their horses being jarred to a halt. Then either from the saddle or on foot, they would continue to whack each other with swords, maces, or anything else they had handy. The crowd loved these single combat jousts and over time they became the prime event.

A century later the organizers of jousts began to make changes designed to protect the players. Unsharpened swords were used, and better armor was devised. In addition, the "Lance of Peace" was adopted: it was about the same size and weight of the standard lance, but the tip was either blunted or replaced with a coronel, a metal head shaped like a crown and designed to disperse the impact of the blow. These modified arms and armor were called *armes a plaisance* (arms of courtesy), as opposed to *armes a outrance*, or arms of war. The latter weaponry was only utilized in serious challenges and combats, the contest ending when one combatant was killed or disabled.

In modern times, jousting and even melee are performed at Renaissance Faires all over the United States. These Faires provide a wonderful glimpse back in time for the visitors, who can sample foods, take in entertainment, listen to music, and enjoy a hearty joust or two—all accurate portrayals of the historic Age of Chivalry.

Photos courtesy of Pennsylvania Renaissance Faire.

The actor-athletes who perform these jousts and duels are all highly trained. They can ride, use a lance, fight with swords and quarterstaffs, and give battle with a degree of realistic enthusiasm that dazzles audiences.

24.2 STAGE FIGHTING

As the term suggests, Stage Fighting is fighting designed for use onstage. The movements, whether a dashing swordfight or a taproom brawl, have to be so tightly choreographed that the fights look real to the audience but manage to stay within the limited confines of the stage. These fights are blocked out in much the same way as a ballet, with each turn and lunge, each leap and fall, carefully planned so that no one crashes into the scenery and no cast members are skewered. Even so, the fight is an exhilarating experience for the audience.

This is not easy to do, and it takes top professionals to bring it off with such deftness and sleight of hand so that when Romeo kills Tybalt, it looks so real that the audience gasps because each of them feels the cold steel and the hot blood themselves.

Peking Opera choreography by Jim Corcoran.

Teaching Stage Fighting to actors is often a serious challenge to a fight choreographer. Though an actor may be talented at his craft, fighting is a completely different art. The fight choreographer is also limited in the time allotted him to prepare the actors. Most plays are rehearsed from only a few weeks to a couple months at the outside, and in that time the actors have to learn their roles, develop their performances, practice the standard stage blocking, and run through the play countless times. All of this leaves little time to learn how to joust with the heroic ease of a Lancelot or fence with the offhand expertise of a Cyrano. So the fight choreographer has to develop the battle and teach the actors the necessary skills to convince a roomful of people who will be watching very closely.

The fight choreographer has to be adaptable in many regards because stages vary in size and space, and actors vary greatly in skill and ability. The fight choreographer needs to be as flexible as a rapier blade.

The trick is to make a fight look totally spontaneous, as though it is being made up before your eyes, like it is a natural occurrence arising from the events unfolding in the drama. Masters of stage fighting use many drills and exercises to help actors develop a feel for whatever method of fighting is called for, and other drills to acquire proficiency in the weapons of choice.

Many theater departments—university and professional—offer classes in Stage Fighting taught by top fight choreographers. The exposure to some of the deeper levels of training raises the bar in terms of possible performance. A choreographer can work wonders with actors who come into a rehearsal already capable of basic stage fighting.

One of the most difficult aspects of the fight choreographer's job is to keep the fight looking real and yet maintain an absolute level of safety. Nothing is of greater importance to a fight choreographer than the safety of his actors.

On a more technical level, the choreographer has to be deeply versed in a great variety of fighting methods and styles, because theater embraces all ages and eras and cultures. When choreographing a sword duel in *The Scarlet Pimpernel,* which is set during the French Revolution, the fighting styles and methods have to suit the era; just as a broadsword battle in a stage version of *Ivanhoe* would have to match the weapons, tactics, and methods of that medieval era. To accomplish this, most fight choreographers study a great number of disciplines, from various methods of European fencing, to boxing, to the martial arts of Asia.

Photo courtesy of Pennsylvania Renaissance Faire.

There are quite a few professional organizations that teach high levels of skill and proficiency to Stage Fight choreographers. Some of the best known, in alphabetical order, are:

The Academy of the Sword

The Academy of Theatrical Combat

American Fight Directors

Art of Combat, Inc.

Atlanta Stage Combat Studio

British Academy of Dramatic Combat

British Academy of Stage and Screen Combat

Fight Directors of Canada

Guild of Fight Masters

International Guild of Swordsmen & Swashbucklers

Nordic Stage Fighting Society

Rapier-Wit.Com

Society of American Fight Directors

Swordplay

The Thrown Gauntlet

Photos courtesy of professional fight choreographer Stephen D. Hyers of Elon University

The process of creating a stage fight always begins with a script (for a play) or the libretto and music (for an opera). Once these have been read and digested, the choreographer does his own research into the specific historical period in which the play is set.

The next step involves discussions between the fight choreographer and the director, who must establish the role of the fight in the director's overall vision of the performance. They also discuss set design, costumes, and casting since these will all play major roles in the completed piece.

Speaking of roles, many fight choreographers are actors themselves and have taken parts in plays, sometimes out of a love of theater and sometimes to add their own combative skills to the choreographed fight. They especially come in handy playing roles of villains. Many fight choreographers are capable stuntmen as well, and by spinning away from punches, getting knocked down, or getting in the way of a sword thrust at just the right moment, they can make the hero of the piece look like a champion fighter.

There are four general rules for creating fighting moves for the stage:

Photo courtesy of Pennsylvania Renaissance Faire.

1. Bigger Is Better: A small, subtle flick of the wrist may work well for Olympic fencers, but on stage such a move would be invisible to the audience. Stage fencing, as well as stage unarmed fighting, must be big—big enough to be seen and understood from the back row in the top balcony—yet believable to even the most jaded theater critic sitting in the front row.

2. Keep It Simple: Actors are not professional fighters, so the more complex the fight the greater the chance someone will miss a cue or, even worse, miss the mark and actually hit the other actors on stage instead of passing close. Besides, a complex fight scene takes longer to learn and the actors still have to concentrate on their lines, their blocking, and the quality of their overall performance, all of which demand much of their time and focus. The fight choreographer has to devise a way to make the fight simple (for the actors) but exciting and unpredictable (for the audience).

3. Understand The Characters: The best fight choreographers get inside the heads of the characters when they are creating fights. By understanding the personality, viewpoint, and motivations of each character who is involved, the choreographer can develop techniques and even fighting styles that are appropriate to each. For example, the way in which a cowardly and secretive character would approach a duel is far different from the way in which a self-assured hero would manage the same fight.

4. Be A Fighter: The choreographer has to think like a fighter when he writes his moves. He has to understand the weapons, the surface on which the fight will occur, the motivations of the characters, and the required outcome. But above all of this he has to be a fighter. The moves he designs need to be logical, appropriate, creative, and possible, and it takes the mindset of a true warrior to do this.

24.3 MOVIE & TV FIGHT CHOREOGRAPHY

Fight Choreography in a TV or movie action sequence can make or break the whole production. A good movie with an obviously phony fight will suddenly jolt a viewer out of the envelope of suspended belief that the show's director has worked so hard to construct. This is true of any TV show or movie with a fight scene, but if action is to be highlighted over all else, then the fights have to come off smoothly and well, and leave the audience gasping.

Whereas in stage fight choreography the fight director has very little time to develop the action and needs to make it broad enough to be seen in the back of the theater, a movie fight choreographer has ten times the latitude for creating action sequences that are either believable or so over the top that they seamlessly blend fantasy and action together. Film and video also allow the use of special effects that are generally not possible on stage, such as wires and digital effects; and this freedom of expression allows the fight choreographers to write larger, longer, and far more elaborate battle sequences.

Fight choreographers have to be versatile because in a single film they may need to stage a gun battle, a desperate encounter between a lone hero and a dozen thugs, a creative escape, and a final fight scene that will be talked about for years. Some of this planning and staging may be done with the director and stunt coordinator, but in many films the fight choreographer is given a fairly free hand. For this reason film critics have come to acknowledge that fight choreographers are an important part of the creative process of movie making.

Fighting in film has evolved greatly from the broad theatrical punches of the early days of cinema, when fights were staged for film in the same manner as for stage. The problem is that film encourages subtlety in movement whereas the stage requires bigger movements. So fight choreographers have had to become students of film as well as various fighting disciplines.

In action films there are usually several fight scenes, each one more elaborate and violent than the last, culminating in a finale that resolves all of the stories' tensions with one knock-the-walls-down fight between hero and villain, or hero and a band of villains. American-made films like *Only the Strong, Exposure, Blade, Blade II, Lethal Weapon, Die Hard II*, and *Uncommon Valor* all featured top notch and exciting fight choreography. On TV, shows like *Buffy the Vampire Slayer, Martial Law, Angel*, and *Alias* feature some of the best small-screen fights ever seen. Each choreographer builds partly on the work of his predecessors and partly on his own innovative thinking and sense of style.

The move toward truly sophisticated fight scenes, however, really blossomed in Hong Kong cinema, which has a long tradition of action in film. Long before the days of Bruce Lee,

Hong Kong films featured Kung Fu and swordplay as de rigueur components. Since the Kung Fu movie explosion of the 1970s, stars of Hong Kong cinema have become household names. Who hasn't heard of Jackie Chan, Sammo Hung, or Jet Li?

And with the growing relationship between Hong Kong and Hollywood, many top stars and fight choreographers from the East are making films here in the West. The dynamic fights in the blockbuster sci-fi hit *The Matrix* were choreographed by Yuen Wo Ping, and action star/fight choreographer Donnie Yen had a small role in *Blade II* and the dynamic fight scenes

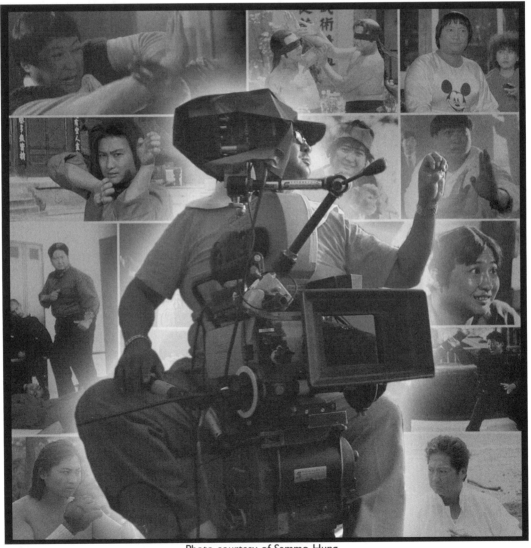

Photo courtesy of Sammo Hung.

in the recent blockbuster *The Brotherhood of the Wolf*, set in Revolutionary France, were staged by fight director Kwok Choi. Action star and fight director Sammo Hung even had a hit TV series in the United States called *Martial Law*, which featured at least one spectacular fight scene every week, and his vast body of film work has established him as the dean of action film choreographers who are also accomplished actors and directors.

Since fight choreographers have had to study many aspects of film making (cinematography, directing, etc.), many of them are moving into the director's chair and helming big budget, highly successful action pictures that sell tremendously well on the international market.

Fight choreography in action films is a true art form, where the actors are given routines to perform as complex as any modern dance, as physically demanding as any ring fight, and as breathtaking as that first drop on a rollercoaster. Some of the most beautifully choreographed fight scenes—scenes that tell of the choreographers' insight, artistry, and imagination —can be seen in the following dynamic battles:

Sammo Hung choreographing fight scenes. Photos courtesy Sammo Hung.

Jet Li versus Billy Chow in *Fist Of Legend*

Jackie Chan versus Ken Lo in *Drunken Master II*

Jackie Chan versus Benny Urquidez in *Dragons Forever*

Randall "Tex" Cobb and Patrick Swayze in *Uncommon Valor*

Zhang Zi Ying versus Michelle Yeoh in *Crouching Tiger, Hidden Dragon*

Mel Gibson versus Gary Busey in *Lethal Weapon*

Lau Kar Leung versus Lau Kar Wing in *Legendary Weapons of Kung Fu*

Jet Li versus Donnie Yen in *Once Upon A Time In China II*

Keanu Reeves versus Hugo Weaving in *The Matrix*

Sammo Hung versus Lau Kar Leung in *Pedicab Driver*

Cynthia Rothrock and Michelle Yeoh versus Dick Wei in *Yes, Madam*

Charles Bronson versus Nick Dimitri in *Hard Times*

Chiu Man Cheuk versus Xin Xin Xiong in *The Blade*

Movie fight choreography is also heavily used for animation, from hand-drawn cartoons to computer generated films. The animation which makes the heaviest use of fight choreography is Japanese Anime, a style of epic adventure film which has developed a hugely popular following around the world.

Anime got its start with the 1945 feature-length film *Momotaro, Divine Sea Warrior*. It has grown in scope, complexity of storytelling, and sophistication of animation ever since, going through phases where episodic TV shows like *Star Blazers* and *The Macross Saga* were its prime forums, to the current crop of highly detailed feature film epics like *Ghost in the Shell*, *Akira*, *Princess Mononoke*, and *Blood: The Last Vampire*. Many of these films feature the usual staples of science fiction and fantasy (heroes, monsters, ray guns, and spaceships), but many also feature remarkably realistic and sophisticated fight scenes.

Computer generated animation is another outlet for fight choreographers. The newest generation of cartoons is not drawn by hand but created by digital wizardry, which allows the widest possible range of freedom for a fight choreographer because anything that can be imagined can now be filmed. From the hilarious take-off on *The Matrix* seen in *Shrek*, to the blazing gun battles in *Final Fantasy*, computer generated graphics allows filmmakers to go anywhere and do anything without limitations of any kind.

Since many of the characters in such films are not

Sequence A: Human movement is used to choreograph animated wolf dogs.

366

even human, fight choreographers have to think way outside the box, imagining how other kinds of creatures might reasonably fight. Miriam Anzovin, a fight choreographer and film-maker for Anzovin Studio, observed, "One of the most interesting things about choreo-graphing fights for animation is the challenge of developing moves for fighters who aren't human. Animal characters like the stylized wolf-dogs [shown in Sequence A] may not have the same joint movements and range of flexibility that humans do. These particular charac-ters can't make a fist, because they don't have functional thumbs. Kicking is basically limited to a back kick, which develops from a canine's natural running movement. Everything is slashing, clawing, biting, or twisting. Some of the moves [we did] evolved from some fun Filipino knife-fighting moves I was working on. We just replaced the knife with claws."

The approach to choreographing computer generated fights is different from live action film. According to Steve Anzovin, "Coming up with plausible combat motion for 3D-animated characters is quite difficult. Most studios employ one or both of the following methods: (1) hiring a martial artist to choreograph reference movements on video, which the animators then follow as they animate the fighting characters, or (2) capturing direct limb-position and joint-rotation data from a martial artist wearing a motion capture [mocap] suit. The mocap method works well when the 3D characters have the same proportions and motion

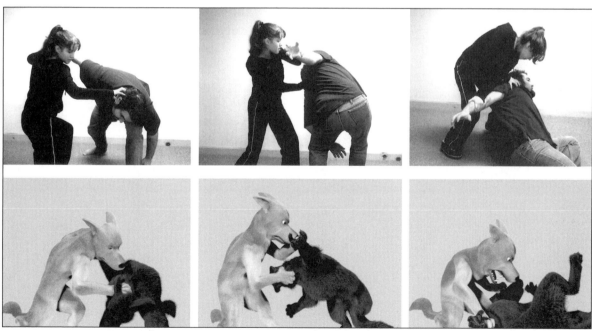

Photos courtesy of Miriam Anzovin and Anzovin Studio;
for further information visit their web site at http://www.anzovin.com/miriam.html

capabilities as the human martial artist—you just apply the motion data to the 3D character. But when the animated character is not built like a human, using human motion data just causes endless trouble. It's better in that situation to rely on well-choreographed reference footage."

Miriam Anzovin adds, "In [Sequence B], a noir-movie parody, all the fighting is done in a 1940s brawl-type situation.

Sequence B. Photos courtesy Anzovin Studio.

Though one character is a cartoon human and the other is a cartoon dog, they both fight the same way - haymakers and uppercuts! - except the dog also bites.

"In animation, where there is basically no limit to the fighting capabilities of a cartoon character, there are endless possibilities for new, original fight choreography. Something I haven't seen done well up till now is a complex, involved fight between a real-life human and a CG (computer graphics) fighter. That would be something to see."

Computer games, especially the action games which feature a variety of exotic fighters, also require very evolved fight choreography, in terms of techniques and diversity of fighting styles. Movie fight choreography legends, such as Jet Li and Cory Yuen, have worked with animators and game developers to create the next generation of video games, such as "Rise to Honor"® from Sony Computer Entertainment America (SCEA) and the many fantastic characters in the various generations of "Tekken."®

Odds are the fight between human and computer generated character is not far off.

APPENDIX ONE
Dictionary of Sparring Terms

KEY: C: Chinese term

J: Japanese term

K: Korean term

A

<u>Armbar</u>: A type of arm lock in which the arm is hyper-extended at the elbow, inflicting sufficient pain to get the opponent to submit or "tap out."

B

<u>Bo</u>: (J) A fighting staff, about 6 feet long and 1 inch in diameter, made of polished wood and used in several martial arts.

<u>Bokken</u>: (J) A wooden sword approximating the katana or longsword used in Kenjutsu (Japanese swordplay). The Bokken is also used by practitioners of Jujutsu and Aikido.

<u>Bout</u>: A match between two competitors that consists of four two-minute rounds, with a one-minute break between rounds.

<u>Break</u>: A referee's command for fighters to break from a clinch. On the command each fighter takes a step back before continuing boxing.

<u>Breakfall</u>: A method of safe falling from trips and throws.

<u>Bridge</u>: (J) A trapping technique that lays one limb over another, blocking the opponent's arm while creating an opening for a strike.

(2) An arched position of the body used in wrestling where the weight rests on the feet and on either the shoulders or head.

<u>Bridge out</u>: A move used to escape an opponent by rolling from a bridge onto the stomach.

<u>Bushido</u>: "The Way of the Warrior." A code of ethics employed by the Samurai and which forms the code of conduct for practitioners of Japanese martial arts.

<u>Bunkai</u>: (J) A study of the techniques and applications in kata.

C

<u>Caution</u>: An admonition from the referee to a fighter. Generally not for serious infringements of the rules. After three cautions, a warning is issued.

<u>Chi (Qi)</u>: (C) "Vital energy"; an electrochemical field of energy that flows through the body along pathways called meridians. It is believed that correct Chi flow promotes good health, which is the basis for acupuncture and acupressure; whereas blocked Chi flow causes sickness and even death, which is the basis for Dim Mak, a destructive substyle of Kung Fu.

<u>Choke</u>: A move blocking the carotid artery in the neck, restricting the passage of blood to the brain. Failing to "tap" can put the victim into a temporary state of unconsciousness.

<u>Clinch</u>: A position in which two fighters are face to face, usually with their arms and upper bodies locked, performed either for a "breather" or to protect against strikes. Some fighters have mastered the art of the clinch for offensive purposes, throwing effective short punches and/or knees from this position.

<u>Coach</u>: The person who trains and teaches the fighter. He also works in his fighter's corner, giving advice and motivation between rounds.

<u>Combinations</u>: Punches thrown in sequence, such as a left jab, followed by a straight right, followed by a left hook.

<u>Control</u>: The deliberate regulation of force and power used in martial arts, either to do a specific amount of damage or to do none at all. Control also extends to moderating one's level of intensity in a match.

<u>Covering</u>: Holding the hands high in front of the face to keep the opponent from landing a clean punch.

<u>Counter-attack</u>: An attack launched after the opponent initiates his attack.

<u>Counter-punch</u>: A blow delivered immediately after an opponent throws a punch. A "counter-puncher" typically waits for his opponent to throw punches, then blocks or slips past them and exploits the opening in his opponent's position.

D

Dan: (J & K) Level, Rank, or Degree. Black Belt rank.

Dantian (Tan T'ian): "Field of Cinnabar." A Taoist term referring to a center of energy located approximately two inches below the navel and inside the lower abdomen. The location roughly corresponds to the center of mass of a person standing in a natural posture, hence it is often referred to as the "center of being." In the internal martial arts, Chi (or Qi) is considered to be stored in the Dantian.

Do: (J) Way or path. The Japanese character for Do is the same as the Chinese character for Tao (as in Taoism). Used primarily as a suffix to denote a method of modern Japanese martial arts (post 1880), such as "Karate-do" or "Judo".

Dobok: (K) Uniform worn in Korean martial arts.

Dojang: (K) Korean word for training hall or school of martial arts.

Dojo: (J) Japanese word for training hall or school of martial arts.

Down: When a fighter touches the floor with anything other than his feet or if he goes outside the ropes from a blow. A fighter is also technically "down," even if he hasn't fallen, if he takes a serious blow or blows to the head and the referee steps in to stop the action.

Drill: An exercise designed to hone skills, generally through repetition.

Drill Based Sparring: See "In-Class Sparring."

E

Embusen: (J) Floor pattern of movement in a kata.

Evasion: A technique to avoid contact.

External: Referring to the use of muscular force or mechanical energy in the physical body; as opposed to Internal, which uses Chi (or Ki, Gi, etc.)

Feint: A blow that is stopped short of the target in order to distract the other player or cause him to move in such a way as to expose himself to a hit.

F

Fish-hooking: The act of "hooking" a finger into an opponent's mouth or ears and pulling much like a fish on a hook. This move is illegal in nearly every form of organized martial competition.

<u>Focus</u>: The controlled regulation of depth of penetration in a hit, selecting whether it hits full power, lightly, or not at all.

<u>Footwork</u>: The way a fighter moves and plants his feet which enables him to be well-balanced for throwing punches and ready to switch easily between defensive and offensive boxing.

<u>Forfeit</u>: A loss caused by committing a serious foul, missing the start of a match or other behavior.

<u>Foul</u>: An infringement of a set of rules, generally based on safety or etiquette.

<u>Freestyle</u>: (1) Sparring without using pre-set or specific techniques. (2) Sparring without adhering to any specific style of martial arts.

G

<u>Gi</u>: (J) Uniform worn in Japanese martial arts. (2) See "Chi"

<u>Grappling</u>: Any of a variety of close-quarters fighting skills involving holds, pins, throws, takedowns, trips, locks and floor matwork.

<u>Grappling Arts</u>: Martial arts that use wrestling, locking, throwing, holding, or pinning as their primary skill area. Grappling arts include Aikido, Judo, Jujutsu, Sumo and others. Also referred to as Scuffle Arts.

H

<u>Hakama</u>: (J) Culottes worn by advanced practitioners in Japanese martial arts.

<u>Head Butt</u>: To strike an opponent using the head. This move is illegal is most forms of competitive fighting.

<u>Hook</u>: A short power punch in which the fighter swings from the shoulder with his elbow bent, bringing his fist from the side toward the center.

<u>House Rules</u>: The rules established by whatever governing body initiates the match. In tournaments these rules are usually based on the style of art the governing body advocates. For in-class sparring, the rules are usually set prior to each match, often to allow players to achieve a specific benefit or work on designated skill areas.

I

<u>In-Class Sparring</u>: Methods of sparring that are used only within a martial arts school and are often quite different from the sparring used in official competitions and tournaments. Also called "Drill Based Sparring"

In-Fighting: Fighting at close range

Ippon: (J) One full point. Most Karate matches are based on a single point, though half and quarter points may be earned to contribute to the full point.

J

Jab: A quick, straight punch thrown with the lead hand. It can be used as a set-up for power punches, as a way to gauge distance, to keep an opponent wary, or as a defensive move to slow an advancing opponent.

Jam: A technique designed to stop the attacker from completing a step, strike or kick.

K

Kata: (J) A form or prescribed pattern of movement used to teach students groups of skills or responses.

Ki: See "Chi."

K.O: An acronym for "knock out," a term typically used in boxing. A KO is the act of a fighter taking a hard blow and temporarily losing consciousness.

Kwangjangnim: (K) Teacher of Korean martial arts.

Kwoon: (C) General term given to any school of Chinese-based martial arts. Also spelled "Guan".

Kuen: (C) A form or prescribed pattern of movement used to teach students groups of skills or responses.

L

M

Matwork: Wrestling techniques performed while one or both partners are lying on the floor.

Mouthpiece: A piece of plastic used to protect a fighter's teeth and prevent him from biting his tongue.

N

<u>Neutral Corner</u>: One of two corners that are not assigned to either fighter.

<u>N.H.B.</u>: An acronym for "No Holds Barred" (see "No Holds Barred").

<u>No Holds Barred</u>: A popular term used to describe "mixed martial arts" events. Due to the evolution of the sport and implementation of safety rules, the term "no holds barred" is out-dated but remains popular among fans.

O

<u>Open Tournament</u>: A tournament that does not place restrictions on the parent style of entrants. For example, an open tournament hosted by a Karate school may still admit prac-titioners of Taekwondo, Kung Fu, etc.

P

<u>Parry</u>: A deflection that redirects a blow rather than attempts to stop it by direct opposition.

<u>Percussion Art</u>: A martial art based primarily (though not always exclusively) on striking and/or kicking; as opposed to a Grappling art.

<u>Point</u>: A unit of measure to determine a winning score.

<u>Poomse</u>: (K) Also spelled "poomsae" A form or prescribed pattern of movement used to teach students groups of skills or responses.

Q

Qi (C): See Chi.

R

<u>Referee</u>: The official who ensures the bout is clean and fair, and to make sure the fighters are physically able to box after taking a punch. The referee can end the bout if one fighter is hurt or over-matched.

<u>Ring Sense</u>: Good competitive judgment usually based on common sense and experience.

<u>Ringside Physician</u>: The doctor who checks the condition of competitors during the bout and determines whether a hurt fighter can continue. The physician has the power to stop a bout at any time.

S

Scoring Blow: A punch that lands cleanly on the opponent's head or torso and is struck with the knuckles, signified by the white stripe on the glove. If three judges agree within a one-second window that the blow was clean, the fighter gets a point.

Scuffle Arts: See "Grappling Arts."

Second: A person aside from the coach who gives a fighter assistance or advice between rounds.

Sensei: (J) Teacher of Japanese martial arts.

Shift: To move one's body abruptly in order to generate power or evade a blow.

Sifu: (C) Teacher of Chinese martial arts.

Slip: An evasion accomplished with little or no footwork.

Small Joint Manipulation: Any variation of submission holds which consist of twisting, popping, or hyperextending a small joint, such as the fingers or toes. Such holds are illegal in most forms of grappling except traditional Jujutsu sparring.

Stance: A method of standing so that the body is ready for both attack and defense.

Standing Eight Count: When a fighter is in trouble, or has been knocked down the referee stops the action and counts to eight. During this time the referee determines if the fighter can continue. If a fighter takes three standing-eights in a round or four in a bout, the contest is stopped and the opponent is declared the winner.

Stand-up Art: Nickname given to any of the martial arts like Karate, Kenpo, Taekwondo, etc., that fight primarily from a standing position, as opposed to floor-based arts such as Wrestling.

Street Real: A technique that is effective in self-defense without significant modification.

Streetfighting: Methods of fighting used for self-defense as opposed to skills acceptable in a competitive match.

T

Taolu: (C) A formally defined posture, movement, or set of movements used to teach coordination and technique to a student of Kung Fu. The basic postures, movements and techniques of a Martial Art are often collected into a form or group of forms for ease of practice and memorization. A group of formal movements may also be called a set. This is essentially the same as the Japanese Kata or Korean Poomse.

Tournament: A formal competition.

Trap: A blocking technique that uses one of the attacker's limbs to limit the use of another of his limbs.

Trick: A deceptive maneuver designed to lure one's opponent into a making a move that is tactically unsound. (2) An early Twentieth Century nickname for a technique, especially a lock, hold, escape, or throw.

U

Uppercut: A powerful, upward punch that comes up underneath an opponent's guard.

V

W

Warning: Given by the referee to the fighter who commits a serious foul, or receives three cautions. When the referee signals a warning the ringside judges can decide whether to give a point to the opponent. Three warnings in a bout mean disqualification.

Weaving: A way of eluding punches by turning and twisting movements.

X

Y

Z

APPENDIX TWO
Guide to First Aid

No matter how careful you are, injuries may still happen, especially in a contact sport. Though it is always best to consult a physician whenever an injury is suspected, it is simply smart to know First Aid techniques for your own safety and peace of mind. First thing to do is obtain a proper First Aid kit and keep one in the training hall and a portable one in your tournament bag. A basic kit should contain the following:

<u>THE ESSENTIALS</u>

1) First Aid Manual (clearly explains how to handle basic problems).

2) Basic Bandages (assorted adhesive bandages, athletic tape, Moleskin, gauze pads, ace bandages, butterfly bandages).

3) Basic Drugs/Lotions (aspirin and/or non-aspirin pain reliever, antiseptic, antacid tablets).

4) Basic First Aid Tools (tweezers, small mirror, razor blade).

5) CPR Shield (covers the mouth to prevent exchange of saliva during mouth-to-mouth).

6) Lotions (burn ointment, skin lotion, Caladryl).

7) First Aid Tools (sling, basic splint, instant ice pack).

GLOSSARY OF FIRST AID TERMS

Asphixiation: loss of consciousness due to insufficient oxygen or too much carbon dioxide.

Concussion: a jostling of the brain within the skull, caused by a blow to the head.

Convulsion: a violent, involuntary contraction or muscle spasm.

CPR: Cardio-Pulmonary Resuscitation.

Dislocation: a bone that has become severely displaced within its joint.

Fracture: a break or crack in a bone.

> Simple Fracture: the bone does not pierce the skin.

> Compound Fracture: the bone pierces the skin.

Heat Exhaustion: condition where body temperature rises above normal and person feels sick and dizzy.

Heat Stroke: very serious condition when the body loses ability to regulate its own temperature and internal temperature rises to a dangerous level (104 F and above).

Hypothermia: body becomes too cold (below 95 F).

Hypoxia: low level of oxygen.

Laceration: rough, ripped wound.

Myocardial Infarction (MI): clinical term for a heart attack.

Shock: insufficient oxygen getting to where it is needed in the body.

Sprain: injury to the ligaments around a joint.

Strain: injury to a muscle or tendon.

Tachycardia: heart beating too quickly.

Unconciousness: interruption of brain's normal activity so that a person is no longer aware of their surroundings.

FIRST AID FOR INJURIES INVOLVING BLEEDING

CUTS

1) Cleanse the area thoroughly with soap and warm water, carefully washing away any dirt.

2) Apply direct pressure to the wound until the bleeding stops.

3) Put a sterile bandage on the wound.

4) If the cut is deep, get to a doctor as quickly as possible.

ABRASIONS

1) Wash thoroughly with soap and warm water.

2) If it bleeds or oozes, bandage it to protect it from infection.

SIGNS OF AN INFECTED WOUND

1) Swelling

2) Redness

3) Pain

4) Pus

5) Fever

NOSEBLEEDS

CAUSES

1) Nose injury

2) Strenuous activity

3) High blood pressure

4) Exposure to high altitudes

5) Blowing the nose too hard

WHAT TO DO IF YOU GET A NOSEBLEED:

1) Sit down

2) Lean slightly forward to prevent blood running into your throat.
   Do not tilt your head back.

3) Place cold, wet cloths on your nose to constrict the blood vessels
   in your nose and stop the bleeding.

4) If blood is coming from only one nostril, press firmly at the top of that nostril.

5) If both nostrils are bleeding, pinch your nostrils together for at least 10 minutes.

6) If bleeding continues, apply pressure for another 10 minutes.

7) If bleeding is the result of direct injury to the nose, only *gentle* pressure
   should be applied.

8) If heavy bleeding persists or if nosebleeds recur frequently, consult a physician.

EXTERNAL BLEEDING

1) Apply direct pressure. Place a clean, folded cloth over the injured area and
   firmly apply pressure. If blood soaks through, *do not remove it*. Instead, cover that
   cloth with another one and continue to apply pressure to the wound for 7 to 10
   minutes. If the bleeding is from the ear, place a clean bandage over the ear, lay the
   victim on his side, and allow the blood to drain out through the bandage.

2) Elevate the injury. Position the wounded part of the body above the level of the
   heart if possible while applying direct pressure to the wound.

3) Know the pressure points. If direct pressure and elevation do not sufficiently slow
   the bloodflow, find a pressure point. Large arteries found close to the skin's surface supply blood to the head and to each arm and leg. The most common pressure points used during first aid are located in the upper arms and in the creases
   above the upper legs. Apply pressure to the closest pressure point to the wound
   so that the artery is pressed between your fingers and the bone directly behind

the artery. If using the pressure point on a leg, you may need to use the heel of your hand instead of your finger.

4) Resort to a tourniquet. On very rare occasions everything listed above may fail. To prevent the victim from dying, you should apply a tourniquet. Once a tourniquet is applied, it should not be loosened or removed until the victim has reached medical help. Use a tourniquet ONLY if everything listed above has failed. If you use a tourniquet, write down somewhere on the victim the time it was applied, so medical personnel will know how long it has been in place.

INTERNAL BLEEDING

Internal bleeding results when blood vessels rupture, allowing blood to leak into body cavities. It could be a result of a direct blow to the body, a fracture, a sprain, or a bleeding ulcer. If a victim receives an injury to the chest or abdomen, internal bleeding should be suspected. He will probably feel pain and tenderness in the affected area.

Other symptoms to watch for:

1) Cold, clammy skin

2) Dilated pupils

3) Dizziness

4) Nausea

5) Pale face and lips

6) Rapid, weak, irregular pulse

7) Shortness of breath

8) Swelling or bruising at the site of injury

9) Thirstiness

10) Weakness or fainting

The more symptoms that are experienced, the more extensive the internal bleeding.

WHAT TO DO FOR THE VICTIM:

1) Check for an open airway and begin rescue breathing (refer to the section on Injuries Involving Breathing and Circulation) if necessary.

2) Call for medical help as soon as possible and keep the victim comfortable until help arrives.

3) The victim may rinse his mouth with water, but DO NOT give a victim of internal bleeding anything to drink.

FIRST AID FOR INJURIES INVOLVING MUSCLES AND LIGAMENTS (SPRAINS AND STRAINS)

SPRAIN: involves injury to the ligaments around a joint.

STRAIN: involves injury to a muscle or tendon.

SIGNS OF A SPRAIN

1) Affected joint begins to swell immediately, possibly looking deformed.

2) Joint may also turn black and blue due to the escaped blood from torn blood vessels.

3) Victim will experience excruciating, shooting pains at the time of the injury because many nerves are injured in a sprain.

TREATMENT FOR SPRAINS

1) RICE treatment (REST - INCAPACITATION - COLD - ELEVATION)

2) Thermotherapy (applying moist heat) promotes healing but should not be applied to a muscle or ligament injury for at least 24 hours because heat will increase the swelling. After the swelling has gone, you should alternate applying cold compresses and moist heat to the injury.

3) To treat the injury with warm, wet packs, place a water-dampened towel in a microwave oven for about 30 seconds. Check to make sure the towel is not too hot before placing it on the skin. If a microwave oven is not available, run a towel under very hot tap water, wring it out, and apply it to the injury.'

4) A sprained arm should be placed in a sling.

5) Most sprains take at least 6-8 weeks to heal.

TREATMENT FOR STRAINS

1) At the time of the injury, begin the RICE treatment.

2) For lower back strain, rest will often bring relief to the strained muscle. If not, alternate cold compresses with moist heat, allowing a time of rest between the treatments.

FIRST AID FOR INJURIES INVOLVING BONES

IF A DISLOCATION IS SUSPECTED

1) Apply a splint to the joint to keep it from moving.

2) Try to keep joint elevated to slow blood flow to the area.

3) A doctor should be contacted to have the bone set back into its socket.

FRACTURE: a broken bone.

SIMPLE FRACTURE: does not pierce through the skin. If it is not cared for properly, it could become a compound fracture.

1) Check for swelling around the affected area.

2) There may be discoloration of the skin.

3) If the victim complains of tenderness and pain in the area or says that he felt or heard a bone snap, see a doctor immediately.

COMPOUND FRACTURE: pierces through the skin. Serious bleeding may occur with this kind of wound. Do not apply pressure to a compound fracture to stop the bleeding. What to do for a compound fracture:

1) Cover the injured part with a sterile pad.

2) Apply a splint to keep the bone from causing further injury to the surrounding tissues.

3) Wait for medical help.

4) Avoid moving the victim, but keep him warm, comfortable, and reassured.

FIRST AID FOR INJURIES INVOLVING BREATHING OR CIRCULATION

FAINTING

Before losing consciousness, the victim may complain of:

1) Lightheadedness

2) Weakness

3) Nausea

4) Skin may be pale and clammy

If a person begins to feel faint, he should:

1) Lean forward

2) Lower head toward knees

3) As the head is lowered below the heart, blood will flow to the brain

TREATMENT FOR PASSING OUT: THE RECOVERY POSITION

1) Keep the victim lying down with head lowered and legs elevated.

2) Loosen any tight clothing.

3) Apply cool, damp cloths to face and neck.

4) In most cases, the victim will regain consciousness shortly after being placed in this position.

After the victim regains consciousness, do not let him get up until you have questioned him (Who are you?, Where are you?, Do you know what day it is?) to be sure he has completely recovered.

HEAT STROKE

1) Cool the body of a heatstroke victim immediately; if possible, put him in cool water, wrap him in cool wet clothes, or sponge his skin with cool water, rubbing alcohol, ice, or cold packs.

2) Once the victim's temperature drops to about 101 F, you may lay him in the recovery position (see Fainting, above) in a cool room.

3) If the temperature begins to rise again, you will need to repeat the cooling process.

4) If he/she is able to drink, you may give him some water.

5) Do not give a heatstroke victim any kind of medication.

6) Watch for signs of shock while waiting for medical attention.

ASPHYXIATION

Asphyxiation is a loss of consciousness due to the presence of too little oxygen or too much carbon dioxide in the blood. The victim may stop breathing for a number of reasons (i.e. drowning, electric shock, heart failure, poisoning, or suffocation). The flow of oxygen throughout the body will stop within minutes if a person's respiratory system fails. Heart failure, brain damage, and eventual death will result if the victim's breathing cannot be restarted.

RESCUE BREATHING/RESPIRATORY RESTORATION (also known as CPR)

A person suffering from asphyxiation should be given rescue breathing. Before you begin rescue breathing, be certain that the victim has actually stopped breathing.

1) Kneel beside the victim, place your ear near his nose and mouth, and watch his chest carefully. You should feel and hear the breaths and see his chest rise and fall if he is breathing. If he is not breathing, continue to step 2.

2) Provide an open airway. Carefully place the victim on his back and open his mouth. If any material is blocking the airway, it must be cleared out. Turn the victim's head to one side and sweep out any contents in his mouth with your fingers.

3) If the victim's breathing is not restored after removing the object, tilt the victim's head back by placing the heel of one hand on his forehead and the other hand under the bony part of his chin to lift it slightly.

4) Straddle his thighs, placing one palm slightly above the navel but well below the breastbone. Cover this hand with the other and interlace the fingers.

5) Without bending your elbows, press sharply on the victim's abdomen 6 to 10 times.

6) If there are no signs of breathing , pinch the victim's nostrils closed. Seal your mouth over the victim's mouth and blow two full breaths. A rising chest indicates that air is reaching the lungs. If the stomach is expanding instead, the victim's neck and jaw are positioned improperly. Gently push on the victim's abdomen with the palm of your hand until the air is expelled, because the extra air in the stomach may cause vomiting.

7) Look, listen, and feel again for signs of breathing. If the victim is still not breathing on his own, continue blowing into his mouth one breath every five seconds until help arrives.

CHOKING

If a person is choking, you should not interfere as long as he is coughing. If coughing does not dislodge the object from the trachea and the victim is breathing with extreme difficulty, or if he turns a bluish color and appears to be choking but is unable to cough or speak, quickly ask, "Are you choking?" A choking victim can nod his head "yes," but will be unable to talk. It is important to ask this question because a person suffering from a heart attack will have similar symptoms, but he will be able to talk.

THE ABDOMINAL THRUST (also known as the Heimlich Maneuver)

If the victim is choking:

1) Stand behind him with your arms around his waist.

2) Place one fist, with the knuckle of the thumb against the victim's midsection, slightly above the navel but well below the breastbone.

3) Hold your fist firmly with the other hand and pull both hands sharply toward you with an upward-and-inward jab.

4) This procedure should be administered continually until either the object is forced out or the victim becomes unconscious.

Note: due to the force with which the abdominal thrust is given, it should be used only in an actual emergency,

CONCUSSIONS

A sharp blow to the head could result in a concussion, which is a jostling of the brain inside its protective, bony covering. A more serious head injury may result in contusions, or bruises to the brain. A period of unconsciousness may indicate brain damage and accompanies many head injuries.

Symptoms to look for if a brain injury is suspected:

1) Clear or reddish fluid draining from the ears, nose, or mouth.

2) Difficulty speaking.

3) Headache.

4) Unequal size of pupils.

5) Pale skin.

6) Paralysis of an arm or leg (opposite side of the injury) or face (same side as the injury).

PROPER CARE FOR CONCUSSIONS

1) While waiting for help to arrive, keep the victim lying down in the recovery position (refer to the section on Fainting).

2) Control any bleeding, and be sure that he is breathing properly.

3) Do not give the victim any liquids to drink.

4) If the victim becomes unconscious for any amount of time, keep track of this information so that you can report it when medical help arrives.

CONVULSIONS

A convulsion is a violent, involuntary contraction or muscle spasm. Also called a seizure, it can be caused by epilepsy or sudden illness. Convulsions are not likely to cause death unless the victim stops breathing. The victim should be checked by medical personnel.

SIGNS OF CONVULSION

1) The victim's muscles become stiff and hard, followed by jerking movements.

2) He may bite his tongue or stop breathing.

3) His face and lips may turn a bluish color.

4) May drool excessively or foam at the mouth.

TREATMENT FOR CONVULSION

1) Clear all objects away from the victim and place something soft under his head.

2) Do not place anything between his teeth or in his mouth.

3) Do not give the victim any liquids.

4) If the victim stops breathing, check to see that the airway is open and begin rescue breathing.

5) Stay calm and keep the victim comfortable until help arrives.

6) Most convulsions are followed by a period of unconsciousness or another convulsion.

ELECTRIC SHOCK

1) Remove the victim from the source of electricity before you touch him directly. Either turn off the master switch to disconnect the power, or use a nonmetal, dry object such as a stick to pull the wire or electrical source away from the victim's body.

2) If he is not breathing, begin rescue breathing immediately; a victim whose heart has stopped breathing needs CPR.

3) If the person is unconscious, but is breathing and has a heartbeat, you should place him in the recovery position (refer to the section on Fainting) and monitor his breathing and heart rate until medical help arrives.

APPENDIX THREE
Basic Anatomy

THE SKULL

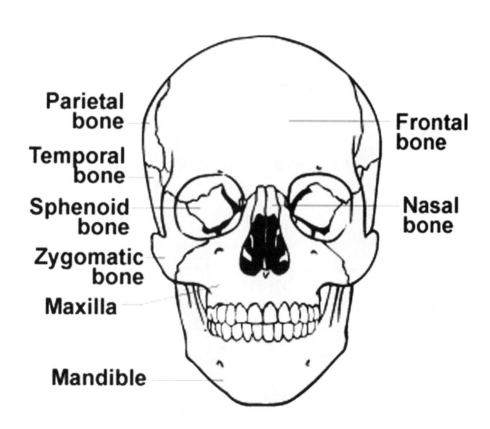

Parietal
bone

Temporal
bone

Sphenoid
bone

Zygomatic
bone

Maxilla

Mandible

Frontal
bone

Nasal
bone

Medical illustrations provided by the American Medical Association.

THE SKELETON - FRONT

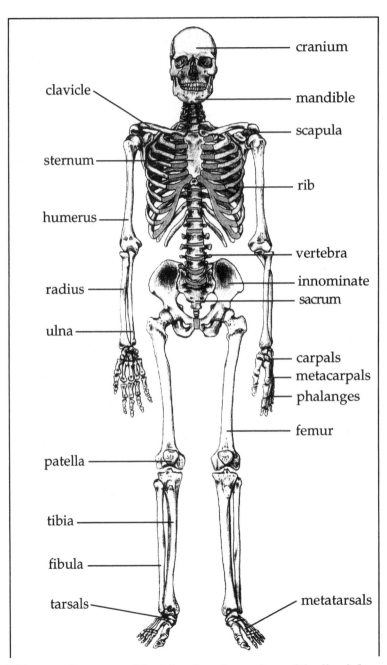

cranium

clavicle

mandible

scapula

sternum

rib

humerus

vertebra

innominate

sacrum

radius

ulna

carpals

metacarpals

phalanges

femur

patella

tibia

fibula

tarsals

metatarsals

Medical illustrations provided by the American Medical Association.

THE SKELETON - BACK

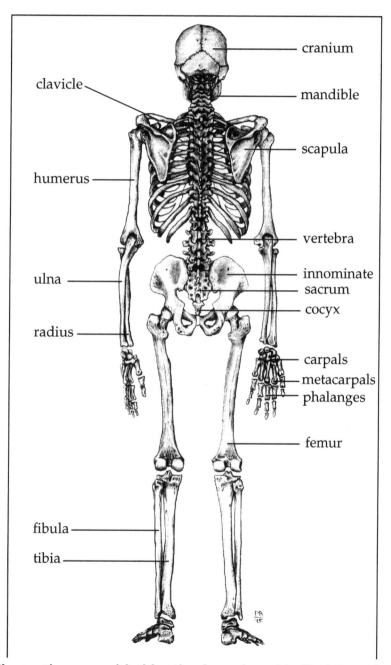

cranium

clavicle

mandible

scapula

humerus

vertebra

innominate
sacrum
ulna

cocyx

radius

carpals
metacarpals
phalanges

femur

fibula

tibia

Medical illustrations provided by the American Medical Association.

THE NERVOUS SYSTEM - FRONT

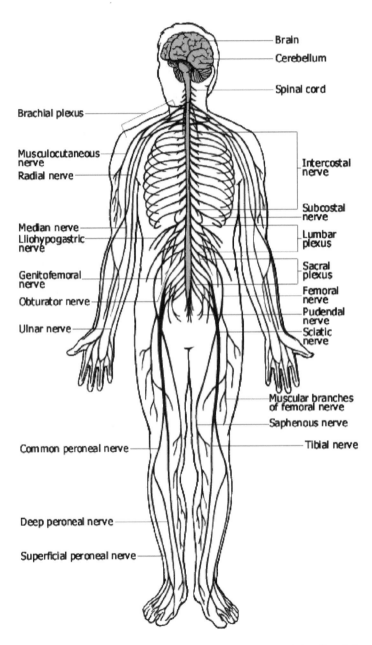

Brain
Cerebellum
Spinal cord
Brachial plexus
Musculocutaneous nerve
Radial nerve
Intercostal nerve
Subcostal nerve
Median nerve
Lliohypogastric nerve
Lumbar plexus
Genitofemoral nerve
Sacral plexus
Obturator nerve
Femoral nerve
Pudendal nerve
Ulnar nerve
Sciatic nerve
Muscular branches of femoral nerve
Saphenous nerve
Common peroneal nerve
Tibial nerve
Deep peroneal nerve
Superficial peroneal nerve

Medical illustrations provided by the American Medical Association.

THE NERVOUS SYSTEM - BACK

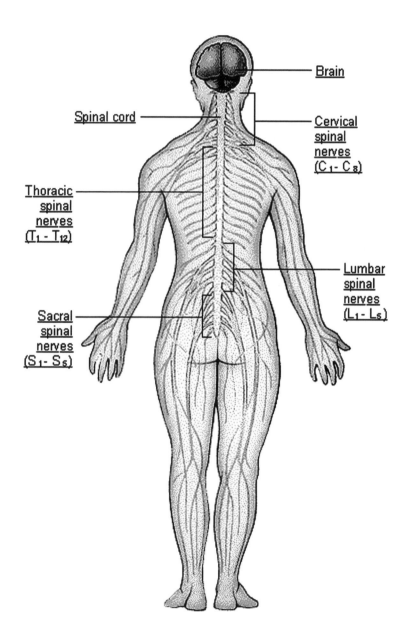

Medical illustrations provided by the American Medical Association.

THE CIRCULATORY SYSTEM - GENERAL

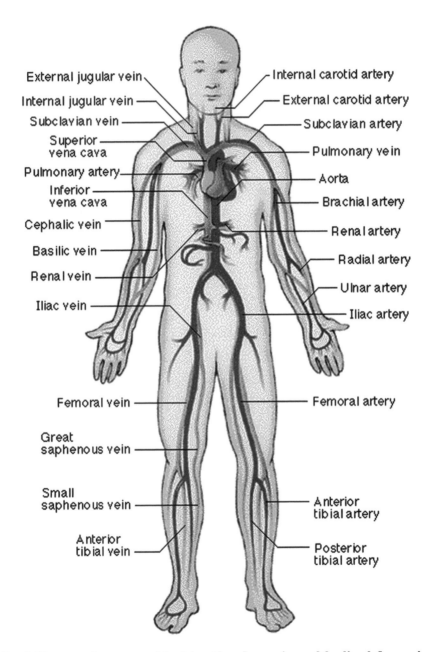

External jugular vein

Internal jugular vein

Subclavian vein

Superior vena cava

Pulmonary artery

Inferior vena cava

Cephalic vein

Basilic vein

Renal vein

Iliac vein

Femoral vein

Great saphenous vein

Small saphenous vein

Anterior tibial vein

Internal carotid artery

External carotid artery

Subclavian artery

Pulmonary vein

Aorta

Brachial artery

Renal artery

Radial artery

Ulnar artery

Iliac artery

Femoral artery

Anterior tibial artery

Posterior tibial artery

Medical illustrations provided by the American Medical Association.

THE CIRCULATORY SYSTEM - VENOUS

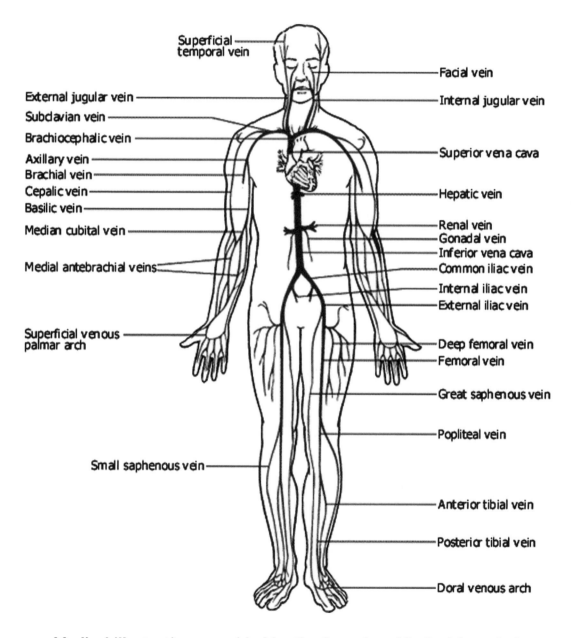

Superficial temporal vein
Facial vein
External jugular vein
Internal jugular vein
Subclavian vein
Brachiocephalic vein
Axillary vein
Superior vena cava
Brachial vein
Cepalic vein
Hepatic vein
Basilic vein
Median cubital vein
Renal vein
Gonadal vein
Inferior vena cava
Medial antebrachial veins
Common iliac vein
Internal iliac vein
External iliac vein
Superficial venous palmar arch
Deep femoral vein
Femoral vein
Great saphenous vein
Popliteal vein
Small saphenous vein
Anterior tibial vein
Posterior tibial vein
Doral venous arch

Medical illustrations provided by the American Medical Association.

THE INTERNAL ORGANS

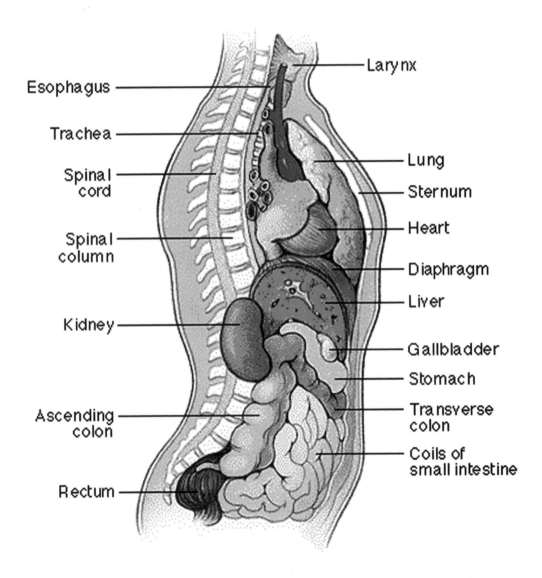

Esophagus

Trachea

Spinal cord

Spinal column

Kidney

Ascending colon

Rectum

Larynx

Lung

Sternum

Heart

Diaphragm

Liver

Gallbladder

Stomach

Transverse colon

Coils of small intestine

Medical illustrations provided by the American Medical Association.

BIBLIOGRAPHY

BOXING

Fleischer, Nat, *Heavyweight Championship: An Informal History of Heavyweight Boxing From 1719 to the Present Day*, New York: G.P. Putnam's Sons, 1949. Highlights important boxers in the history of boxing. Provides nice explanations of the boxers and their background, and also compares their style to other boxers, of the same and different eras.

Johnson, Christopher, "British Championsism: Early Pugilism and the Works of Fielding," *Review of English Studies: A Quarterly Journal of English Literature and the English Language*, 1996.

Lynch, Bohun, *Knuckles and Gloves*, New York: Henry Holt & Co, 1923. Provides a comprehensive history of boxing and pugilism, gives detailed descriptions of important fights, while also discussing the social settings of the fights.

Mendoza, Daniel, *The Art of Boxing*, Dublin: M. O'Leary, 1792.

Wignall, Trevor C., *The Story of Boxing*, New York: Brentano's, 1924. Provides detailed description of important boxers, highlighting their strengths and weaknesses. Also includes detailed pictures of the boxers.

CAPOEIRA

Almeida, Bira, *Capoeira: A Brazilian Art Form: History, Philosophy, and Practice*, Berkeley: North Atlantic Books, 1983.

"Capoeira," *New Yorker*, 15 May 1989.

Capoeira, Nestor, *The Little Capoeira Book*, Berkeley: North Atlantic Books, 1995.

Capoeira: Roots of the Dance Fight Game, Berkeley: North Atlantic Books, 2002.

Desch, T.J.O., <u>Knocking and Kicking, Ladya, and Capoeira: Resistance and Religion in the African Martial Arts of the Black Atlantic</u>, 1994. Unpublished thesis, Ph.D. dissertation.

Gilbey, John, "The Capoeira Champion," *The Way of the Warrior*, Berkeley: North Atlantic Books, 1982.

Kubik, Gerhard, *Angolan Traits in Black Music Games and Dances of Brazil: A Study of African Cultural Extensions Overseas*, Lisboa, 1979.

Lewis, J. Lowell, *Ring of Liberation : Deceptive Discourse in Brazilian Capoeira*, University of Chicago, 1992.

Tigges, Gabriela, The History of Capoeira in Brazil, Thesis (Ed. D) Brigham Young University, 1990.

CHINESE MARTIAL ARTS

Hsung, Li, *China's Ninja Connection*, Paladin Press, 1984.

Ming, YangJwing, *Tai Chi Chuan Aplicaciones Marciales*, Karma 7, 2001.

Webster-Doyle, Terrence, *Karate: The Art of Empty Self*, Atrium Publications, 1989.

FENCING AND SWORDFIGHTING

Aylward, J.D., *The English Master of Arms*, London: University of Del. Press, 1991.

Barth, Dr. Berndt (Autorenkollektiv), *Fechten, Ein Lehrbuch fur die Grundausbildung im Florett-, Sobel- und Degenfechten*, 255 S., Sportverlag Berlin (Ost) 1975.

Barth, Dr. Berndt and Dr. Joachim Wargalla, *Fechten - Rahmentrainingskonzeption fur Kinder und Jugendliche im Leistungssport*, Landessportbund Nordrhein-Westfalen 1995

Beck, Emil, *Tauberbischofsheimer Fechtlektionen*, 175 S., DSB Bundesausschuszlig zur Forderung des Leistungssports, Trainerbibliothek Band 17, Bartels & Wernitz 1978

Beck, Emil, *Fechten - Florett, Degen, Sobel*, 88 S., Falken Sport 1988

Beck, Emil, *Richtig Fechten*, 95 S., BLV Sportpaxis 1990.

Berry, Herbert, *The Noble Science: A Study and Transcription of Sloan MS. 2530, Papers of the Masters of Defence of London*, London: Routledge and Kegan Paul, 1956. Gives detailed accounts of various method and teachings of English Masters of Arm from the Twelfth through the Twentieth Centuries.

Bower, *Foil Fencing*, Iowa: Brown & Benchmark, 1993.

Burke, Sheehen, *Fencing Is For Me*, Lerner Publications, 1982.

Civrny, Cestmir, *Modernes Sportfechten*, Anleitungen Frbungsleiter, 199 S., Bayerischer Fechterverband 1982.

Civrny, Cestmir, *Florett*, 191 S., Selbstverlag (Dr. Cestmir Civrny, Heitwangerstr.52, 8000 Munchen 70), 1992.

Chrudimak, Franz, *Vom Duell zum Sport: Handbuch Fechten*, Bd.1-2, 290 u. 280 S., Uhlen Verlagsges Wien 1988.

Curry, Nancy L., *The Fencing Book*, New York: Leisure Press, 1984.

De Silva, Henry, *Fencing: The Skill of the Game*, Crowood Press 1991.

Domenico, Angelo, *The School of Fencing: With a General Explanation of the Principal Attitudes and Positions Peculiar to the Art*, London: [S.N], 1787.

Evered, D.F., *Sabre Fencing*, Duckworth, 1982.

Garret, Maxwell R., Emmanuil G. Kaidanov and Gil A. Pezza, *Foil, Saber and Epee Fencing. - Skills, Safety, Operations and Responsibilities*, 221 S., The Pennsylvania State University Press 1994.

Gaugler, William M., *Fencing Everyone*, Munich, 1983.

Gray, Edmund, *Modern British Fencing. - History of Amateur Fencing Association 1964 - 1981*, Amateur Fencing Association, London, 1984.

Hope, Sir William, *Hope's New Method of Fencing; or, The True and Solid Art of Fighting with the Back-Sword, Sheering-Sword, Small-Sword, and Sword and Pistol; Freed From the Errors of the Schools*, Edinburgh: Printed by James Watson, 1714.

Huhle, Henner and Helma Brunck, *500 Jahre Fechtmeister in Deutschland*, 120 S., Kleine Schriften des Historischen Museums Bd. 34, Frankfurt; Histor. Museum, 1987.

Kogler, Aladar, *Preparing the Mind: Improving Fencing Performance Through Psychological Preparation*, Pennsylvania:. Counter Parry Press, Lansdowne, 1993.

Lukovich, Istv·n, *Fencing*, Budapest: Corvina, 1986.

Martinic, Albert, *Kevey und Seine Fechtschule*, Eigenverlag, Graz, 1983

Moll, Richard, *Die Fechtlegende von Tauberbischofsheim*, 200 S., Laub Etztal, 1987.

Morton, E.D., *A to Z of Fencing*, Macdonald Queen Anne Press, 1986

Nadi, Aldo, *On Fencing*, Laureate Press, 1994.

Nagy, Lazlo, *Bibliographie des Fechtens: Allgemeine Chronologische Bibliographie Ober die Fechtliteratur*, 200 S., Akademie der Fechtkunst sterreichs, Graz, 1987.

Nostini, Renzo, *Die Kunst des Florettfechtens*, Berlin: Weinmann, 1984.

Page, Thomas, *The Use of the Broad Sword. In Which is Shown, the True Method of Fighting with That Weapon, as it is Now in Use Among the Highlanders*, Norwich, Printed M. Chase, 1746.

Pardoel, Henk W., *A Bibliography of the Art and Sport of Fencing*, Ontario 1995. For more information see: http://www.ii.uib/~arild/fencing/book/fenrefs.html

Paschel, Bernd, *Fechten*, Limpert, 1981.

Pepper, William, *Treatise on the New Broad Sword Exercise*, London: Pater-Noster-Row, 1798.

Pitman, Brian, *Techniques of Foil, Epee and Sabre*, Crowood Press, 1988.

Pitman, Brian, *Know the Game: Fencing*, A & C Black 1987.

Selberg, Charles A., *The Revised Foil*, Oregon: Ashland, 1993.

Skipp, Alan, *Teachers Handbook of Foil Fencing*, Leon Paul, 1987.

Stratton, Max M. and Warren K. Simpson, *Fencing*, Boston: American Press, 1985.

Szabo, Laszlo, *Fencing and the Master*, Budapest: Corvina, 1982.

Tein, Horst H., *Mit dem Fechten auf Du,*, Eigenverlag, 1994.

Theuerkauff, J6rgen, *Fechten*, Sport - Gymnasiale Oberstufe, Cornelsen Schwann, 1988

Vass, Imre, *Degenfechten*, Budapest: Corvina-Verlag, 1969.

Wojciechowski, Ziemowit, *Theory, Methods and Exercises in Fencing*, British Amateur Fencing Association.

JAPANESE MARTIAL ARTS

Birrer, R.B., "Back to Japan," *Shadows of Iga Society Journal* 15 no. 5 (Sept-Oct 1991).

Chiu, John C. and Johnny C. Chiu, *The Mystic Arts of the Ninja and Shuriken -Do, A Training Manual*, Mind & Body Publishing, 1991.

Cleary, Thomas, *Classics of Strategy and Counsel: Thunder in the Sky, the Japanese Art of War, the Book of Five Rings, Ways of Warriors, Codes of Kings*, Shambhala Publications, 2001.

Draeger, Donn F., *Classical Bujutsu*, Weatherhill, 1996.

Draeger, Donn F., *Classical Budo*, Weatherhill, 1996.

Herrigel, Eugen, *Zen in the Art of Archery*, Random House, 1999.

Otake, Risuke, *The Deity and the Sword*, Vols. 1-3, Japan: Minato Research and Publishing Co., 1977.

Ratti, Oscar and Adele Westbrook, *Secrets of the Samurai: A Survey of the Martial Arts of Feudal Japan*, Boston, MA: Charles E. Tuttle Co., 1991.

Sasamori, Junzo and Gordon Warner, *This is Kendo: The Art of Japanese Fencing*, Boston, MA: Charles E. Tuttle Co., 1964.

Tsunemoto, Yamamoto, William Scott Wilson (Translator), *Hagakure : The Book of the Samurai*, Kodansha International, 1992.

Watanabe, Tadashige, *Shinkage Ryu Sword Techniques*, Vols. 1 & 2, Tokyo, Japan: Sugawara Martial Arts Institute, Inc., 1993. A good technical book for Shinkage Ryu afficionados. Covers techniques and kata ("The First Five" and "The Nine Kinds") through pictures. Little text.

MEDICINE

Birrer, Richard and Christina Birrer, "Unreported Injuries In the Martial Arts," *British Journal of Sports Medicine* 17 no. 2, pp. 131-134 (June 1983).

Fuller, J. R., "Martial Arts and Psychological Health," *British Journal of Medical Psychology* 61 no. 4, pp. 317-28 (Dec. 1988).

Gleser, J.M., "Physical and Psychosocial Benefits of Modified Judo Practice for Blind, Mentally Retarded Child: A Pilot Study," *Journal of Perceptive Motor Skills* 74, pp. 915-25, 1992.

Madorsky, J. G. and J. R. Scanlon, "Kung Fu: Synthesis of Wheelchair Sport and Self-Protection," *Archives of Physical Medicine and Rehabilitation*, 70 no. 6, pp. 490-492 (June 1989).

"Martial Arts Injuries: The Results of a Five-Year National Survey," *American Journal of Sports Medicine* 16 no. 4 (1988).

Nowicki, D., *Gold Medal Mental Workout For Combat Sports: Boxing, Fencing, Judo, Karate, Kick-Boxing and Wrestling*, Stadion Publishing Company, 1993.

MILITARY STRATEGY

Feng, Gea-Fu and Jane English, translators, *Tao Te Ching: A New Translation*, New York and Toronto: Vintage Books, 1972.

Godfrey, John, *Treatise Upon the Useful Science of Defense*, 1747.

Hanzhang, General Tao and Yuan Shibing (translator), *Sun Tzu's Art of War: The Modern Chinese Interpretation*, New York: Sterling Publishing Company, Inc., 1990.

The Militia Man: Containing Necessary Rules for Both Officer and Soldier. With an Explanation of the Manual of Exercise of the Foot, London, c. 1740.

The Soldier's Companion: Containing Instructions For the Drill, Manual, and Platoon Exercise, Intended For the Use of Volunteers, Ornamented With Figures, London, 1798.

Tzu, Sun and R.L. Wing (translator), *The Art of Strategy: A New Translation of Sun Tzu's Classic, The Art of War*, Doubleday, 1988.

Tzu, Sun, Samuel B. Griffith (Introduction), *The Art of War*, Oxford University Press, 1984.

Tzu, Sun, Thomas Cleary (translator), *The Illustrated Art of War*, Shambhala Publications, 1998.

Tzu, Sun, *El Arte de la Guerra*, S.A.: Editorial Edaf, 2001.

MISCELLANEOUS

Browning, Barbara, "Headspin," *Samba: Resistance in Motion*, Indiana University Press, 1995.

Bussy, Robert A., *Basic Skills and Techniques*, Bushing Publishing Company, 1987.

Cleary, Thomas (translator), *The Book of Change*, Boston: Shambhala Pocket Classics, 1992.

Corcoran, John, *The Martial Arts Companion*, New York: Mallard Press, 1992.

Crompton, Paul, *The Complete Martial Arts*, London: McGraw Hill Publishing Company, 1989.

Frederic, Louis, *Diccionario Ilustrado de Artes Marciales*, French & European Pubns, 1989.

Thomas, Raymond, *Diccionario del Budo Artes Marciales*, French & European Pubns, 1978.

PHILOSOPHY AND RELIGION

Daniels, Kevin and E. Thorton, "An Analysis of the Relationship Between Hostility and Training In the Martial Arts," *Journal of Sports Sciences* 8, pp. 95-101 (1990).

Hyams, Joe, *Zen in the Martial Arts*, New York: Bantam Press, 1979.

Kepka, Bukkyo Dendo, *The Teaching of Buddha*, 86th revised edition, Tokyo, Japan: Kosaudo Printing Co., Ltd., 1984.

Kraft, Kenneth, ed., *Zen, Tradition & Translation*, New York: Grove Press, 1988.

Morgan, Forrest E., *Living the Martial Way*, Fort Lee: Barricade Books, 1992.

Okuse, Heishichiro, "Authentic Empowerment," *Shadows of Iga Society Journal* 15 no. 6 (Nov-Dec1991).

Seeger, Elizabeth, *Eastern Religions*, New York: Thomas Y. Crowell Company, 1973.

Seitz, F.C. and G.D. Olsen, "The Martial Arts and Mental Health: The Challenge of Managing Energy," *Journal of Perceptive Motor Skills* 70 no. 2, 459-64 (1990).

Tsu, Chung, Gea-Fu Feng and Jane English (translators), *Inner Chapters*, New York and Toronto: Vintage Books, 1974.

Wing, R. H., *The Tao of Power: A New Translation of the Tao Te Ching*, New York: Doubleday, 1986.

Yu-han, Fung, Derk Bodde, ed., *A Short History of Chinese Philosophy*, New York: The MacMillan Company, 1948.

STICKFIGHTING

Docherty, Frank, "A Brief History of the Quarterstaff," web site article, http://ejmas.com/jwma/jwmaart_docherty_0501.htm.

Lacaze, Pierre, *Du Duel a L'Escrime*, Paris 1991.

Manuel, Bruno, *Passion Escrime*, Prieur 1990.

Revenu, Daniel, *Initiation a L'Escrime: Un D'marche Pour l'Ecole*, Vigot, Paris, 1985

Revenu, Daniel and R. Thomas, *Que sais-je? L'Escrime*, Presses Universitaires de France, 1992.

WEBSITES
Contributors To This Book

Alliance Martial Arts: www.alliancemartialarts.com

Allied Independent Wrestling Federation - Great Britain: www.britishwrestling.vze.com

American Heritage Fighting Arts Association: www.ahfaa.org

Association for Historical Fencing: www.ahfi.org

Batuque Capoeira Group: www.batuque.2y.net

Brazilian Jiu-Jitsu: www.bjj.org.

Cabales Historical Photos: www.geocities.com/TheTropics/Bay/1216/cabales/cabales.html

Counterstrike Kenpo www.counterstrikekenpo.com

Egyptian history, photos by Su Bayfield: www.egyptsites.co.uk

Escrima Arnis Forum: www.topica.com

Extreme Martial Arts and Fitness Academy of Philadelphia: www.extrememartialarts.tv

Journal of Western Martial Arts: www.ejmas.com/jwma/jwmaframe.htm

Miriam Anzovin and Anzovin Studio: www.anzovin.com/miriam.html

Shinowara-ryu Jujutsu: www.shinowara.com

Southern California Naginata Federation: www.scnf.org

Strider Nolan Publishing, Inc.: www.stridernolan.com

Tan Shin Kai Kendo Dojo of Philadelphia: www.tanshinkaidojo.org

Tony Cecchine's Catch Wrestling: www.catchwrestle.com

United Seated Armwrestling Association (USAA), www.geocities.com/armstrength/index.html

Western Martial Arts Workshop: www.wmaw.org

World Escrima Kali Arnis Forum: www.wekaf.com

The World Shuai Chiao Society: www.shuaichiao.org

INDEX

By Jonathan Maberry, 7th degree black belt
With Jolie Bookspan, Ph.D., Christine Borofsky, Mary Parshelunas, Ph.,D., and Robert Wilsbach, P.O. Ret.

THE MARTIAL ARTS STUDENT LOG BOOK

The Martial Arts Student Logbook is the perfect resource to keep track of your life in the martial arts! This unique book is part diary, part ledger and part reference guide for students of ALL martial arts.

With The Martial Arts Student Log Book you can keep track of:
- Belt Tests and Promotions
- Rank Requirements
- Class Dues and Fees
- Your Tournament Record
- Your Martial Arts Book and Video Libraries
- Important Numbers and Emergency Contacts
- School History
- Guest Lecturers, Workshops and Seminars

Helpful Appendices include:
- Glossaries of Japanese, Korean and Chinese Martial Arts
- The Philosophies of the Martial Arts
AND MUCH, MUCH MORE.
This is the perfect resource for anyone studying martial arts, from first-day white belt to senior black belt master.

ULTIMATE JUJUTSU: PRINCIPLES AND PRACTICES

Ultimate Jujutsu: Principles and Practice presents a deeper look into the principles and practices of Jujutsu than has ever appeared in print outside of Japan. Includes:
- The Creation and Evolution of Jujutsu
- Vital Movement Strategies, including Circular Motion and Zero Distance
- How to create force: Muscular Power vs. Postural Power vs. Soft Power
- Training methods for the Dojo and the street
- Rare strikes and kicks, never before taught outside the Jujutsu Dojo
- Defense against multiple attackers
- The use of weapons, including Hadaka Korosu: the skill of using everyday objects as weapons

TO ORDER CALL 1-877-877-8665 OR LOG ON TO
WWW.STRIDERNOLAN.COM